P9-EDH-749

EYES
OF THE
CROCODILE

EYES
OF THE
CROCODILE
and Other Bite-sized Devotions for Juniors

CHARLES MILLS
AND FRIENDS

REVIEW AND HERALD® PUBLISHING ASSOCIATION
HAGERSTOWN, MD 21740

Copyright © 2000 by
Review and Herald ® Publishing Association
All rights reserved

The author assumes full responsibility for the accuracy of all facts
and quotations as cited in this book.

Unless otherwise noted, texts are from the *Holy Bible, New International
Version.* Copyright © 1973, 1978, 1984, International Bible Society. Used by
permission of Zondervan Bible Publishers.
Texts credited to NKJV are from the New King James Version.
Copyright © 1979, 1980, 1982 by Thomas Nelson, Inc. Used by permission.
All rights reserved.
Verses marked TLB are taken from *The Living Bible*, copyright © 1971 by
Tyndale House Publishers, Wheaton, Ill. Used by permission.

This book was
Edited by Gerald Wheeler
Copyedited by Delma Miller and James Cavil
Cover/interior design by Trent Truman
Desktop Technician: Tina M. Ivany
Cover illustration by Extraordinair Art Inc./Gary Fasen
Typeset: 11/13 Cheltenham

PRINTED IN U.S.A.

04 03 02 01 00   5 4 3 2 1

R&H Cataloging Service
Mills, Charles Henning, 1950-
    Eyes of the crocodile and other bite-sized devotions for juniors,
by Charles Mills and friends.

    1. Teenagers—Prayer-books and devotions—English. 2. Devotional
calendars—Juvenile literature. I. Haffner, Karl Mark, 1961-   .
II. Chase, Jane. III. Humphrey, Art. IV. Humphrey, Patricia L.
V. Title.

                        242.6

ISBN 0-8280-1519-8

To Dorinda
My BEST Friend

WELCOME TO *YOUR* JUNIOR DEVOTIONAL!

We've got tons of terrific stories, fascinating bits of information, great advice, and some surprises waiting for you.

This year the Review and Herald has added an exciting new feature to your book. Sprinkled throughout the pages, you'll discover stories and poems written by real, honest-to-goodness, library card-carrying juniors—kids just like you! You're going to enjoy what they have to say.

Here's how we have divided your book:

Sunday is *Gracelink* day. Begin your week with thought-provoking stories and stimulating ideas based on the theme from your Sabbath school lesson quarterly.

Monday says, *Let's Go Retro.* Start the day with a faith-strengthening story from past *Guide* magazines. There's some neat stuff here!

Tuesday offers loads of *Great Advice.* You can't be too rich or too smart. Increase your brainpower with some timely tips on love, relationships, and surviving school.

Wednesday will make you gasp, *That's Amazing!* You won't believe some of the things you'll read during this journey into the wondrous world of the unexpected.

Thursday slips you *More Great Advice,* this time centered on spiritual matters. It will discuss God, heaven, sin, and the church, and offer lots of helpful suggestions for fighting evil on your own terms.

Friday is *Mission Critical*, timeless stories from the front lines of missionary work around the world. Prepare to be awed!

Sabbath provides a quiet time to *Meet Your Saviour.* Walk with Jesus through His earthly ministry as you read the words of those who knew Him best.

Your devotional boasts many writers. Lawrence Maxwell, former editor of *Guide* magazine, introduced the stories in *Let's Go Retro* and *Mission Critical* to young readers years ago. You'll find them just as fascinating today. *That's Amazing!* includes some of his nature adventures as well as astounding insights provided by Jane Chase, a Minnesota-based writer known to all *Guide* readers for her *Factory* articles.

Karl Haffner, senior pastor at Walla Walla College church in Washington state, and Art and Pat Humphrey of Texas serve up timely guidance in your *Great Advice* and *More Great Advice* pages.

My name is Charles Mills. From my home in West Virginia I had the privilege of editing this one-of-a-kind book as well as adding some ideas of my own in the advice sections and introducing you to Jesus in the *Gracelink* and *Meet Your Saviour* pages. (If something doesn't have a name after it, you can assume that I wrote it.)

You'll find junior writers too as you move through the year. Their names will appear with their beautiful stories and poems.

OK. Enough chitchat. It's time to begin your journey through your devotional. May God bless you as you learn more about Him each day.

Forgiveness

When we hate,
You forgive.
When we are jealous,
You forgive.
When we abuse our bodies,
You forgive.
When we sin,
You forgive.
What a merciful God we worship!

—*Devin Darrough, 15, Alaska*

THORN IN HIS FOOT

No one knows his name. We have learned that he was a shepherd boy in ancient Greece and lived 350 years before the birth of Christ.

One day he was watching his sheep when in the distance he saw the glimmer of sun on metal. "The Persians," he gasped. "Their army is on the move, and I'm the only one who knows." Then he stiffened. "If I don't warn the city of Athens, many will die and my country will be lost forever."

He got up to leave, then hesitated. "My sheep. Who will watch them?" But the thought of his beautiful country falling into the hands of Persian invaders was stronger than his concern for his flock. Sheep could be replaced. People couldn't.

Leaving his hilltop perch, the boy began running toward the city. Stones bruised his bare feet. Twigs and grass cut into his skin. But on he ran, gasping for breath.

Passing through a forest, he stepped on a large thorn and felt new pain surge up his leg. Bending down, he broke off the thorn and continued running with part of it still embedded in his sole.

At long last he reached the city and stumbled to the government building. Bursting into the senate chamber, he shouted, "The Persian army is in the valley, and they're headed here." Then he collapsed on the floor.

Like America's Paul Revere, he'd delivered the warning in time to save many lives.

Today, as you go about your business, keep an eye open for the advancing forces of evil. When you see them, sound the warning. Sound it long and loud!

HOW DOES LOVE FEEL?

Q: I'm a boy, 14 years old. I have a girlfriend I like a lot. The problem is that I'm not sure how you're supposed to feel when you're in love. What is true love? How do you know when you're in love? My girlfriend claims she's in love with me, so I feel guilty not being in love with her.

A: Have you ever heard a guy who has just seen a beautiful girl remark "I'm in love"? Is that love? No, it's infatuation. Infatuation is normal. It involves many of the same feelings and emotions as love.

So what's the difference between love and infatuation? Basically, love stands the test of time—tough times. First, true love takes time to grow and mature. It's estimated that teenagers "fall in love" at least five times in high school. Don't be in a hurry—true love develops over time. And don't feel guilty if you're not sure it's love. Second, true love survives tough times. True love is more than fuzzy feelings. It likes to give, not just get. I suggest you use 1 Corinthians 13:4-7 as a measuring stick to help you determine whether you are really in love.

Karl Haffner

BIRDS OF A FEATHER

The swan had no way of telling how low the temperature would drop that night as it made itself comfortable on a little pond in Clydebank, Scotland.

Midnight approached. The temperature continued its nosedive, and ice began forming on the surface of the water. By morning a thick crust encased the pond. When the bird awoke, it found itself trapped tightly in nature's frozen grip.

Swans need to eat constantly. They don't have large reserves of body fat as mammals do. If it didn't have a good, hearty breakfast soon, it would perish. That's when Ned McCaffery, a truck driver who happened by, saw an amazing thing. A seagull flew over the pond, swooped down to inspect the trapped bird, then left. But not for long. Soon it was back carrying a fish that it placed within reach of the swan.

Can birds talk to each other? Apparently so, because that gull formed a "Friends of the Trapped Swan Society." In a matter of minutes other seagulls arrived, each carrying its own life-sustaining gift for the unfortunate flier.

That afternoon the sun heated the water enough so that the ice melted and the well-fed and thankful swan rose under its own power and flew away.

Someone found an owl by railroad tracks in Sussex, England. It had been injured and couldn't fly. But surrounding it were piles of dead mice. It seemed that every owl in England had pitched in to help.

We Christians could learn a lot from our feathered friends, don't you think?

POPULATION BOOM

Q: How many people will be in heaven?

A: Have you ever tried to count snowflakes? One winter day I looked out my window as a few flakes drifted past. Then more fluttered by. Absentmindedly I began to count, just for fun. I think I gave up around 150. By then they were beginning to fall too fast. If I'd kept at it, I'd have gone crazy. We had a blizzard that day.

I wonder if John had the same problem when he was writing chapter 7 of Revelation. God was showing him what would happen at the end of time. Here's how he described one of the scenes he was shown. "After this I looked and there before me was a great multitude that no one could count, from every nation, tribe, people and language, standing before the throne and in front of the Lamb" (verse 9).

That's a lot of people.

But even with such a multitude singing praises, God will know it if you're not there. Or if I'm not there. He'll be searching the throng for your face and mine. And when He sees us He'll smile.

John also wrote: "And I heard a loud voice from the throne saying, 'Now the dwelling of God is with men, and he will live with them. They will be his people, and God himself will be with them and be their God. He will wipe every tear from their eyes. There will be no more death or mourning or crying or pain'" (Revelation 21:3, 4). Let's look forward to heaven together.

EYES OF THE CROCODILE

It was a hot, sticky afternoon in central Africa as the missionary walked a dusty road. "I wish I could find a water hole," he gasped, wiping perspiration from his face.

In this wild, desolate country, trails sometimes skirted small pools left by passing rains. Turning a corner, he noticed a beautiful pond beyond the bushes, its waters sparkling in the bright sun.

"Finally!" the missionary exclaimed. Since no one was around, he began to remove his clothes.

Suddenly a voice said, "Don't go in!" The weary traveler glanced about to see who was talking. *That's odd*, he thought. *This hot weather is making me hear things.* Reaching down to pull off his shoes, he heard the voice again. "Don't go in!"

I'd better hop into that water quickly, he chuckled to himself, *before this heat makes me completely crazy.* He stood on the water's edge. "Don't go in!" This time the voice sounded urgent.

Something's strange about this, the missionary mused. Then, because he was a Christian, he paused. *I wonder if God is trying to warn me about something.*

He didn't plunge into the cool waters, as he'd intended. Instead, he walked around the edge, peering behind every bush and shrub. Next he sat down and watched the surface for several minutes. All seemed calm and peaceful. Then the water rippled just the tiniest bit as two round orbs stuck up above the glassy surface.

The missionary recognized what they were. Had he put so much as a toe into the pool, he would have died violently. Falling to his knees, he prayed, "Thank You, God. Thank You for saving my life!" The eyes of the crocodile watched him dress and leave.

JOSEPH'S DREAM

Many call it "The Greatest Story Ever Told." It begins with a dream. Let's invite Gospel writers Matthew, Mark, Luke, and John to tell us the story of how a God became a man and a baby became a Saviour.

This is how the birth of Jesus Christ came about: His mother Mary was pledged to be married to Joseph, but before they came together, she was found to be with child through the Holy Spirit. Because Joseph her husband was a righteous man and did not want to expose her to public disgrace, he had in mind to divorce her quietly.

But after he had considered this, an angel of the Lord appeared to him in a dream and said, "Joseph son of David, do not be afraid to take Mary home as your wife, because what is conceived in her is from the Holy Spirit. She will give birth to a son, and you are to give him the name Jesus, because he will save his people from their sins."

All this took place to fulfill what the Lord had said through the prophet: "The virgin will be with child and will give birth to a son, and they will call him Immanuel—which means, 'God with us.'"

When Joseph woke up, he did what the angel of the Lord had commanded him and took Mary home as his wife. But he had no union with her until she gave birth to a son. And he gave him the name Jesus.

Matthew 1:18-25

SETTING OUT

The Lord had said to Abram, "Leave your country, your people and your father's household and go to the land I will show you." Genesis 12:1.

I know what it's like to do what Abram did—left everything familiar to follow what he determined to be an invitation from God.

Years ago I climbed on board an airliner at San Francisco International Airport. After stowing my stuff in the overhead bin and fastening my seat belt, I sat for a long moment with my thoughts. Then I gasped. "Charles, what are you doing!"

It had seemed to be a good idea at the time—take a break from college and spend a year as a student missionary teaching conversational English in Osaka, Japan. But as I sat there, surrounded by strangers, listening to the mysterious sounds of the aircraft preparing to follow the setting sun westward, I wavered. I was leaving everything and everyone I cared about behind me—family, friends, my great job at the college radio station.

Just then a little girl, maybe 5 years old, peeked at me from above her seat a few rows ahead. She smiled sweetly as if to say, "Hey, mister, are you going to fly in this airplane too? Isn't it exciting?"

Suddenly all my fears and uncertainties vanished. I wasn't really leaving anything. Japan would be filled with people who could be my friends and serve as my temporary family for 12 months. And all of them—perhaps even that little girl—needed to learn about Jesus.

I settled back for the long flight. Yes, this was going to be exciting after all!

REVENGE OF THE SEAS

When Sir Richard Grenville told his crew that their ship, the *Revenge*, was about to take on 53 Spanish ships single-handedly, they cheered. The year was 1591, and England was at war with Spain.

Grenville reviewed the situation. He had only a few hundred cannon shot and scarcely enough gunpowder. Half of his men were too sick to leave their hammocks. The other vessels in his fleet had escaped, and now 53 enemy warships were bearing down on him in two long lines. It was fight or flight.

"Steer straight down the middle," he ordered. "Tell the men to fire as soon as we come into range."

The Spanish almost laughed when they saw the little *Revenge* turning to fight. But the small size and agility of the boat surprised them, and its ferocity caused them to grow concerned. Within an hour two of their warships sailed away, badly damaged. Others scattered, fearing for their own safety.

Up and down the line the *Revenge* sailed until it had run out of ammunition. An enemy ship's huge sails cut off the wind, and the little boat stopped. Spaniards tried to board it, but the determined men of the *Revenge* fought them off until night fell. Sir Richard was shot twice but managed to stay at his post.

Dawn illuminated an incredible sight. The *Revenge* was in shambles, its men sick or dead, and the ammunition exhausted. But there it sat, still afloat, encircled by nearly 50 enemy vessels, their crews in awe of the courage and tenacity of their little foe.

Facing a challenge? Don't let the odds keep you from giving it your best shot.

ADDICTED TO BASEBALL CARDS

Q: I'm addicted to baseball cards. Every time I go to the store I want some. What should I do? I'm 12.

A: Here's a simple way to help fight any addiction. Think of the word CARD and remember:

Choose your limit. It's not bad to buy baseball cards if you control it. Set a reasonable limit each month.

Avoid. Once you've bought your quota, try to avoid going near those places where you know you'll be tempted to buy cards.

Reward. If you stick to your limit, reward yourself by buying something you've been wanting with the money you saved.

Depend on God. He cares about you and will help you if you ask.

Karl Haffner

SNOW SCOOP

Wilson Bentley loved looking at snowflakes. But they would always melt before he could get a good look at them. So when he received a microscope for his fifteenth birthday, the first thing he did was figure out how to combine it with his camera equipment, thus inventing the photomicrograph camera.

Wilson spent the next 50 years taking thousands of microphotographs of snowflakes. For each photo he had to go outside and catch a falling snowflake on a blackboard. Next he checked it with a magnifying glass to make sure he had a decent specimen. Then he carefully transferred it to a microscope slide, pressed it flat, and positioned it in the center of the glass. Cold work, but worth it to Wilson.

He studied each flake to decide for sure if it was worth having its picture taken. If so, he centered the slide under the camera lens of the photomicrograph camera. He pointed the camera to the sky for a solid, clear background and took the picture. The photograph now preserved the flake forever.

Where do snowflakes come from? High in the air a tiny dust particle drifts through a cold cloud of water vapor. As the particle makes its way toward earth, vapor droplets stick to it and freeze. The molecules of frozen water arrange themselves in intricate patterns, giving birth to a snowflake.

A patch of snow two feet square and 10 inches deep contains about 1 *million* snowflakes! The odds of two snowflakes being alike are about 1 in 105 million.

With so many varieties, God has made sure we won't get bored with winter precipitation!

Jane Chase

ZERO HOUR

Q: When is Jesus coming?

A: We've all heard the Bible texts describing what the world will be like when Jesus comes: Wars and rumors of wars, earthquakes, pestilence, people's hearts failing them for fear, people running to and fro on the earth, natural affections turning cold, anger, hate, lust.

Sound familiar?

Even the people alive right after Jesus lived on this earth believed the world was ripe for His quick return. When He didn't show up, Peter wrote, "First of all, you must understand that in the last days scoffers will come. . . . They will say, 'Where is this "coming" he promised? Ever since our fathers died, everything goes on as it has since the beginning of creation'" (2 Peter 3:3, 4).

Ever feel that way? Where is He? Why hasn't He come back?

No one knows the day or hour when Jesus will return the second time. God says so in the Bible. But we can be ready today, or tomorrow, or the next day. We can begin to prepare for our future life in heaven with Jesus so when He does return, we can say, "Lo, this is our God; we have waited for him, and he will save us" (Isaiah 25:9, KJV).

When it will happen is not important. If it were, God would have told us. *That* it will happen should fill our hearts with gladness and set our lips to singing. He's coming—He's coming. You can count on it!

THE BULLETPROOF MULE

Pastor Seidel slumped into a chair and sighed. The journey had been long, but he and his faithful mule Penicillin had made it through the jungle all in one piece.

Not all journeys had been so successful. Poisonous snakes had bitten the missionary three times in the Amazon basin. For protection, he'd purchased a rifle, which he always kept in Penicillin's backpack.

Pastor Seidel discovered that the family he'd come to visit wasn't interested in hearing about God. "We don't need Him," the father said. Then he changed the subject.

While the visiting pastor prepared for supper, his host noticed the rifle lying on the porch. *Nice gun*, he thought to himself. *Telescopic sight and everything*. He positioned the weapon by his chin and peeked through the scope. *Wow. I've got a closeup view of ol' Penicillin—*

Bang! By accident the gun fired, sending a slug right into the head of Pastor Seidel's faithful companion. The mule began to shiver and shake. "What happened?" the missionary gasped as he ran from the hut. Seeing the gun and the shaking mule, he instantly figured it out.

"I'm so sorry!" cried the man.

"My mule!" the missionary exclaimed, thinking about those jungle miles between him and home and his poor four-legged friend, who now had a bullet in his brain.

"O God," Pastor Seidel prayed aloud. "Save my mule. Please!" The mule shook for several days, then got well.

The man who'd fired the gun decided that if God could heal a mule, He could save him and his whole family from their sins. They were all baptized.

A CHILD IS BORN

So Joseph also went up from the town of Nazareth in Galilee to Judea, to Bethlehem the town of David, because he belonged to the house and line of David. He went there to register with Mary, who was pledged to be married to him and was expecting a child. While they were there, the time came for the baby to be born, and she gave birth to her firstborn, a son. She wrapped him in cloths and placed him in a manger, because there was no room for them in the inn.

And there were shepherds living out in the fields nearby, keeping watch over their flocks at night. An angel of the Lord appeared to them, and the glory of the Lord shone around them, and they were terrified. But the angel said to them, "Do not be afraid. I bring you good news of great joy that will be for all the people. Today in the town of David a Savior has been born to you; he is Christ the Lord. This will be a sign to you: You will find a baby wrapped in cloths and lying in a manger."

Suddenly a great company of the heavenly host appeared with the angel, praising God and saying, "Glory to God in the highest, and on earth peace to men on whom his favor rests."

When the angels had left them and gone into heaven, the shepherds said to one another, "Let's go to Bethlehem and see this thing that has happened, which the Lord has told us about." So they hurried off and found Mary and Joseph, and the baby, who was lying in the manger.

Luke 2:4-16

GOD CAN DO IT

I cannot do it," Joseph replied to Pharaoh, "but God will give Pharaoh the answer he desires." Genesis 41:16.

Have you ever faced a situation for which you were *totally* unprepared? I sure have.

When I arrived in Tokyo, Japan, as a student missionary, I met a bunch of other Adventist college students who'd chosen to spend a year teaching conversational English in that country. Some went north to Hokkaido, some stayed in Tokyo, but a large number of us boarded the speedy Bullet Train and headed south toward Hiroshima and Osaka.

Once we'd settled into our apartment in Kobe, my roommate and I headed to the Adventist evangelistic center in nearby Osaka to be trained for our new jobs. Then, just a few days later, I stood before a classroom filled with eager students waiting to learn how to speak understandable English. I'd never done anything remotely similar to this. Would I fail? Would my students end up jabbering in a language *no one* could comprehend?

"Lord, help me," I prayed silently.

Then I remembered the story of Joseph and Pharaoh. "I can't interpret your dreams," the frightened young man had told the powerful Egyptian leader. "But God can."

All at once I felt calm and assured. Missionaries don't have to have all the answers or possess every talent to serve God. They just have to have faith in the power that God offers.

"Open your textbooks to page 10," I said with growing confidence. As my students spent our first evening together learning about English, I spent it learning about God.

RESCUE THE ENEMY

Bullets pounded the deck inches above John Elliott's head. Bombs exploded, and dying men cried. When the day was over, America was at war with Japan and the naval shipyards in Pearl Harbor, Hawaii, lay in ruins.

Four years later Elliott was a Navy lieutenant commanding a cargo ship off the coastal waters of China. The war that had begun so violently was over, but images of death and destruction at Pearl Harbor still seared his thoughts.

BOOM! The percussion of an explosion shook the bridge. Up ahead he could see fire and smoke billowing from a Japanese freighter loaded with refugees. An underwater mine left over from the war had ripped a hole in its bow.

"Change course and rescue those people!" John ordered.

"But sir," one of his officers protested, "there may be more mines. Besides, you were at Pearl Harbor where Japanese forces tried to kill you."

Elliott turned to his subordinate. "That boat has men, women, and children on it," he said sternly. "We must save them!"

The officer grinned. "That's what we hoped you'd say, Lieutenant." The American ship raced to the rescue, lashed itself to the sinking vessel, and saved 4,300 doomed persons.

John never told the refugees his name or asked for thanks. But 17 years later the people of Japan tracked him down and sent him many gifts, including the Third Order of the Rising Sun, their country's highest award for foreigners.

The Bible says, "If your enemy is hungry, feed him; if he is thirsty, give him something to drink" (Romans 12:20). Jesus declared, "Love your enemies" (Matthew 5:44). John Elliott put those words into action.

I WORRY A LOT

Q: I am a boy 12 years old. My biggest problem is I worry about everything. I worry something will go wrong when I baby-sit my sister. I worry when my parents don't get along. I worry about not getting good grades. I worry all the time. What can I do?

A: Worry is a natural part of life. (I worry sometimes that my advice isn't as good as it ought to be!) We should not, however, let worry overwhelm us.

Jesus preached a sermon once in which He talked about worry. In Matthew 6:25-34 He gave three ways we can stop worrying.

1. Trust God. In verse 32 Jesus says wicked people should worry, but Christians don't need to worry about anything, because God will take care of them.

2. Seek God first. Next, in verse 33, Jesus says to put your energy into finding God's kingdom. If you do that, Jesus tells us, you don't have to worry about anything else.

3. Live one day at a time. Finally, in verse 34, Jesus tells us just to live one day at a time. Don't sweat what could happen tomorrow—just pay attention to today!

Karl Haffner

WALK ON THE CEILING

Some afternoon when you have nothing else to do, try this. Hold a ball at arm's length and let go. Chances are very good that it will fall to the floor.

Ask your mom or dad if the same thing happened when they were juniors. Check with your grandparents, too.

Some people say, "The Bible is old-fashioned. We don't have to obey those old laws spoken by Moses—the Ten Commandments. They applied to people a long time ago, not to us." When you hear such statements, tell them, "Go drop a ball."

You see, what makes that ball fall is something called *gravity*. Legend claims that one day a falling apple thumped Sir Isaac Newton on the head. *Hey, there must be a force that drove that apple from that tree down onto my cranium,* he thought. So he did some studying, talked to a few other scientists, walked around with his hands clasped behind his back, and came up with something he called "the law of gravity." Newton didn't create it. He just named it.

Fact is, gravity has been around for a long time. Astronomers report that it's been controlling the movements of stars for billions of years. Newton just wrote it down.

The Ten Commandments aren't *Moses'* laws either. Like gravity, they're laws of God. Moses just put them in writing.

So if it's true that God's laws get old, that they don't apply to us, then the law of gravity, being so old, must be *really* out of date. Surely it doesn't apply anymore.

Well, there's a way to find out. Go drop a ball. Or try walking on the ceiling!

FORGIVEN BUT GUILTY

Q: I'm 12 years old and am kinda messed up. I know God forgives and all that, but I still feel guilty. Can you help?

A: Sometimes it's hardest to forgive ourselves—we pay for our mistakes for a long time after we make them. However, that doesn't mean God has not forgiven us.

A priest in the Philippines, a much-loved man of God, felt very guilty because of a secret sin he had committed many years before. He asked God again and again to forgive him, but still he felt guilty.

In his church was a woman who deeply loved God and claimed she talked to Him and He talked to her. The priest, however, didn't believe it. To test her he said, "The next time you talk to God, I want you to ask Him what sin your priest committed while he was in seminary." The woman agreed.

A few days later the priest said, "Well, did you talk with God?"

"Yes, I did," she replied.

"And did you ask Him what sin I committed?"

"Yes, I did."

"Well, what did He say?"

"He said, 'I don't remember.'"

If you ask God to forgive you, He does! And then He forgets it!

Karl Haffner

SAVAGE RAIN

Missionary Paton knew that if he didn't act fast, all that he and the others had worked for would be destroyed. The church was already burning, and the attackers would soon set the house ablaze.

The devil doesn't like the good news of salvation spreading around the world and often fills innocent minds with thoughts of violence against those who preach His Word.

"I'm going out," the missionary told his companions hiding in the safety of their simple, modest home. "I've got to try to save the buildings. Lock the door behind me so no one can get in."

Sending one last prayer heavenward, he stepped into the night. Running to the wooden fence connecting the two structures, he tore out a section, trying to keep the flames from spreading to the house. That's when he noticed shadows creeping about him. Glancing up, he saw the dark forms of the local people, their angry faces lit by the crackling fires.

"Kill him!" one of them ordered.

Missionary Paton lifted his hand. "My God is stronger than fire and spears and anger," he said in their language. "If you hurt me, you're hurting my heavenly Father."

Suddenly, as if to underline his words, a great wind swept through the forest and raced across the clearing. A torrential rain, the type that's common in that part of the world, immediately followed. In seconds it extinguished the fires, leaving behind a very astonished, very wet mob. Panic seized the people. Dropping their torches and spears, they ran back into the night.

Missionary Paton returned to his companions, and together they thanked God for the wind and the rain and the power of His presence.

A TEMPLE BLESSING

When the time of their purification [circumcision] according to the Law of Moses had been completed, Joseph and Mary took him to Jerusalem to present him to the Lord. . . . Now there was a man in Jerusalem called Simeon, who was righteous and devout. He was waiting for the consolation of Israel, and the Holy Spirit was upon him. It had been revealed to him by the Holy Spirit that he would not die before he had seen the Lord's Christ. Moved by the Spirit, he went into the temple courts. When the parents brought in the child Jesus to do for him what the custom of the Law required, Simeon took him in his arms and praised God, saying:

> "Sovereign Lord, as you have promised,
>   you now dismiss your servant in peace.
> For my eyes have seen your salvation,
>   which you have prepared in the sight of all people,
> a light for revelation to the Gentiles
>   and for glory to your people Israel."

The child's father and mother marveled at what was said about him. Then Simeon blessed them and said to Mary, his mother: "This child is destined to cause the falling and rising of many in Israel, and to be a sign that will be spoken against, so that the thoughts of many hearts will be revealed. And a sword will pierce your own soul too."

Luke 2:22-35

I WILL TEACH YOU

The Lord said to [Moses], "Who gave man his mouth? Who makes him deaf or mute? Who gives him sight or makes him blind? Is it not I, the Lord? Now go; I will help you speak and will teach you what to say." Exodus 4:11, 12.

Moses didn't want to face Pharaoh to demand the release of God's people, who'd endured slavery in Egypt for generations. But God had other ideas. In the above verse He was saying, "Hey, Moses. I could've created you deaf and blind, but I didn't. I gave you a mouth and eyes so you can use them in service to Me!"

One of the first things we did at the Evangelistic Center in Osaka was hold a series of revival-type meetings. Every student missionary had to prepare a sermon as well as help out in the music and promotion departments. I played the piano and organ, so making a joyful noise to the Lord was not a problem. But preach a sermon? In front of a bunch of people? Me?

"You can do this," Bruce, our student missionary leader, encouraged. "Just let the Lord speak through you."

Speak through me? How do I do that?

When the big night arrived, I delivered my sermon, wondering if anyone was interested in what I was saying. After the meeting, several of my students came to me and said, "Charles, you really helped me understand God better. Thanks."

That's when I knew they hadn't been listening to me at all. No, they'd been hearing what God said through me. I'd rattled their eardrums. But God had touched their hearts.

"GET OUT!"

As night spread a dark blanket over northern Luzon in the Philippines, Bill dug a hole three feet wide and six feet long. Opening a stretcher, he placed it across the bottom to form a mattress. Then he climbed in to catch some sleep.

Bill was a medic with the United States Army. World War II raged across the Pacific islands, and blood and screams had filled his day. But night brought some relief. Occasionally sniper fire or the deep-throated boom of an American cannon would rouse him, but he'd become accustomed to the sounds of war.

"Get out of this foxhole and go back to the surgical tent!"

The voice seemed so real that Bill lifted himself on one elbow and looked around to see who'd spoken. Seeing no one, he lay back down and was about to drift away when the command came again.

Bill was a Seventh-day Adventist Christian as well as a soldier and knew that God might be trying to impress on his mind something important. So he rolled up his bedding, left the foxhole, and spent the remainder of the night in the nearby surgical tent.

In the morning he returned to the foxhole to retrieve the stretcher and gasped in amazement. A sniper bullet had pierced the stretcher in the exact location where his head would have been had he remained in the foxhole.

Bill survived the war, returned to America, and began writing articles for *Guide* magazine. His last name was Anderson, and his friends called him Andy. For many years he was the author of Andy's Gadget Magic.

A GIRL MAKES ME NERVOUS

Q: I'm a 10-year-old boy. I like a girl in my class, but I'm not sure if she likes me. Whenever I try to say hi or talk to her, I get real nervous. What should I do in order for her to like me?

A: I know what you mean about getting nervous when you try to talk to the girl you like. I remember talking to my "dream girl" when I was 10—I stuttered like a guilty criminal on the witness stand. Now I'm convinced that being nervous is part of being a guy!

As for getting her to like you, that's her choice. Give it lots of time. Don't get carried away with her, but rather get to know lots of different girls. As you start feeling comfortable talking to different girls, you will find it easier to talk with the one you have special feelings for. Practice at it and take your time!

Karl Haffner

BANDIT AND THE BULLDOG

Occasionally life seems to turn miraculous. While we know that angels seldom appear to us in the physical world, they certainly keep busy trying to get others to come to our aid. Listen to this amazing story from Alberta, Canada:

It was the summer of 1998. I was at my cabin with my friend Ashley Woods. That summer I was having trouble believing in God.

Ashley and I walked to a nearby candy store with my dog, Bandit. When we arrived, we tied Bandit to a bench and went in. Then we came out and were sitting on the bench enjoying our treats when, all of a sudden, a big bulldog attacked Bandit. We tried to stop the fight, but couldn't. Both of us started to pray.

A moment after we prayed, a man appeared in front of us. He was wearing a long, black trench coat and a cowboy hat. The attacking dog walked away when the man came. I looked at Bandit and then turned to say "Thank you," but the man was gone! It was as if he had disappeared into thin air.

As Ashley and I walked home, neither of us spoke a word. We were both thanking the Lord for sending that man to save the life of Bandit. The stranger was like an angel in disguise!

Ashley Woods and Kim Kilkenny,
Canada

Wow! What a beautiful illustration of what God can accomplish through willing helpers.

WRONG PLACE, WRONG TIME

Q:
Why does God let some people live and other people die?

A:
Not long ago I watched an interview with a young woman who'd survived a terrible airplane crash. Many passengers had lost their lives. She and a few others had miraculously walked away without a scratch.

"God must have something important planned for my life," she said with tears in her eyes. "That's why He let me live."

My immediate reaction to her statement was "Does that mean God had nothing important planned for the people who *didn't* survive? He just let them die because He was through with them?"

How we answer your question reveals the basis for our entire belief in God. It has to do with His *will*—that means His set of wants for our lives. Jesus said: "For my Father's will is that everyone who looks to the Son and believes in him shall have eternal life" (John 6:40). The apostle John, who learned to love at Jesus' feet, wrote: "I wish above all things that thou mayest prosper and be in health, even as thy soul prospereth" (3 John 1:2, KJV).

God's will centers on life, not death. He wants us to enjoy a healthy, prosperous existence, spiritually *and physically.* Don't ever think your heavenly Father is sitting around waiting to pull the plug on your existence when He thinks you've lived long enough. That young woman survived because she was sitting in the right place at the right time. The others died because they weren't.

CHANGE OF PLANS

We've got to stop those Adventists and their lies," shouted the leader of the group.

"Yeah, but none of us can fight," someone said. "We can't drive them out alone."

"How 'bout Aadly," yet another chimed in. "He's so strong he may be going to the Olympic Games as a wrestler. If anyone can throw those bums out, he can."

"I'm your man," Aadly responded when asked to deal with the "situation." "I'll show those Adventists that they can't waltz into our town and mess with our religion."

It just so happened that the preacher and his team were planning an evangelistic meeting that very night. As the pastor stood to deliver his talk, the back door flew open and in walked Aadly, muscles bulging and fists clenched.

"We'll begin with prayer," the evangelist said. All heads bowed. To be honest, Aadly was glad for the moment of calm. He needed to plan his attack.

"Our topic tonight is on Revelation with its many beasts and dreams," the preacher announced as everyone sat down.

H'mmm, Aadly thought. *Beasts and dreams? Sounds interesting. Maybe I'll just listen for a few minutes before pulverizing the preacher.*

He listened—and listened. While he sat there, the Holy Spirit whispered in his ears, calming his violent thoughts, allowing him to see for the first time the beauty of Jesus.

He came back the next night. And the next. In the end, the man given the task of driving the Adventists out of town wound up being lowered under the waters of baptism by the very man he'd come to beat up.

ROYAL VISIT

After Jesus was born in Bethlehem in Judea, during the time of King Herod, Magi from the east came to Jerusalem and asked, "Where is the one who has been born king of the Jews? We saw his star in the east and have come to worship him."

When King Herod heard this he was disturbed, and all Jerusalem with him. When he had called together all the people's chief priests and teachers of the law, he asked them where the Christ was to be born. "In Bethlehem in Judea," they replied, "for this is what the prophet has written: 'But you, Bethlehem, in the land of Judah, are by no means least among the rulers of Judah; for out of you will come a ruler who will be the shepherd of my people Israel.'"

Then Herod called the Magi secretly and found out from them the exact time the star had appeared. He sent them to Bethlehem and said, "Go and make a careful search for the child. As soon as you find him, report to me, so that I too may go and worship him."

After they had heard the king, they went on their way, and the star they had seen in the east went ahead of them until it stopped over the place where the child was. When they saw the star, they were overjoyed. On coming to the house, they saw the child with his mother Mary, and they bowed down and worshiped him. Then they opened their treasures and presented him with gifts of gold and of incense and of myrrh.

Matthew 2:1-11

THE WAY TO LIVE

Teach them the decrees and laws, and show them the way to live and the duties they are to perform." Exodus 18:20.

When Moses' father-in-law, Jethro, came to visit him right after the children of Israel left Egypt, he sat him down and gave the reluctant leader some good advice. "Get organized," he said. "Don't try to do everything yourself, and remember why you're here."

Being a student missionary requires organization and loads of teamwork. I learned very quickly that in areas in which I wasn't talented or experienced, someone else was. We worked as a team and enjoyed the fruits of our labors as a team.

After our revival meetings, we asked if anyone would like to be baptized. One of our students raised her hand. Wow! Talk about excited. God had used us to reach someone, and we were thrilled beyond words.

On the day of her baptism we all stood proudly to watch her being lowered under the water by the center pastor who'd been studying with her for some time. As a group we had talked to her, sang to her, taught her things she didn't know before, expressed God's love and forgiveness, prayed for her, and encouraged her. Now, as a group, we welcomed her into the Seventh-day Adventist Church.

When we asked her why she'd decided to be baptized, she said, "I'd heard and read about God ever since I was a little kid. But here at the center you *showed* God to me, and that made all the difference."

Kinda humbling, huh?

LIFE PRESERVER

Religion is for babies," Harvey announced as he tossed aside the Christian tract his friend John had given him. "He-men don't need it."

World War II raged across the Pacific as the two seamen stood at the railing of their battleship. John had hoped that his buddy would want to learn about Jesus, but the man wasn't interested.

"Man your battle stations!" The voice over the loudspeaker sounded urgent. Suddenly the air was filled with roaring guns, screaming airplanes, and the sharp whine of ricocheting bomb fragments. The two friends quickly hurried to their positions, hoping to ward off the attack. But a torpedo found its mark and ripped a hole in the side of the ship. Water poured in, and the vessel began to list heavily.

"Abandon ship!" the captain ordered. As they were rushing toward the lifeboats, John noticed that his friend Harvey didn't have his life preserver. He must have lost it during the attack. Without one, he'd surely die with the rapidly sinking ship.

"Here!" John shouted. "Take my preserver. I've given my life to God and am ready to die. You aren't. Take it!" He thrust the vest into his friend's hands and vanished in the rush of terrified sailors.

The ship slipped under the waves, taking John with it. His life preserver kept Harvey afloat until rescuers arrived.

Months later a humble seaman appeared at the door of an Adventist church. "I want to be a Christian like my friend John," he said softly. "He died for me."

Someday there's going to be a reunion in heaven between two old friends. One gave his life. The other found his—in Jesus.

HOW DO I GET HER?

Q: I am 11 years old and I like a girl who likes me, but she also likes a seventh grader. I do nice things for her whenever I can, but not too much, because I don't want to scare her away. I don't know if she is going to go for me or for this other guy in our school. How do I know? And what do I do to get her?

A: You seem to be moving cautiously and slowly—that's smart!

Be certain that you are not doing these kind things just to snag a girlfriend, but that you do nice things for everyone simply because you want to. In the long run, if you keep looking for ways to do kind things for others, you'll have a lot of friends.

As for what to do to "get her," remember, you can never force anyone to like you. You can simply work on yourself and try to be likable. It sounds like you're doing that.

Karl Haffner

KINK IN THE TAIL

Alipo didn't see the leopard until it sprang onto the back of one of his cows.

Herding can be a very boring job. You lead the animals out of their pens in the morning, watch them munch grass all day long until the sun hangs low in the west, then you lead them back home again. That's the way it had been for Alipo during the dry season in northern India. But a leopard attack certainly didn't qualify as "business as usual" in the cow-watching profession.

"Hey!" the boy shouted, hoping that the sound of a human voice might scare the leopard away. Nope.

He began throwing rocks at the beast, striking it repeatedly on the back. Nothing.

Racing to the predator, he began jabbing his fists into the legs of the determined creature, trying to dislodge it. The leopard simply sank its claws deeper into the bellowing cow's back. Alipo knew that if it bit into the neck where the great nerve ran down the spine, he'd be less one cow that night.

That's when Alipo did an incredibly brave thing. He grabbed the leopard's tail with both hands and bent it. He bent it hard! The cat let out a scream of pain, released its grip on the cow, and raced out across the meadow as fast as it could go.

By the way, if you find the devil on your back today, ask Jesus to help you think a few kind thoughts and do a few kind deeds. It's just like bending Satan's tail.

THREE IN ONE

Q: I have a hard time praying to the Holy Spirit. I know He's God. Am I supposed to start my prayer like "Holy Spirit, come into my life today . . ."?

A: Here's something to try. Instead of speaking to one particular member of the Godhead, why don't you just pray to "God"? You can be sure that all three—the Father, the Son, and the Holy Spirit—are listening intently to your prayer. They'll know which one should respond.

The idea of three persons being one God is confusing until you learn more about Them. The Father, Son, and Holy Spirit are one in thought (They are in complete agreement with Each Other), but They do different things. The Son, Jesus, is the Creator. He made everything. And because He died for us, He's the God who can forgive us when we sin.

The Holy Spirit works in us by nudging our conscience when we've done something bad. He makes us want to be good, to act kind, to love others. Giving us the power to forgive those who mistreat us, He kindles hope when all seems lost.

God the Father serves as our Judge. Don't think He's out to condemn us. Hardly. He works constantly to make sure that Satan doesn't accuse us wrongly. Instead of the title "Judge," perhaps a better label for the Father would be "Protector."

When God says, "Call to me and I will answer you and tell you great and unsearchable things you do not know" (Jeremiah 33:3), He means it. So when you whisper your prayer, the greatest power in the universe is listening. That's power times three!

PARAMILIK

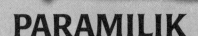

The South Pacific sparkled in the warm night as the scent of orchids drifted with the quiet tide. A canoe sliced through the waters, following the trail of the moon.

Snore!

The man at the bow closed his eyes in frustration.

Snore!

He'd recently married the woman at the other oar. Although he liked her fine, his new stepson had a definite problem.

Snore!

He snored.

The Solomon Islander had had enough. He reached back, grabbed the sleeping child, and tossed him into the ocean. The mother screamed and tried to wrestle the boat about, but her new husband leaned into his oar and propelled them away from the thrashing boy.

When they reached the island, the desperate mother hurried along the beach, hoping that her son had been able to swim to safety. Sure enough, she found him washed ashore and alive. But she couldn't take him home. That would be dangerous. Then she remembered the mission run by people called Adventists. Her sister had joined their church. Maybe they'd care for her son.

The people at the mission welcomed the boy and gave him a new name. "We'll call you Paramilik," the director announced. "That means 'no father or mother, drifting alone at night.'"

Later, an Adventist missionary visited the mission. He found Paramilik a bright, happy boy full of energy and joy. Each day the missionary received gifts from the child—papaws, tomatoes, beans, and other things. "This is my way of saying 'Thank you,'" the youngster explained. They were heartfelt words from the boy who had drifted alone in the sea at night.

HIDING IN EGYPT

And having been warned in a dream not to go back to Herod, [the Magi] returned to their country by another route.

When they had gone, an angel of the Lord appeared to Joseph in a dream. "Get up," he said, "take the child and his mother and escape to Egypt. Stay there until I tell you, for Herod is going to search for the child to kill him." So he got up, took the child and his mother during the night and left for Egypt, where he stayed until the death of Herod. And so was fulfilled what the Lord had said through the prophet: "Out of Egypt I called my son."

When Herod realized that he had been outwitted by the Magi, he was furious, and he gave orders to kill all the boys in Bethlehem and its vicinity who were two years old and under, in accordance with the time he had learned from the Magi. Then what was said through the prophet Jeremiah was fulfilled:

> "A voice is heard in Ramah,
> weeping and great mourning,
> Rachel weeping for her children
> and refusing to be comforted,
> because they are no more."

After Herod died, an angel of the Lord appeared in a dream to Joseph in Egypt and said, "Get up, take the child and his mother and go to the land of Israel, for those who were trying to take the child's life are dead."

So he got up, took the child and his mother and went to the land of Israel.

Matthew 2:12-21

SAVING THE LOST

F or this son of mine was dead and is alive again; he was lost and is found." Luke 15:24.

When Jesus told the parable of the prodigal son, He may as well have been speaking to a group of student missionaries, because "lost" is how we viewed the whole world.

One night we heard a great commotion in a town near Osaka, and a group of us went to check it out. It was a festival of some sort with drums pounding, brightly lit lanterns, and colorfully dressed people dancing in the streets. "What's going on?" I asked a Japanese friend.

"It's a celebration," he announced.

"Who for?"

He clapped his hands to the beat of the music. "For the dead," he said. "Our ancestors like it when we sing and beat our drums for them."

Not everyone in Japan believes that dead ancestors enjoy such festivities, but many still do. As a matter of fact, some worship the dead, asking them for guidance in their daily lives.

Jesus compared such people as these Japanese to sons and daughters who've wandered far from home and become lost in a world of confusion and lies created by Satan. Missionaries who travel to foreign lands or simply talk to a neighbor across the backyard fence have one central goal—to save the lost, to bring them into a true understanding of God. In this case, we know that the Bible says dead people sleep and cannot listen to pounding drums.

I watched my friend enjoy the festival and secretly asked God to help me find ways to invite prodigal sons and daughters back home again.

SUICIDE PILOT

The following pilots are ordered to crash their planes directly into the side of an American bomber. Shomiko, Toshi, Sakae . . ."

"That's me!" Sakae announced with a happy grin. "Finally, I'm going to die for my emperor."

American and Japanese military forces had been at each other's throats for four years. Hundreds of thousands of young men had joined the armies of both sides, eager to fight for their country and win the war.

As the worldwide conflict ground on, Japanese forces had begun using a rather desperate measure to stop the American advance. They ordered pilots to turn their airplanes into lethal missiles by ramming them at full speed directly into attacking bombers and ships. To the fliers, it was an opportunity to die for their much-loved emperor and enjoy the rich rewards waiting for them in the afterlife.

Sakae bounded to his plane, started the engine, and waited for the order to take off.

Suddenly the lineman ran to his plane and waved for him to stop the engine. "The war is over," he called excitedly. "Japan has surrendered."

Sakae groaned in disappointment and left his aircraft. Hard times followed. His house and family were gone, victims of American bombing.

Then he met a young woman who happened to be a Christian. She introduced the bitter ex-pilot to the God of his enemy. In time he changed his allegiance from the emperor of Japan to the Emperor of heaven, attended a religious college, graduated, then married the girl and spent the remainder of his life as a pastor in a church near Tokyo.

OLDER SISTER BLUES

Q: I am 10 years old and have an older sister who is always arguing and fighting with me. Sometimes I hate her and want to belt her good. But sometimes she is cool. What would you do?

A: I know what you mean. I have an older sister too. Sometimes I wanted to rip her lips off. But as you mentioned about your sister, she could also be pretty cool at times.

Sometime when you and your sister are both in a good mood, sit down and list all the times you can remember when you were really mad at each other. Write down what happened before each fight. Is there a pattern that leads to the quarreling? The trick is to be aware of the beginning stages of arguments and try to stop the fight before it grows into a doozy.

Another good method I have found for handling arguments is to frankly admit my wrongs and ask for forgiveness. It is amazing how quickly this can calm the storm. A little secret about this technique: it will frustrate your sister to no end, because there's nothing more for her to argue about!

Karl Haffner

BLIND "DRAGONS"

Johann crept forward carefully, his torch casting weird shadows on the stalagmites and dripstone formations of the Yugoslavian cave. It was 1689, and the villagers believed that dragons lived in the caves. Johann kept a sharp watch for the beasts.

He gazed around the damp cavern, as furtive creatures scuttled in the dark. A white shape caught his eye. He picked up his torch and knelt by a stream flowing from a crevasse. A small creature about a foot long waved its shovel-shaped snout at him. Its pale skin shimmered with moisture, and its feathered gills waved as it breathed.

Johann stared. "It's a dragon," he whispered. He studied the creature intently as it cautiously approached on tiny white legs. Johann Valvasor recorded the first discovery of *Proteus*, calling it "a new, pint-sized species of dragon."

Proteus, a blind amphibian of European caverns, breathes through feathery gills like a fish, has legs that look like little human arms, two-toed feet, and a long silky-white body. But *Proteus* isn't a weird fish or reptile, and certainly not a "dragon." It's a salamander.

While God gives blind salamanders everything they need to live underground—a metabolism that keeps them alive on a starvation diet, toes that grip slimy rock, and a specialized lung/gill system to breathe—He also provides them the means to survive above ground if necessary. When you raise baby blind salamanders above ground, they don't grow up white and blind. Instead, they become dark-colored and develop normal sight. God uses His creative power to provide for the salamanders in *all* circumstances!

Jane Chase

CLOSER TO GOD

Q: I am a 12-year-old boy, and my question is How can I get closer to God?

A: Ex-basketball superstar Michael Jordan and I aren't buddies or anything, but my hunch is that if you asked him how to be a better basketball player, he would tell you to master the basics.

The same principle is true if you want to improve your friendship with God. I still remember a sermon I heard four years ago in which the preacher answered your question of how to get closer to God. He suggested the STP treatment.

S–Study. You can get closer to God only if you take time each day to learn more about Him. Set aside time daily to study God's Word.

T–Tell others. You strengthen your spiritual muscles only with exercise. If you want to be closer to God, do things for others and share His love with them.

P–Pray. Again, it's back to the basics. If you want to get closer to someone, you have to talk with him or her. Take time daily to talk with God, and you will get closer to Him.

Karl Haffner

"I DON'T KNOW YOU"

Pastor Watson couldn't find his ticket. He'd looked in his coat pocket, pants pocket, suitcase, and briefcase. Then he remembered. At the hotel he'd placed it in a box he planned to carry onto the plane. But in the hustle and bustle of getting members of his youth group on their respective aircraft, he'd shipped the box on an earlier flight.

"I've made a mistake and sent my ticket to England," he told the agent at the counter. "If you'll look in your computer, you'll see that I'm supposed to be on the next flight to London."

The man nodded. "Your name is here. But that only means that you made a reservation."

Pastor Watson sighed. He was getting nowhere fast.

"Look, mister," said the agent sympathetically but firmly, "I don't know you. I don't know if you bought a ticket. Without one, you can't fly."

The young minister thought for a moment, then reached into his pocket and pulled out a program folder from the youth congress that had just taken place in the city. "I was one of the participants at this," he said, holding up the paper.

The agent's face lit up. "I heard about that congress. Say, do you happen to be a Seventh-day Adventist?"

"Yes," Watson responded.

"That's different," the agent said, reaching for a ticket form. "I've had Seventh-day Adventist young people working for me. They're honest and trustworthy. I know I can trust you, too."

Pastor Watson flew home to England lifted not only by the air under the wings but by the trustworthiness of Adventist young people he'd never met.

"MY FATHER'S HOUSE"

And the child grew and became strong; he was filled with wisdom, and the grace of God was upon him.

Every year his parents went to Jerusalem for the Feast of the Passover. When he was twelve years old, they went up to the Feast, according to the custom. After the Feast was over, while his parents were returning home, the boy Jesus stayed behind in Jerusalem, but they were unaware of it. Thinking he was in their company, they traveled on for a day. Then they began looking for him among their relatives and friends. When they did not find him, they went back to Jerusalem to look for him. After three days they found him in the temple courts, sitting among the teachers, listening to them and asking them questions. Everyone who heard him was amazed at his understanding and his answers. When his parents saw him, they were astonished. His mother said to him, "Son, why have you treated us like this? Your father and I have been anxiously searching for you."

"Why were you searching for me?" he asked. "Didn't you know I had to be in my Father's house?" But they did not understand what he was saying to them.

Then he went down to Nazareth with them and was obedient to them. But his mother treasured all these things in her heart. And Jesus grew in wisdom and stature, and in favor with God and men.

Luke 2:40-52

MANY ROOMS

I n my Father's house are many rooms." John 14:2.

The Seventh-day Adventist Osaka Evangelistic Center in downtown Osaka fairly vibrated with activity each and every weeknight. All of us student missionaries loved the energetic aura of the place. The something-is-always-happening feeling radiated from every doorway and down every hall.

My classes were mostly on the second floor where my students would practice saying the simple sentences I tossed their way again and again and again. "I'm going to town." *"I'm going to town."* "You." *"You're going to town."* "She." *"She's going to town."* "They." *"They're going to town."*

Such banter echoed throughout the second and third floors. Down in the auditorium, groups of students sat with earphones on their heads, repeating prerecorded words and phrases only they could hear.

In other rooms the sounds of pianos, guitars, and singing mixed with the muted bedlam as student missionaries and willing students prepared for upcoming Sabbath school and church musical specials. Add to all of this the occasional tap-tap-tap of a typewriter, jingling telephones, and bursts of laughter, and—well, you get the idea.

When I read John 14:2, I have no trouble visualizing the "many rooms" in my Father's heavenly mansion. My Father's house is no lonely palace filled with distant echoes and the creaking and groaning of decaying wood. It's a place of light and happiness, brimming with joyous activity and endless pleasant sounds. Listen. Can't you just hear it? "We're in heaven." *"We're in heaven."* "They." *"They're in heaven."* "She." *"She's in heaven."* "I." *"I'm in heaven."*

GIVING UP

Ageneration ago America was involved in a terrible foreign war. The fighting on the battlefield was intense and violent. Sometimes American soldiers found themselves completely surrounded and had to lay down their weapons and surrender.

One such soldier was Bob Heinrich. He and many others found themselves in a prisoner-of-war camp. Bob felt humiliated, helpless, homesick, and terribly lonely. So one day he sat down facing the wall in one corner of his cell, wrapped a blanket about him, and stayed there unmoving until he finally dropped over . . . dead.

Four out of every 10 American prisoners did exactly the same thing during this conflict. Many others cooperated with the enemy to save their skin! Why? Because, this particular war didn't have any goals or objectives. The men had no idea why they were fighting. They were just told to shoot their guns and fire their cannons and the next day do it some more.

The enemy didn't have to guard their prisoner-of-war camps very much. Few tried to escape. Others took Bob's way out of the war. On the other hand, Americans had a tough time keeping their prisoners in check. They tried to escape every chance they got. They had to have many more guards. You see, enemy prisoners knew what they were fighting for and wanted to get back to protecting their homeland.

You're a soldier in a war—a war between Christ and Satan. Take time to discover why your life is important to God and what He wants you to do while you're here on earth. Then if Satan takes you prisoner, you won't give up. You'll escape—*now!*

EXPRESSING FRIENDSHIP

Q: My name is Michael. I'm 11 years old. I go to church, and very often a girl comes to our church. I like her a lot, but don't know how to express it. I'm afraid if I do it the wrong way, she'll never like me. What should I do?

A: Girls can be tough to understand, can't they? But for starters, don't sweat too much about her never liking you simply because you expressed yourself in the wrong way. If a girl holds a lifelong grudge against you simply because one time you were awkward, she's not a whole lot more desirable than a piece of moldy cheese. I'm not sure you'd be interested in a girl like that anyway. So don't be afraid about slowly letting her know how you feel—even if it's not the "right" way.

There are dozens of ways to express interest in someone. For example, put a note in a fortune cookie and give it to her, share your favorite book with her, help her with homework, give her a couple 50-cent gift certificates for Baskin-Robbins, or write her a note and leave it on her desk with some M&Ms. The ways you can let others know you care about them are limitless.

Let me encourage you, however, not only to work toward showing this girl you care about her, but to make it a habit to show everyone that you care for them. You do that, and you'll never be hurting for friends—boys or girls.

Karl Haffner

JUMPING SNOW MAN

What about that one?" Harry de Leyer asked, pointing at a horse in the delivery truck.

The driver laughed. "I'm taking all these critters to the dog-food factory. Ain't none of them worth anything, if you ask me."

"But he's got his ears up and looks like he might be ambitious. Will you take $70?"

"Sold!"

So it was that Snow Man, a no-good horse destined for the dog-food factory, came to be the pet of Mr. Leyer's children. A year later a doctor made a nice offer for the animal, and it changed hands again. But not for long. "This horse keeps jumping my fences, no matter how high I build 'em. I want my money back!"

Mr. Leyer brought Snow Man home again, but on the way began to think. *Horses don't like jumping over things. But here's one that seems to enjoy it.*

Snow Man had no pedigree. No one knew who his father and mother were—important information in horse trading. But he could jump.

To make a long story short, Mr. Leyer trained Snow Man carefully and then entered him in the three biggest horse-jumping contests in the country. The animal won them all! At the end of the last show someone offered $100,000 for the horse, and Snow Man's story appeared in a national magazine.

Been feeling a little down on yourself lately? Report card a bit embarrassing? Strike out in the last baseball game? Hey, if a no-good horse can become a champion, what can you, a son or daughter of God, accomplish in your life?

BLACK AND WHITE

Q: Is God black or white?

A: Would it make a difference to you if He was one or the other? Think about it. And does it make any difference to Him whether you're black or white?

Fact is, we don't know what color God is, because we haven't seen Him. No human being has.

Jesus was born into a Jewish family. Jews usually have lighter skin tones, but some are darker than others, depending on the ancestral line.

So to the question "Is God black or white?" I'd have to answer, "Yes." He's also brown, and pink, and yellow, and golden. God's the color of all nations, all people, all boys and girls.

Consider this text: "And I will put my Spirit in you and move you to follow my decrees and be careful to keep my laws" (Ezekiel 36:27). It reminds me of the words to a song we've all sung many times. "Into my heart," we harmonize, inviting Jesus to take up residence in our lives. In this simple tune, not only do we ask our Saviour to come in "today," we also request that He come to "stay."

When you allow God to live in your heart, He becomes exactly the same color as you.

STRANGERS IN THE MUD

Mrs. Grayson grabbed her husband's arm as their car slid out of control and slammed into a ditch. Then all was silent.

Getting out to survey the damage, they saw mud oozing around the axles. Their predicament would be bad enough on a busy road. But it was a lonely part of Nigeria, Africa.

"I'll have to walk to Lassa," Mr. Grayson announced. "It's too far for you. You'll have to wait here."

"That's OK," his wife responded with a lot more confidence than she felt.

Soon after her husband left, night descended, filling her ears with the sounds of the jungle. A screech owl screamed. Hyenas moaned. Jackals barked.

Suddenly she heard voices. Flicking on the headlights, she noticed two men walking toward her. They paused by the car, asked who she was, then left. *What are they up to?* Mrs. Grayson wondered.

Soon the men returned, accompanied by two women carrying bundles of wood. The concerned missionary watched as her mysterious visitors spread blankets on the wet ground, lit the wood into a blazing fire, and sat down. "Come join us," they invited.

Timidly, Mrs. Grayson took her place by the fire and soon warmed to the friendliness of the group. "Who are you and why have you come to keep me company?" she asked.

"Three years ago your husband drove through our village and stopped to talk to us," one explained. "My little daughter was ill, and he took her in this car to a mission hospital, where she got well. We've been waiting to thank him."

And they did, all that lonely night.

WILD MAN OF JUDEA

In those days John the Baptist came, preaching in the Desert of Judea and saying, "Repent, for the kingdom of heaven is near." This is he who was spoken of through the prophet Isaiah: "A voice of one calling in the desert, 'Prepare the way for the Lord, make straight paths for him.'"

John's clothes were made of camel's hair, and he had a leather belt around his waist. His food was locusts and wild honey. People went out to him from Jerusalem and all Judea and the whole region of the Jordan. Confessing their sins, they were baptized by him in the Jordan River.

But when he saw many of the Pharisees and Sadducees coming to where he was baptizing, he said to them: "You brood of vipers! Who warned you to flee from the coming wrath? Produce fruit in keeping with repentance. And do not think you can say to yourselves, 'We have Abraham as our father.' I tell you that out of these stones God can raise up children for Abraham. The ax is already at the root of the trees, and every tree that does not produce good fruit will be cut down and thrown into the fire.

"I baptize you with water for repentance. But after me will come one who is more powerful than I, whose sandals I am not fit to carry. He will baptize you with the Holy Spirit and with fire. His winnowing fork is in his hand, and he will clear his threshing floor, gathering his wheat into the barn and burning up the chaff with unquenchable fire."

Matthew 3:1-12

CHRISTMAS CALL

For I am convinced that neither death nor life, neither angels nor demons, neither the present nor the future, nor any powers, neither height nor depth, nor anything else in all creation, will be able to separate us from the love of God that is in Christ Jesus our Lord. Romans 8:38, 39.

Christmas can be a lonely time for someone far from home. When that special day rolled around during my student missionary year in Japan, I picked up the phone and placed a transoceanic call to the little town of Collegedale, Tennessee, where my family lived and worked.

It was evening in Japan but morning in Tennessee when the phone rang in our house on Surrey Drive.

"Hello?"

"Dad? It's me."

"Well, hello, Charlie Boy! Let me call mother and Susie to the phone."

For 10 wonderful minutes we passed words of love and affection between countries, reminding one another of how much we missed being together. I didn't have to say, "Hey, Dad and Mom, do you still love me?" All of that was understood. Even though we were miles apart, our family bond was as strong as ever.

If we human beings can love from afar, don't you think that God is totally capable of loving us from His home in heaven?

After I hung up, I cried for a little while, not because I was sad, but because I was so happy to know that when my year in Japan was finished, I'd be going to a place where love waited, and where familiar voices and comforting arms would welcome me home.

TWO SUITCASES

C hile is a prosperous South American country filled with modern cities and rich farmland. But not long ago something happened under the earth that affected the lives of thousands of Chile's citizens, three of whom were named Don, Pedro, and Mr. Henrico.

Don and Pedro had heard about God's love from a preacher who also warned that our old world is getting more unstable as the time for Christ's return nears. Scientists had sent warnings about the tension building up between two giant earth plates running under their country. "They're pushing against each other," the researchers had said. "Something has to give."

When the earthquake struck, Don and Pedro rushed out of their house and were terrified to see buildings collapsing and a crack forming down their street.

Mr. Henrico was a wealthy man. When the ground began to tremble, he ran around his house collecting valuables and stuffing them into a suitcase. When one filled up, he grabbed another. Soon he was huffing and puffing toward the front door, trying to drag his two suitcases to safety. But there simply wasn't enough room for him and his possessions to slip through.

The town rested on the Pacific coast. The shaking ground emptied the beaches, but the water soon returned in the form of a giant wave that crashed down on the hapless man as he struggled to get out of his house. Don and Pedro saw it happen from higher ground. The boys shook their heads, remembering the words of the preacher, "What good is it for a man to gain the whole world, yet forfeit his soul?" (Mark 8:36).

How about *you?* Are you holding on to any suitcases?

SOCKS ON AN OCTOPUS

Q: I'm a 10-year-old boy. I like a girl who's in my class. I don't know if she likes me. I want to make her like me, but I don't know how. I know her pretty well, and I guess she knows me pretty well too.

But another boy in my class also likes her and is always getting in the way of things and showing off in front of her. Since he's there, it's going to be harder to get her to like me or even be with her, because he'll be in the way of things. I need help!

A: You're talking about doing something as difficult (or impossible!) as putting socks on an octopus. Case in point: You can't "make" somebody like you. Also, there's not much you can do to prevent the other boy from showing off. So with that in mind, let's talk a bit about how to at least control the octopus.

Don't try too hard! Sometimes show-offs work too hard to attract someone's attention, and it backfires. Give time a chance to let the situation settle. Take your time, and don't force anything—it won't work.

Also, concentrate on making and improving lots of friendships with lots of different guys and girls. I wouldn't advise focusing too much of your energy on one person. You may think that's what you want, only to discover later you have an unwanted octopus on your back!

Karl Haffner

INTRUDERS FROM OUTER SPACE

In 1954 Mrs. Hewlett Hodges was asleep on her couch when a deafening *boom!* shook her awake. She jumped to her feet and looked around. Something had ripped a round hole in the ceiling, the radio lay smashed on the floor, and among the debris from the roof lay a softball-sized rock.

When the woman bent to pick it up, she felt a pain in her left hip and hand. The rock was much heavier than she expected, and warm.

Specialists confirmed that a meteorite had hit her, but it was only a glancing blow. Before hitting her in the hip, the nine-pound meteorite had crashed through the roof and ceiling of her house and then bounced off her radio.

Anytime you walk across a field, down a trail, or along a mountain path, you are probably stepping on meteorites. That's because hundreds of thousands of them have been landing on the earth for thousands of years, and most of them haven't been found.

Most meteorites are asteroids that have strayed from their orbit between Mars and Jupiter. Others are actually pieces of Mars or the moon. When an asteroid hits one of these bodies, it throws rocks into space. The rocks get caught in Earth's gravitational pull and land on our planet.

One of the most spectacular meteorite showers took place on November 13, 1833. Experts estimate that 240,000 meteorites were visible in a nine-hour period. Seventh-day Adventists and many other Christians believe it was a direct fulfillment of Matthew 24:29, 30. Take a moment and read the texts and discover the truth about those intruders from outer space.

Jane Chase

GOD HEARS

Q: Why does it seem that sometimes when you pray, God doesn't hear you?

A: Because that's what the devil wants you to think. "You're not important enough for God," he'll whisper in your thoughts. "He's not interested in your stupid problems. And you're too sinful, or selfish, or mean. God listens to only nice people who say the right words and smile all the time."

Listen to what David—that's right, Mr. Giant-Killer himself—once prayed. "How long, O Lord? Will you forget me forever? How long will you hide your face from me? How long must I wrestle with my thoughts?" (Psalm 13:1, 2). Sounds as though he was having a slight communication problem as well.

But David finally overcame his doubt. He wrote: "Come and listen, all you who fear God; let me tell you what he has done for me. I cried out to him with my mouth; his praise was on my tongue. If I had cherished sin in my heart, the Lord would not have listened; but God has surely listened and heard my voice in prayer. Praise be to God, who has not rejected my prayer or withheld his love from me!" (Psalm 66:16-20).

It doesn't matter what the devil says. God hears every prayer from every mouth. And that includes yours and mine. As a matter of fact, God's even one up on you—"For your Father knows what you need before you ask him" (Matthew 6:8). How's that for hearing what you have to say?

So when you pray, ignore those feelings the devil tries to plant in your mind, and continue talking to your friend Jesus.

PREACHER IN CUT-DOWN CLOTHES

Johnn was 17 years old when he heard a minister proclaim that Jesus was coming soon. The teenager grabbed his Bible and looked up the texts. Sure enough, it was true!

"I'm going to go out and preach," the determined young man announced. Then he paused. "But I can't. I'm too sick."

That also was true. His sickness made him slow at whatever he did, so finding a job was next to impossible.

"I'm going to preach no matter what!" John stated emphatically. His determination made him feel better immediately. Then he paused again. "Wait. I don't have any money!"

A kindly neighbor heard of John's desire and offered him a job cutting wood. He could work as slowly as he needed to. No one would care, as long as the job got done. So John cut wood and managed to save a dollar.

"I don't have any preaching clothes," the teen moaned, studying the contents of his closet.

"Not to worry," the same neighbor announced. "With a little creative cutting and sewing, a pair of my trousers will fit you. I'll throw in a vest, too." John's brother lent him an overcoat, which he shortened into a suit jacket by cutting around the bottom.

That's how John Loughborough, a great Adventist pioneer, began his ministry. He went from town to town, preaching in cut-down clothes, telling anyone who would listen that Jesus was coming back soon. Hundreds believed and invited Christ into their lives.

In our day and age of high-tech satellite evangelism and Internet communications, it's still the *message of hope* we Adventists proclaim that catches ears and transforms hearts.

WATER AND A DOVE

Then Jesus came from Galilee to the Jordan to be baptized by John. But John tried to deter him, saying, "I need to be baptized by you, and do you come to me?"

Jesus replied, "Let it be so now; it is proper for us to do this to fulfill all righteousness." Then John consented.

As soon as Jesus was baptized, he went up out of the water. At that moment heaven was opened, and he saw the Spirit of God descending like a dove and lighting on him. And a voice from heaven said, "This is my Son, whom I love; with him I am well pleased."

Matthew 3:13-17

Many juniors ask, "Why do I need to be baptized? Isn't loving and obeying God enough?" If that were true, Jesus certainly didn't need to visit John by the Jordan. There wasn't a sin in His body, and His love for God was undeniably strong! He was baptized, not because he *needed* to, but because he *wanted* to. Jesus longed to show the people on the shore how much He loved His heavenly Father. He desired to demonstrate by this simple act that He was willing to live as God wanted Him to.

When we allow ourselves to be lowered under the waters, we're saying to the world, "I'm deciding to place my life in the hands of my heavenly Father. I'm choosing to be a part of His army of witnesses."

If you've been baptized, good for you! If you haven't yet, why not ask your pastor to do the honors? Join Jesus by the waters and make your choice today.

UPWARDLY MOBILE CLASS

Am I now trying to win the approval of men, or of God? Galatians 1:10.

"Hey, Charles, you wanna earn a few extra yen?"

"Sure. What do I have to do?"

"Teach English to a movie star."

Wow! Not only was I going to rack in some extra gas money for my much-used-and-abused Yamaha motorcycle, I was going to have the privilege of teaching classes to a roomful of corporate clients, one of whom was a model and much-admired movie star in Japan.

Have you ever heard the word "yuppie"? Although people don't use it as much anymore, it means "Young, upwardly mobile professional," and that certainly describes my added collection of students. These young men and women had one goal in mind—to make a million dollars before they turned 30.

You could see it in their eyes and hear it in their voices. They wanted to learn to speak English so that they could close big-ticket deals with American businesses. Each of them desired to have their pronunciation so perfect that they could compete head-to-head with U.S. competitors.

There's absolutely nothing wrong with wanting to be rich and working toward the goal *as long as* you remember that you've also got a life to live that must include family, friends, and God. This group didn't seem to have that concept in mind.

I often wonder what happened to them. I'm certain they won the approval of fellow human beings and probably made their millions, too. But did they remember the God I tried to introduce with my smile and encouraging words? Only time will tell.

DYING FOR THE KING

Leonard Woolley and his fellow diggers couldn't believe their eyes. There, lying in neat rows in the ancient tomb they'd just uncovered near the ancient city of Ur, were six men and 68 women. The women wore fine clothes and were decked out in expensive jewelry, their hair done up with colorful ribbons. It looked as if everyone were going to a party!

You might expect that people would fight tooth and nail when told they must get ready to be buried with their king. But they didn't run. They didn't hide. Instead, they got dressed up and gladly walked into the tomb, perfectly willing to be buried with the monarch.

Evidence showed that once everyone was in place in the tomb someone passed a powerful poison around. As the lethal drug took hold, they grew sleepy, lay down next to each other, and died.

Why? They thought their king was a god and would live forever in some other world beyond the grave, a world filled with happiness and peace. So they dressed up and drank their poison fully believing that they'd live again in Paradise.

They weren't totally wrong. There *is* a Paradise filled with happiness and peace. But those men and women followed the wrong king to the grave. He was just a man.

We know better. Our King, Jesus Christ, is the one true God. All who die with Him will live again in heaven. Yet many of us are still afraid of death and wonder what's beyond the grave.

Could it be that the pagans in Ur's royal tomb had more faith in their king than we have in ours?

GRUDGE HOLDER

Q: I'm 14 years old. There's a girl in my class that I really like, but she won't have anything to do with me because of something real stupid I said almost a year ago. I've told her I'm sorry, but that turned her off even more, and for some reason all the other girls won't have anything to do with me either.

I've tried hard to be nice to them, but it doesn't seem to matter. (I'm not considered one of the more "fine" guys in the class, nor the most energetic.) I need help bad!

A: I can relate. I was never one of the "fine" guys in my class either. I did discover, however, the ABCs of getting along with girls, and hope my suggestions will help you.

1. Avoid trying too hard. When guys are too eager, it turns girls off.

2. Be yourself. Someone once told me, "If you're a nerd, be a nerd, and people will like you." I have found this to be true. Don't try to impress this girl by pretending to be someone else. Be yourself.

3. Continue on. If this girl holds a grudge because of something you said in the past, that's her problem, not yours. You need to continue on with life and make the best of it. Don't dwell on the past; just keep going.

Karl Haffner

BIRD IN THE WALL

Ten-year-old Alex sat watching the builders working on his dad's new garage. They had poured the foundation the day before and were now cementing large cinder blocks into place.

Suddenly the boy saw a small bird land atop the unfinished wall and then drop out of sight. At that moment a workman carried a freshly prepared block to the spot, ready to slip it into place.

"Stop!" Alex called. "There's a bird in the wall!"

"What are you talking about, kid?" the man responded.

The two peered down between the freshly laid cinder blocks. Sure enough, a baby robin sat looking up at them from the foundation.

"Hey, Hank," the workman called. "See if you can reach down here and pull out this bird. My arm's too thick." But Hank's arm was too broad to fit between the blocks, too. Alex tried, but his arm was too short.

"Guess we'll just have to leave him there," the workman announced.

"No!" Alex blurted. "He'll die."

Everyone was standing around trying to come up with a solution when Alex brightened. "Sand," he gasped. "Please bring me some sand."

As the block layers watched, he carefully poured sand down the hole. The grains washed over the feathers of the baby bird and began forming a pile at its feet. Ever so slowly, the pile grew higher and higher as the bird lifted its legs to keep from being buried. In about an hour Alex was able to reach down and retrieve the helpless creature and return it to its mother.

Hey, grown-ups don't always have all the answers!

I STILL FEEL GUILTY

Q: I did something two years ago when I was 11 that I know was a sin. Nobody knows about it. I've asked God to forgive me a bunch of times, but I still feel guilty. Has God forgiven me?

A: Suppose you have a pet Saint Bernard named Bozo. Now suppose I run over Bozo in my Chevy 4 X 4 and kill him. Naturally I feel terrible and knock on your door and in tears tell you, "I've killed your pet. Can you forgive me?" You feel sad, but you understand that these things happen, and you say, "I forgive you." We bury Bozo and go our separate ways.

Now suppose that every night after that I feel so guilty that I get out of bed and go dig up Bozo and drag him to your front door and wake you up to tell you how sorry I am that I killed your dog. For a few nights you may tolerate it, but in time you'd probably bonk me on the head (or at least you'd want to!) in order to tell me you have forgiven me.

You didn't mention whether you wronged somebody else. If so, you may need to go to that person. But know this: God has forgiven and buried whatever sin you committed two years ago. Leave it buried.

Karl Haffner

CHICKENS' VERDICT

Now we'll find out who's responsible," Abu whispered to his friend Bella as they made their way to the chief's hut. "Our witch doctor understands secret things."

"The chief says it's the new teacher with his Jesus talk," Bella responded. "Our gods are angry and have destroyed our crops because we listened to him."

The whole village believed in the power of the witch doctor. If the teacher was to blame, they would punish him.

"Our gardens have dried up," announced the chief. Next to him sat the witch doctor and the missionary teacher. "I've asked our village shaman to find out whose fault it is."

The witch doctor, dressed in his finest attire, rose and held up a bag filled with dried bones. He mumbled mysterious words, then tossed the contents of the bag onto the ground. After studying the scattered bones, he moaned, "The gods will speak through a chicken."

Someone quickly brought a hen. With a flick of the wrist, the witch doctor sliced the head off the hapless fowl and then let its body run around on the ground. "Where it stops is where the blame must be placed," the shaman intoned.

The chicken ceased its flailing and dropped motionless before . . . the chief. A gasp escaped every throat. It couldn't be!

They quickly caught another chicken. It too met the same fate as the first. After running around, flapping its wings, it came to rest before . . . the chief.

The witch doctor, totally embarrassed and humiliated, slunk away into the night.

"The new teacher is right," Abu whispered. "Our gods have no power. I'm going to worship *his* God." And he did. So did Bella and the entire African village.

TEMPTATIONS!

Then Jesus was led by the Spirit into the desert to be tempted by the devil. After fasting forty days and forty nights, he was hungry. The tempter came to him and said, "If you are the Son of God, tell these stones to become bread."

Jesus answered, "It is written: 'Man does not live on bread alone, but on every word that comes from the mouth of God.'"

Then the devil took him to the holy city and had him stand on the highest point of the temple. "If you are the Son of God," he said, "throw yourself down. For it is written: 'He will command his angels concerning you, and they will lift you up in their hands, so that you will not strike your foot against a stone.'"

Jesus answered him, "It is also written: 'do not put the Lord your God to the test.'"

Again, the devil took him to a very high mountain and showed him all the kingdoms of the world and their splendor. "All this I will give you," he said, "if you will bow down and worship me."

Jesus said to him, "Away from me, Satan! For it is written: 'Worship the Lord your God, and serve him only.'"

Then the devil left him, and angels came and attended him.

Matthew 4:1-11

Did you notice that Satan tempted Jesus three ways? He tried to make Him doubt who He was, took advantage of His hunger, and pulled the ol' *I-will-make-You-rich* trick. Didn't work. Each time Jesus answered with "The Bible says . . ." That's how we should face temptations too.

GENEROUS HEARTS

And the people continued to bring freewill offerings morning after morning. So all the skilled craftsmen who were doing all the work on the sanctuary left their work and said to Moses, "The people are bringing more than enough for doing the work the Lord commanded to be done." Exodus 36:3-5.

The Seventh-day Adventist Osaka Center, busy enough during the week, seemed to fairly burst with activity whenever Sabbath rolled around—and for good reason. As student missionaries we hadn't left our colleges, universities, and homelands just to teach English. We had a much more important work to do. Each of us had come to Japan to share the love of God with those who sat before us in our daily classes.

The auditorium served as ground zero for our spiritual attack on the lies Satan had been telling a whole nation of wonderful people. We played the piano and organ, sang quartet, duet, and solo songs behind the microphones, showed pictures on the slide projector, passed out colorful Christian literature and freshly printed Bibles, pounded out sermons on the electric typewriters, played soft background music over the sound system, and enjoyed the comfortable pews in the cool air-conditioned room.

Like Moses' sanctuary in the desert, our little auditorium was filled to overflowing with evangelistic equipment made possible by the generous hearts of Japanese Adventists as well as loyal members of our church family from around the world. Without these tools, our outreach would have been less effective and more difficult to achieve.

When your church makes a special offering request, think of Moses in the desert and student missionaries far from home.

BROTHERS IN THE FIRE

Jack Bamford knew if he didn't act fast, his two brothers would die. "I'm going back in," he called as he ran toward their burning house before his parents could stop him. "I'll throw 'em out," he shouted, then disappeared into the billowing smoke.

Dad positioned himself below the second-story window and waited.

When Jack stumbled into the bedroom, he found the walls aflame and his little brothers clinging to each other, terror-struck. Coughing violently, barely able to see, Jack grabbed Roy and rushed to the window. "Catch!" he shouted to his dad and hurled the little form into space.

Turning to retrieve the other child, he was horrified to see that, crazy with fear, the youngster was running into the searing flames. Jack's shirt was on fire and his shoulders were badly burned and blistered, but he couldn't let his little brother die.

Running after him, he grabbed the trembling child and dragged him to the window. The father saw a second bundle drop in his direction. That left Jack alone in the house.

Swinging a leg over the windowsill, the brave 15-year-old prepared to lower himself away from the flames, but smoke overcame him. He slumped unconscious where he sat. For an agonizing moment, the burning body remained motionless. Then slowly, gravity pulled it from the window and sent it falling toward waiting arms. He eventually revived at the hospital.

Big brother Jack risked his life to save his siblings. Did they love him for his bravery? Oh yes! You have a Big Brother who gave His life to save you. Do you love Him for what He did? Tell Him so today.

NOT POPULAR

Q: I'm 12 years old and not very popular. I don't like who I am and wish I could be more like the other guys in my class. Can you help me?

A: It is very normal to feel inadequate at times. We all struggle with it—even the "other guys" in your class at times feel they aren't worth much.

Realize, first of all, that you have the potential to become whatever you want to—if you let God's power control you. Remember Moses? He had a speech problem and told God he wasn't good enough, but God used him to lead the Israelites. With God, it's your *avail*ability, not your ability, that counts. Make yourself available to God, and you will do something great in your life.

Finally, sometimes we don't like ourselves because we are preoccupied with ourselves. TV makes us feel inferior by telling us that our lives are not as exciting as those of celebrities. This is a lie. The best way to stop feeling sorry about your lot in life is to start putting others first.

Hang in there. God created you, He loves you, He cares about you, and He died for you. He loves you just as you are and not as you wish you could be.

Karl Haffner

CLIFF-HANGERS

Standing on top of the rocky cliff beside Niagara Falls, Professor Douglas Larson can see trees far below and the distant outline of the Toronto skyline. He makes sure his climbing harness is securely fastened, then lowers himself down the cliff face.

He picks his footing carefully as he works his way toward a small cedar tree. The tree is only a few feet tall, and its bare branches prove that it has been dead a long time. Small stones crumble from beneath the botanist's feet during his descent. As he edges around a jutting boulder, he keeps a wary watch for bobcats and snakes.

Then the tree is within reach. Bracing his feet against the cliff wall, Larson pulls out a small collapsible saw. He slices a round disk, called a cookie, from the trunk. He slips the saw and cookie into his pack and climbs back to safety.

It's all in a day's work when you're studying the cedars of the cliffs.

When cedars live on flat sod they grow 50 feet in 90 years—a normal growth rate for a cedar. But when they sprout on the rocky cliffs, they become the slowest-growing trees in the world. When Professor Douglas Larson cut the first slice off the trunk of a dead tree and took it to his laboratory to study, he discovered these cedars are like no other trees in the world. They grow more slowly and have a root system that is completely unique.

Sometimes God hides amazing mysteries in the most ordinary places. Who knows what wondrous things are still waiting to be discovered, even in your own backyard?

Jane Chase

PETS IN HEAVEN

Q: Will our animals go to heaven?

A: People and animals were never supposed to be separated. In Eden God told Adam: "Rule over the fish of the sea and the birds of the air and over every living creature that moves on the ground" (Genesis 1:28). "[God] brought [the animals] to the man to see what he would name them; and whatever the man called each living creature, that was its name" (Genesis 2:19).

Not only did the Creator ask Adam to care for the animals, He even let him name each and every one of them! God was not just forming a passing relationship between people and nature—He designed it to be an everlasting bond.

Sin really messed things up. It created enemies where there used to be friends, distrust where there had been harmony, and introduced to both human being and beast the most heartbreaking result of evil—separation from God through death.

I still miss a dog I had when I was a kid. His name was Toodles. A fox terrier-beagle mix, he was my best friend in all the world. Now he lives only in memory and fading photographs.

I believe that someday, when God has wiped sin from the universe and Eden has been restored as the Bible promises, the everlasting people-animal bond will be reestablished, and my little Toodles will run by my side through the meadows and mountains of the new earth. No, I have no Bible text to prove it one way or the other. But since God says He's preparing a home for me, He's got to know what I long to have waiting at the front door of my heavenly mansion. And God can do anything.

SWORD AGAINST SWORD

Adelina and Marta, two teens living in Central America, had to make a decision. Would they defy their parents and keep attending church? They were learning about a God who loved them, and they didn't want to miss a meeting. Father warned that if they went again, he'd beat them. But hadn't Jesus faced persecution too? Could they do any less to show their love for their Saviour?

Night after night they went. And night after night they were beaten. Before long they couldn't even sit down at the meetings, their legs so badly bruised by the impact of the dull side of their father's machete.

"We want to be baptized," they told the minister. "But don't tell our parents."

"They must know," the preacher explained. "It wouldn't be right without their knowledge."

When he and the girls stood before the father, the man was furious. "If you baptize my daughters," he said, "you'll feel this!" He held up the sharp end of his machete.

Adelina and Marta went to the baptism. So did their parents. So did the machete. When the minister raised his hand to begin the service, the father raised the knife. "Heavenly Father," the preacher prayed, "help this man to know Thee."

The angry visitor's hand began to tremble as he watched his first daughter lowered under the water. Suddenly his arm fell to his side, and the machete splashed harmlessly into the river. Unmoving, he watched his second daughter dip under the waves, touched by her determination.

Eventually he and his wife also joined God's church. The Sword of Truth had faced the sword of vengeance. Truth won. It always does.

REJECTED!

Jesus] went to Nazareth, where he had been brought up, and on the Sabbath day he went into the synagogue, as was his custom. And he stood up to read. The scroll of the prophet Isaiah was handed to him. Unrolling it, he found the place where it is written:

"The Spirit of the Lord is on me, because he has anointed me to preach good news to the poor. He has sent me to proclaim freedom for the prisoners and recovery of sight for the blind, to release the oppressed, to proclaim the year of the Lord's favor."

Then he rolled up the scroll, gave it back to the attendant and sat down. The eyes of everyone in the synagogue were fastened on him, and he began by saying to them, "Today this scripture is fulfilled in your hearing."

All spoke well of him and were amazed at the gracious words that came from his lips. "Isn't this Joseph's son?" they asked.

Jesus said to them, "Surely you will quote this proverb to me: 'Physician, heal yourself! Do here in your hometown what we have heard that you did in Capernaum.'"

"I tell you the truth," he continued, "no prophet is accepted in his hometown.". . .

All the people in the synagogue were furious when they heard this. They got up, drove him out of the town, and took him to the brow of the hill on which the town was built, in order to throw him down the cliff. But he walked right through the crowd and went on his way.

Luke 4:16-30

GOD OF THE HEART

But will God really dwell on earth? The heavens, even the highest heaven, cannot contain you. How much less this temple I have built!" 1 Kings 8:27.

When King Solomon dedicated his new Temple to God, he made a comment in his dedication prayer that reminds me of something I learned while serving as a student missionary.

Solomon wondered that if the heavens can't contain God, how could his lowly, human-made Temple ever hope to house the King of the universe? Then, just a few verses later, he spoke these beautiful words: "Hear the supplication [prayers] of your servant and of your people Israel when they pray toward this place. Hear from heaven, your dwelling place, and when you hear, forgive" (verse 30).

The truth of the matter is that God doesn't require a sanctuary or temple or church or mountaintop in order to dwell with us. He just needs us.

Occasionally our Japanese students would invite us to their homes for a visit. Or maybe we'd head out to an interesting restaurant. We told jokes, kidded one another, and basically acted silly trying to communicate in the language they were trying to understand. But they were also watching us, seeing how we reacted to different situations, slowly learning about our God through our words and actions.

One young person said to me, "You teachers are different. You seem to care about us. We like that."

That's why student missionaries dedicate themselves to God. They know He longs to dwell not only in evangelistic centers, but in hearts as well—including yours.

SLEEPING IN A SMOKESTACK

Thomas staggered out of the club. The night air felt cool on his face but didn't do enough to clear his beer-soaked brain. He wanted to go home, but where exactly *was* home?

Weaving down the street, he grew weary. "I gotta find a place to sleep," he told himself.

Seeing an open doorway, he shuffled through. In the darkness, he found another doorway, this one much smaller, and crawled into a confined space. "Got the whole place to myself," he triumphed, closing the door behind him. In moments he was snoring loudly.

Toward morning Thomas awoke with a start. What was that smell? Strange noises surrounded him, and a mysterious glow seemed to be illuminating one end of his enclosure. More alarming than that was the stream of burning, hissing air rushing past him, getting hotter by the second.

He tried the little door, but it was locked. The only way of escape seemed to be . . . up! A metal ladder led to a distant light. Reaching the top, he stuck his head out of what he discovered to be a smokestack! Below was the train station serving his town. Then he understood. The hot blast rushing by was coming from the coal-burning furnace used to heat the terminal.

He caught the attention of a workman who quickly instructed him that the only way to escape was out the little door far below.

The ladder blistered his hands and hot air seared his lungs as he descended. By the time he scrambled out the now-unlocked entrance, an ambulance was waiting. At the hospital doctors heard him saying, "No more beer. No more beer!"

Better late than never!

INTERFAITH RELATIONSHIP

Q: I am 12 years old. I am real good friends with a Mennonite girl. I feel that she is the right girl for me. But I don't know if she feels that way toward me.

A: I would be cautious regarding a couple things. First of all, I am assuming you are not of the Mennonite faith. If this is true, I encourage you to be careful of getting into any serious long-term relationship with someone of another faith. Most serious interfaith relationships just don't work. You certainly want to remain friends and should work on becoming better friends with her, but if you are talking about a lifelong commitment, that's something different. I suggest extreme caution.

The second area of concern involves her being "the right girl." I think there are many right girls for you. In time you will meet one of them and eventually wish to settle down. Don't be in too big a hurry. Enjoy lots of friendships with lots of girls. Don't rush it. One of the right ones will come along at the right time. But that's much later. For now, keep getting to know lots of girls.

Karl Haffner

AMAZING ARACHNIDS

If you've ever been tempted to drop a spider down a friend's neck, wait. These critters are much more interesting to watch in the wild.

The wolf spider becomes a school bus when her eggs hatch. She takes the children everywhere she goes, letting them off only for a drink by a stream.

Fisher spiders sit on riverbanks with two legs stretched forward on the water. When a small fish swims by, they plunge in, grab their prey, and haul it up on shore. (They probably lie about its size to their friends, too.)

Raft spiders sew leaves together and go boating down a river, getting off whenever they see something to eat.

Jumping spiders sneak up on their prey, then leap catlike upon it. Crab spiders change color. Spitting spiders wait until a fly comes near, then spit a sticky gum all over it. Cowboy spiders put a blob of glue on the end of a short piece of silk, then twirl it over their heads and lasso passing moths.

Mating is pretty dangerous for male spiders. If they aren't careful, the female may invite them over for a meal in which they become the main course. Yuck!

Web spinning is incredible to watch. If you're fortunate, you might see a spider spinning its delicate trap in the woods by your house. Toss in a grasshopper or fly and watch the webmaster go to work.

Spiders aren't the terrible creatures most people think they are. God gave them amazing abilities. But you won't see any of them if you drop them down someone's neck!

FUTURE SINNERS

Q: How did God know before Adam and Eve were born that they were going to sin?

A: God knows everything. Somehow He can peek into the future. How? I haven't a clue.

But don't forget some of the other things God knew before Adam and Eve were born—things terrifying and sad. The Father saw His precious Son suffering from hunger and loneliness on earth. He watched Him ridiculed and rejected, tormented and hurt. And imagine the horror He felt as visions of Christ's death filled His perfect, sinless mind.

Yet knowing what He did, He went ahead and created Adam and Eve anyway. Why? Because He wanted *you* to live with Him forever in heaven. That's right. The same powerful eyes that could see what sin would do also witnessed what the plan of salvation was capable of. And by peering just a little further into the future, God saw you and me running up to Him in heaven to thank Him for allowing us the opportunity to live forever.

"For God so loved the world, that he gave his only begotten Son, that whosoever believeth in him should not perish, but have everlasting life" (John 3:16, KJV).

God knew before we were born that *we* were going to sin. But He also knew how lonely He'd feel without us in His kingdom. So here we are, struggling with this old world because God peeked into the future and saw how happy we'd be living with Him in heaven.

TIRED BULLETS

Missionaries do a *lot* of traveling. It's part of their job. Sometimes what's going on within the country affects the journey. Such was the case when Kimber's dad found himself on an old Douglas DC-6 aircraft flying between the island of Singapore and Saigon, the capital of South Vietnam.

A war raged below. Saigon happened to be the prime target of enemy forces this particular night as the missionary's airplane lumbered through the hot, humid air. Weeks before, ground fire had hit a commercial jetliner, knocking out an engine, but the plane had managed to reach the safety of the airport. Kimber's father knew the DC-6 flew lower and slower than the jet!

Just as the pilot radioed the tower for permission to land, enemy forces on the ground began firing up at the plane. Machine guns clattered. Tracer bullets streaked upward like fingers of fire reaching out to catch the aircraft. All that Kimber's dad could do was sit and watch as the deadly bullets approached closer and closer.

Then a strange thing happened. Even though the plane was low, the bullets seemed to grow tired and fade away before they reached it. When the pilot botched the first landing, they had to go around and try another approach. More machine guns. More bullets. But this time the enemy soldiers couldn't seem to aim straight, and their shots veered off in wild angles. Soon they simply gave up.

When the airplane's wheels chirped onto the pavement, pilot and passengers breathed prayers of thanksgiving. Those bullets weren't the only tired things in Saigon that night.

DEMONS!

Then he went down to Capernaum, a town in Galilee, and on the Sabbath began to teach the people. They were amazed at his teaching, because his message had authority.

In the synagogue there was a man possessed by a demon, an evil spirit. He cried out at the top of his voice, "Ha! What do you want with us, Jesus of Nazareth? Have you come to destroy us? I know who you are—the Holy One of God!"

"Be quiet!" Jesus said sternly. "Come out of him!" Then the demon threw the man down before them all and came out without injuring him.

All the people were amazed and said to each other, "What is this teaching? With authority and power he gives orders to evil spirits and they come out!" And the news about him spread throughout the surrounding area.

Jesus left the synagogue and went to the home of Simon. Now Simon's mother-in-law was suffering from a high fever, and they asked Jesus to help her. So he bent over her and rebuked the fever, and it left her. She got up at once and began to wait on them.

When the sun was setting, the people brought to Jesus all who had various kinds of sickness, and laying his hands on each one, he healed them. Moreover, demons came out of many people, shouting, "You are the Son of God!" But he rebuked them and would not allow them to speak, because they knew he was the Christ.

Luke 4:31-41

TREASURES IN THE DUST

But your dead will live; their bodies will rise. You who dwell in the dust, wake up and shout for joy. Your dew is like the dew of the morning; the earth will give birth to her dead. Isaiah 26:19.

One warm summer day a group of us student missionaries from Osaka decided to pay a visit to our coworkers in the city of Hiroshima. So we jumped on our motorcycles and headed west along the North Pacific Ocean.

Hiroshima is a beautiful city filled with hardworking people and friendly smiles. But on August 6, 1945, the world's first atomic bomb exploded over its peaceful streets and canals, instantly killing thousands. Many simply vanished in the brilliant flash of the bomb.

There's a park near where the weapon exploded. In the park we found a large, heavy iron bell. One by one, we rang it and listened as its low, sad tone echoed out across the peaceful park and drifted among the branches of the trees. So many people. So many lives. So much humanity hidden in Isaiah's dust.

As I stood there I imagined another event that will someday rock that city. This time it won't be a bomb exploding, but a King returning. The dust will give up its hidden treasures, and those so long vanished will reappear to welcome their Saviour.

During our ride to Osaka, we each determined to double our efforts to spread the wonderful news that Jesus is coming back to gather His righteous from the rubble of sin. Praise God for that blessed hope!

BACKWARDS BOB

Bob Namwen did everything backwards. He even spelled his name that way. In reality, he was the son of the town's bank manager, Mr. Ralph Newman. Get it?

Bob dressed backwards. His tie hung down his backbone. His winter cap pointed the opposite direction than everyone else's, and his coat hung closed in the front, open in the back.

He ate backwards, too, holding spoons and forks by the wrong end. When friends said, "Hey, Bob, you're doing that wrong," he'd get angry and tell them to mind their own business.

Things were going pretty good for Bob until one day he tried to drive his father's car—backwards. He took out the front seat and installed a kitchen stool so he could swivel around and face where he'd been. With one hand he gripped the steering wheel and with the other, positioned a mirror by his face so he could see where he was supposed to go. Then he stretched a leg back to the accelerator and headed for McDonald's.

At an intersection he got all mixed up. Which way should he go? Is right really right or is right left in the mirror? That's when he also discovered he couldn't reach the brake pedal, drove off the road, and wrecked his whole day.

Silly story, huh? No one would be that foolish! Well, you haven't met Scott.

Scott knows what the Bible says about stealing and dishonoring his parents, yet he does both. Or Jessica? Although she has read in the Bible about guarding what enters her mind, still she watches filth on television. Tyler understands how important Bible reading is, but he'd rather cruise the Internet.

Kind of like driving backwards.

DISRESPECTFUL HABIT

Q: I am a boy 11 years old. I am very disrespectful to my mom, and it is a habit. How do I stop being disrespectful?

A: Habits are difficult to break—but not impossible. In fact, bad habits are made to be broken! So how do you do it?

First of all, keep a small notepad handy and after a clash with your mom jot down the events that occurred just before the blowup. Just by being more aware of the situations leading up to the event, you can often prevent it from happening.

Sometime when you and your mom are both in a good mood, sit down and talk openly about your habit of showing her disrespect. Discussing it with her will probably be the most helpful thing you can do. I think you'll find her to be quite understanding if you are sincerely trying to show her more respect.

Don't give up if you temporarily fall back into your old habit. Hang in there and keep working at it.

Finally, think of the rewards of forming a new habit of respect toward your mother. A helpful text you may wish to memorize is Ephesians 6:1-3: "Children, obey your parents; this is the right thing to do because God has placed them in authority over you. Honor your father and mother. This is the first of God's Ten Commandments that ends with a promise. And this is the promise: that if you honor your father and mother, yours will be a long life, full of blessing" (TLB).

Karl Haffner

"AUTO" MIRACLES

Fasten your seat belts! Here's a couple *mis*adventures from thankful juniors.

Last winter we were in a rainstorm on our way to visit my aunt Sharon. My dad was driving my mom's Volkswagen convertible. Suddenly Dad ran over a large puddle of water and, since we were moving about 55 miles per hour, the car did something that my dad calls "hydroplaning." This means that our car started to float over the road on a layer of water.

Dad lost control, and we skidded to the middle of the road, then started spinning around. We went over the edge of the road and down into a ditch. Our car was facing backward when we stopped. We thank God that the car did not roll over or get damaged in any way.

Andy Murray,
10, California

One dark night my mom and I were on our way home from the truck stop where my mom parked her truck. When we got to an intersection, an old white station wagon driven by a drunk driver rammed into us. I was lying on the back seat with my head about two inches from the door. The car hit the door where my head was. If I'd been any closer, I'd be dead.

The Lord works in everyone's life in different ways. I'm glad that God sent one of His angels to be with me. Someday I want to be one of His angels, too.

Teneira Pressly,
14, California

PK PROBLEM

Q: I'm a pastor's kid, but I don't feel like it. Ever since I was baptized, I've been meaner than ever to my brothers! I want to do what's right, but it seems that I keep doing wrong. What should I do?

A: Have you read the book *P.K. the Great?* The main character was a preacher's kid who wanted to prove that he was the greatest. Like lots of pastors' kids, he probably felt pressured to be smarter, more spiritual, and nicer than everybody else. Fortunately, the story has a happy ending. Yours can too.

Maybe you're thinking that baptism suddenly makes us into good people. But it's not the *baptism* itself that changes us. It's the *relationship* with our friend Jesus. Only He can transform us into the kind of people He wants us to be.

What's the secret of a changed life? Tell God you're sorry for the way you've acted toward your brothers and that you *want* to change. Trust Him to give you the power. Ask for it, believe He will give it, and claim it. Remember, we can't change ourselves. If we could, why would we need God?

Art and Pat Humphrey

WATER WALKER

Mrs. Mable Hillock, a missionary to India, witnessed an event that only deepened her determination to spread the Word of God throughout that country.

It seems that a Yogi (someone who practices the art of Yoga) announced throughout Bombay that he was going to walk on water. Expensive tickets for the great event went on sale, and 500 people bought them.

On the promised day ticket holders crowded into an auditorium and sat looking down at an above-ground pool that had been prepared for the Yogi. He soon appeared to thunderous applause and warmed up the spectators by swallowing some broken glass followed by a plate of iron tacks. He finished his meal with a refreshing drink of nitric acid and then strolled barefooted across a bed of burning coals.

All eyes watched as he prepared for the main event—walking on water. The Yogi climbed over the side of the pool and stepped into the water. Notice the word "into." He stood up to his neck in the pool and proceeded to amble slowly through the water to the other side.

What was going on? Anyone can do that! "What happened?" someone shouted. The Yogi shook his head. "I fell yesterday and broke my right thigh," he said. "Now I can't hold enough air in my body to make myself lighter than the water."

Here's the amazing part. No one complained! They all seemed satisfied with his answer and were happy to have witnessed the Yogi enjoying his strange meal and walking on burning coals.

Ignorance—that's one of the greatest enemies of the good news of salvation. Remove ignorance, and Christianity begins to make a lot of sense.

THE CALL

As Jesus was walking beside the Sea of Galilee, he saw two brothers, Simon called Peter and his brother Andrew. They were casting a net into the lake, for they were fishermen. "Come, follow me," Jesus said, "and I will make you fishers of men." At once they left their nets and followed him.

Going on from there, he saw two other brothers, James son of Zebedee and his brother John. They were in a boat with their father Zebedee, preparing their nets. Jesus called them, and immediately they left the boat and their father and followed him.

Jesus went throughout Galilee, teaching in their synagogues, preaching the good news of the kingdom, and healing every disease and sickness among the people. News about him spread all over Syria, and people brought to him all who were ill with various diseases, those suffering severe pain, the demon-possessed, those having seizures, and the paralyzed, and he healed them. Large crowds from Galilee, the Decapolis, Jerusalem, Judea and the region across the Jordan followed him.

Matthew 4:18-25

How do you know if Jesus has "called" you to work for Him? First of all, God has something for everyone to do for Him. Everyone. So don't sit around waiting for a voice from heaven to tell you to get busy.

Second, God does not ask us all to do the same work. He gave you skills to develop, talents to refine, and desires to fulfill. You want to be a firefighter? Great. Be a *Christian* firefighter. See yourself as a biologist? Fine. Be a *Christian* biologist. That's all it takes to answer the call.

FALSE GODS

K ing Nebuchadnezzar made an image of gold, ninety feet high and nine feet wide, and set it up on the plain of Dura in the province of Babylon. Daniel 3:1.

Golden images—a fairly common sight in long-ago Babylon—are also a fairly common sight in Japan today. While no one gets thrown into a fiery furnace for not bowing down to them (a welcome fact that has saved more than one student missionary's neck), these great likenesses still demand respect and homage from those who believe in their supposed power.

Several such images resided in the lovely city of Kyoto, not far from our home in Kobe. These large, rather well-fed-looking "Buddhas" sat solemnly in tall wooden buildings surrounded by tinkling bells and white-robed monks. The faithful would come each day, stand before the lifeless statues, clap their hands together, and bow in prayer, asking for health, prosperity, and guidance. The images sat and stared down at the visitors with lifeless eyes, just as they had for centuries.

Student missionaries in every part of the world know that their first job is to shift the gaze of their friends and students from the lifeless faces of such creations. A favorite song, one that we sang often, contained an invitation for everyone to turn their eyes upon Jesus and look full in *His* wonderful face. Only one God has *real* power.

Shadrach, Meshach, and Abednego understood that God wasn't in Nebuchadnezzar's image, and they were willing to face the punishment for refusing to bow down to it. Imagine their surprise when they found God in the fire!

RESCUE AT SEA

T hey won't see us," Mike shouted. "Even if they did, they won't stop in a storm like this."

Nicolas ignored his friend and kept waving, hoping against hope that someone on the British Navy tanker would notice his desperate plea for help.

Earlier that day Mike and two fishing partners had headed across the calm Mediterranean Sea in search of a good catch. They had been caught in a sudden storm. Crushing waves had destroyed their boat. Now it looked as if the giant swells would claim their lives. That's when they saw the lights of the tanker.

A call echoed from the lookout. "Strange object in the water, sir," the watchman announced. "Looks like a man waving."

Bells rang in the engine room as the captain ordered, "All stop!" Searchlights flickered on as the ship twisted and turned in the heaving seas. Mike and Nicolas saw ropes falling toward them and heard shouts of encouragement high overhead. In minutes they were safe.

But the doomed boat had had *three* fishers. The third man was too weak to respond to his rescuers. "I'm going after him," the captain called out. He and another sailor leaped into the waves, found the floundering victim, and skillfully brought him back to safety. "No captain in the queen's navy is afraid of personal risk when another man's life is in danger," the brave commander told his men.

Sound familiar? Listen to these amazing words: "Rarely will anyone die for a righteous man, though for a good man someone might possibly dare to die. But God demonstrates his own love for us in this: While we were still sinners, Christ died for us" (Romans 5:7, 8).

WRITER'S CRAMP

Q: I'm 14, and I've been writing to lots of girls for a couple years, but now I want to stop writing to some of them. The problem: I don't want to hurt any of their feelings. Can I stop writing to them and yet not be rude?

About a month ago I wrote a letter to one girl and mentioned I was writing to some other girls. When she wrote back, she called me a rude name. She comes from a divorced family.

A: First of all, yes, I think you can stop writing to some of the girls and not be rude. I've found it works best to be honest and straightforward with people. Tactfully explain why you can no longer write as much. If you're open and direct, yet gentle and sensitive, my hunch is they'll understand.

The girl who became angry because she discovered you were writing to other girls strikes me as being possessive of you. She is uncomfortable with you developing other friendships with girls because she probably fears you will opt for other friends and leave her hanging (and hurting). The fact that she comes from a divorced family tells me that she has seen abandonment and rejection firsthand. That helps me understand why she would respond to you in a possessive manner.

I don't see any problem with continuing to write her. Like my dad used to tell me—have lots of friends.

Karl Haffner

BARREL IN THE BASEMENT

What's that?" Kisha asked, pointing at a mysterious barrel resting in the basement.

Mother glanced up from her unpacking. "Oh, just something the previous owners of the house forgot to take. They'll probably pick it up later."

Kisha nodded and loaded her arms with sheets and pillowcases for a trip upstairs. Moving was a hassle. She'd be glad when all the boxes scattered about their new home were empty and life could get back to normal again.

During the days that followed, the little family discovered that some of their clothes were beginning to have little holes in them, such as Kisha's favorite wool skirt. "Moths!" Dad gasped. "We've got moths." Those little critters began to cost the family a great deal of money as they attacked the couch fabric and garments hanging in closets.

"Where are they coming from?" Mother moaned.

One day Kisha and her mom were in the basement storing some boxes when they saw a moth flit out of the barrel. "Daddy, come quick," Mother called. "We need to see what's in that barrel."

When the man opened the container, hundreds of moths rose in a brown cloud. Inside the barrel was an old woolen coat, a breeding ground for the destructive pests. When they removed the coat and barrel, the moth problem vanished.

It doesn't do us any good to change our bad habits when there's sin in the basement of our hearts. Some juniors spend their lives doing repairs to their reputations but never facing the cause of the damage. If something's hiding in your heart, confess it. Clean it out. Then allow Jesus to transform you into a new person. Go ahead. Lose the barrel!

HEAVENLY BABIES

Q: In heaven, will people still have babies?

A: One day a group of men asked Jesus a difficult question. They intended it to make Him look foolish, but the situation ended up the other way around.

They reminded Christ of an ancient law Moses wrote requiring that when a man's brother died and left a wife with no children, he was supposed to marry the grieving widow.

"Let's say," they suggested, "that the man had seven brothers, and one by one each died right after marrying the widow, leaving the next brother to take his place, exactly as Moses directed."

Wow. Talk about a streak of bad luck!

"Then," they pressed, "after all the brothers had married the woman and died, she dies too. At the resurrection, whose wife will she be, since all seven were married to her?"

Jesus answered their question—and yours. "Are you not in error because you do not know the Scriptures or the power of God?" He asked them in Mark 12:24. "When the dead rise, they will neither marry nor be given in marriage; they will be like the angels in heaven" (verse 25).

The answer to your question is no. But keep in mind another statement from God's Holy Book. "No eye has seen, no ear has heard, no mind has conceived what God has prepared for those who love him" (1 Corinthians 2:9). As exciting as having a baby may be, heaven holds even greater mysteries—and joys.

KISS OF PARDON

Evangeline Booth stood outside the courthouse watching the prisoners leave. Presently she heard screaming and cursing and saw guards dragging a woman through the door. Her face was contorted in fear, her hair matted and dirty. Torn clothes hung from her narrow shoulders. The woman had just been convicted and was being carted off to prison.

What could be done for her? Evangeline knew she had no time to preach a sermon or give her money or even sing. On impulse, she rushed over to the smelly, filthy, cursing woman and kissed her.

"Who did that?" the prisoner cried out. "Who kissed me? No one has kissed me since my mother died!" Then she lifted her tattered apron to her face and burst into tears. Like a gentle lamb, she let the officers lead her away.

Days later Miss Booth went to the prison to visit her. There she learned the whole tragic story. "When I was a baby, my father died," the woman told her. "When I was 7, my mother and I were living in the slums when she fell ill. On her deathbed, she took my face in her hands and said, 'My poor little girl. O God, have pity on my little girl and look after her when I'm gone.' Then she kissed me and died."

Evangeline explained that God loved her so much that He went to the cross and bore her sins so that He could put the kiss of pardon on every sinner's face. The woman, touched by Miss Booth's kindness and God's undying affection, gave her heart to Jesus.

JESUS' WEDDING MIRACLE

Awedding took place at Cana in Galilee. Jesus' mother was there, and Jesus and his disciples had also been invited to the wedding. When the wine was gone, Jesus' mother said to him, "They have no more wine."

"Dear woman, why do you involve me?" Jesus replied. "My time has not yet come."

His mother said to the servants, "Do whatever he tells you."

Nearby stood six stone water jars, the kind used by the Jews for ceremonial washing, each holding from twenty to thirty gallons.

Jesus said to the servants, "Fill the jars with water"; so they filled them to the brim.

Then he told them, "Now draw some out and take it to the master of the banquet."

They did so, and the master of the banquet tasted the water that had been turned into wine. He did not realize where it had come from, though the servants who had drawn the water knew. Then he called the bridegroom aside and said, "Everyone brings out the choice wine first and then the cheaper wine after the guests have had too much to drink; but you have saved the best till now."

This, the first of his miraculous signs, Jesus performed at Cana in Galilee. He thus revealed his glory, and his disciples put their faith in him.

John 2:1-11

If you ever doubt God's feelings about marriage, just remember where Jesus performed His first miracle! By the way, some say Jesus created alcoholic wine when He changed the water. Alcohol requires fermentation. Fermentation is a fancy word for "rotten." Do you think Jesus would ever create something rotten?

DREAMS, HOLIDAYS, AND PAGES

Listen to these hopeful words written by a future student missionary:

We're living in a dream of sadness, living like there's no tomorrow. But that's not true. Yes, our world will end, but when it does, God will come to earth and take us home to where He lives, and we'll be with Him. In heaven life will be like living a wonderful dream, but instead of waking up in your bedroom, you'll find yourself in a more beautiful place than your wildest dreams can comprehend.

Let me put it this way. Say you're not too good at school. Living here is like going to school, but living with God is like the best summer holiday ever, one that goes on and on forever. Can you beat that?

Here's another idea. The story of our lives, which we're living now, is only the beginning of a book that's filled with joy and happiness. Each chapter is more beautiful than the one before. This book goes on forever. Our life and adventures here on earth are only the cover page! God will come to get us, and when He does we'll live the rest of the book. There will be joy, peace, no sin, no sadness, no death, and eternal life.

So when in doubt, just remember that this school term will end and the holidays will begin. This bad dream will vanish, and Jesus will come and start turning the pages of our life.

Meghann Lyons,
grade 5, Canada

STICKY SITUATION

Mr. Thomson wanted to go home, but was too sleepy. The day at the factory had seemed endless. The last thing he wanted to do was drive while fighting drowsiness.

"I'll catch a quick nap," he said to himself as he looked around for a place to stretch out. "Then I'll be much safer."

He discovered several sheds right behind the factory. Feeling his way into one of them, he groped for a level place. "Here," he yawned as his hands felt what seemed to be a tabletop. "This is perfect."

With a sigh, Mr. Thomson lowered himself onto the flat surface and folded his hands above his stomach. "This table even seems soft," he mumbled. Then, with another lung-expanding yawn, he drifted into sleep.

Two hours later he awoke. Yes, he felt better. Now he could drive home. He started to get up, then stopped. He couldn't raise his head, or his arms, or his legs! Some unseen force held him tightly to his makeshift bed.

"Help!" he repeatedly called.

Finally, someone appeared at the door. "I'm stuck!" Mr. Thomson explained.

The man disappeared and soon returned with several others who had flashlights. They shone their beams on the hapless napper, then gasped. Mr. Thomson had fallen asleep atop a container of tar. His body heat had melted the material just enough to fasten him securely. They had to cut the helpless man's clothes off to free him.

Sin is like tar. We get comfortable with it and zap, it's got us! That's when we need Jesus to cut us free and forgive us for what we've done. He's great at getting people out of sticky situations.

TEASING TRAGEDY

Q: My class has someone who gets teased a lot. I feel sorry for him when they tease him, but when I try to stand up for him they tease me and tell me to join in teasing him. I don't know what to do. I am 13.

A: It seems as if every classroom has someone who gets teased a lot. One of my best friends growing up was like the person you describe. He was always the scapegoat for practical jokes.

My friend's story ended in tragedy. He committed suicide. I realize most stories don't end that way, but it is something to think about. I have often wanted to go back in time and treat him differently.

Jesus said the way you treat that person who often gets picked on is the same way you treat Him. Stand up for the kid who gets teased. Who cares what the other kids think?

Karl Haffner

FATHER'S TEST

Aprosperous man was growing old and wanted to leave his business and wealth to one of his three sons. He loved them all equally. Which one would use the wealth wisely after he was gone? To find out, he devised a test.

To each son he gave a small sum of money with the instruction "You're to buy something that will fill this room. Spend it all, but no more. Be back by sunset."

The three brothers headed out, wondering what they should do.

When evening came, the first appeared with a bale of straw and scattered it about the room, almost covering two walls. "Not bad!" his father said proudly.

After they removed the mess, the second son brought in his purchase: a large sack of thistledown that, when fluffed, half filled the room with floating thistle. "Nice work!" the father responded.

The third and last son hung his head. "Father," he said, "I was walking to market when I saw a hungry child, so I bought him some food. I passed the church and went in to pray, leaving more of the money for missions. I had only enough left to purchase this." He held up a small candle that he placed on the table. Since it was getting dark, he lit the wick, and a warm glow reached to the farthest corners of the room.

The father smiled. "Son," he said, "you have filled this room not only with light, but with kindness and unselfishness. I can see that whatever you have, you will always use it to bless others. My business and wealth will be yours."

GOD LOVES EVERYONE

Q: My uncle is going to die of AIDS any day. Is he going to go to heaven when Jesus comes? He's gay.

A: Your uncle must make that decision. You see, God loves everyone. He wants *all* people to go to heaven. As a matter of fact, if your uncle chooses not to become a citizen of the new earth, God will be lonely for him throughout the ceaseless ages of eternity.

Let's stop for a minute and think this through. Heaven will be a re-creation of Eden. The animals live peacefully together, there's no violence or pain, no anger and sadness. Everything is as it was in the beginning, including God's ideal for human relationships. Homosexuality didn't exist before sin entered the world, nor will it be in heaven. It's simply not a part of God's eternal plan for our happiness.

So as things are now, your uncle would hate heaven. He'd be lonely, feel like an outcast, and be uncomfortable around God—the very same feelings he's lived with on this earth. People who maintain a gay lifestyle will not be in heaven because God knows they'd be miserable there. And misery, loneliness, and uncomfortableness cannot exist in God's new earth. Those are the results of sin, and God will have erased sin from the universe.

But if your uncle chooses to accept the future as God has designed it and asks his loving Saviour to make some changes in his life, heaven *will* be his home when Jesus comes. He'll find it a joyous place, filled with thousands who've fought the same battle he's fought and won their own victories with Jesus' help.

RUNNING ON FUMES

Pastor Alex Thomson steered his 45-foot mission launch over the pounding waves. He and his crew were caught in a violent riptide off northern Tanna in the New Hebrides (now Vanuatu). Captain Thomas knew that if they got sideways to the waves, the boat would capsize and put everyone's life in jeopardy.

Suddenly the engine began making a frightening noise. The engineer knew at once that not enough fuel was getting to the carburetor. He and the pastor hurried to see what they could do.

"Filter's clogged," the engineer called out. "Second filter shot too. Dirt is blocking the flow."

"Remove the fuel line and fix it, quickly!" the captain ordered. Then he sent a prayer heavenward. "Please, God, keep the engine running."

With the fuel line disconnected, fuel had absolutely no way to get to the engine. The men worked furiously, knowing that the chugging, clunking motor was using up any gas left in the carburetor and feeder lines. At any moment the engine would die, leaving the launch powerless to maneuver in the fast-flowing tide. But it kept running and running, slowly, with just enough push to keep the rudder effective against the rush of water under the stern.

"Got it," shouted the engineer. As he slipped the pipe back into place, the engine coughed, became silent, and then roared to life as fresh fuel flowed into the carburetor.

Pastor Thomson breathed normally again, thanking God for the engine that ran "without fuel."

"GET OUT OF HERE"

When it was almost time for the Jewish Passover, Jesus went up to Jerusalem. In the temple courts he found men selling cattle, sheep and doves, and others sitting at tables exchanging money. So he made a whip out of cords, and drove all from the temple area, both sheep and cattle; he scattered the coins of the money-changers and overturned their tables. To those who sold doves he said, "Get these out of here! How dare you turn my Father's house into a market!"

His disciples remembered that it is written: "Zeal for your house will consume me."

Then the Jews demanded of him, "What miraculous sign can you show us to prove your authority to do all this?"

Jesus answered them, "Destroy this temple, and I will raise it again in three days."

The Jews replied, "It has taken forty-six years to build this temple, and you are going to raise it in three days?" But the temple he had spoken of was his body. After he was raised from the dead, his disciples recalled what he had said. Then they believed the Scripture and the words that Jesus had spoken.

John 2:13-22

Talk about raising a fuss! Jesus wanted to make a point, and He sure did. God's house—the place where people come to worship the Creator—is special. It's not supposed to be used as a business or a place to party, but is a sacred space sheltering the presence of God.

When you attend church, enter with reverence and keep in mind that God is there with you enjoying the praise and the prayers.

BITTER CUP

My Father, if it is possible, may this cup be taken from me. Yet not as I will, but as you will." Matthew 26:39.

When Jesus prayed these words, He knew that in a matter of hours He'd be nailed to a cross and killed. I certainly don't blame Him for wanting such a horrible event not to happen. But then He spoke a phrase echoed by countless missionaries around the world: "Not as I will, but as you will."

God's will is that we obey Him and become like Jesus. It allows us to take advantage of the salvation Christ freely offers.

I learned firsthand that—sometimes—obeying God makes things a bit uncomfortable. I once told an employer that I couldn't work on Sabbath. Even though we'd been through this when he hired me, he got so mad at my stubborn resolve to keep the seventh day holy that he punched me right in the face. It hurt. But so did the cross.

Other times I've been among friends who made fun of me when I refused to go places or do things that they wanted to do. That hurt too. But so did the cross.

Being a Christian means taking responsibility for your beliefs. It may also involve being laughed at, fired from jobs, ridiculed, or even thrown in jail. Sure, God is with you to help you deal with the situations, but it's still not fun.

Determine today to stand for what you know to be right, come what may!

JUST A COUPLE FARMERS

The president of Harvard University looked up to see two people entering his office. Visitors were always stopping by to visit, to gab, to complain. *I never can get anything done,* the man sighed in frustration.

His latest disruptions appeared to be simple farmers. Well, he'd show them how busy he was. He picked up a letter and began reading. Out of the corner of his eye, he watched his visitors seat themselves and then wait. Good. Farmers should wait.

He read slowly, deliberately. Only when he'd finished did he speak. "Well," he snapped, "what do you want? Hurry. My time is extremely limited."

The farmer stood and bowed courteously. "We're sorry to interrupt," he said. "Since you're so busy, we shouldn't take your time." He smiled at his wife. "We'll be going."

Good riddance, the president thought as he watched the couple leave. *That's the way to treat farmers. Now I can get back to my important work.*

The president was right. His visitors were farmers. They also owned 9,000 of the finest and most productive acres in California. The man in worn work clothes had been governor of that state and would soon be one of its senators. He'd built the western end of the transcontinental railroad and had come to give the university president several million dollars for his university. But the man behind the desk had been too busy to listen to his donors.

Instead, those two "farmers" went back to California and started their own college as a memorial to their son, Leland Stanford, Jr. Stanford University is one of the most respected institutions of higher learning in the world today. Millions of dollars—if the president had just been polite!

BANANAS

Q: My classroom has three boys that all the cool guys exclude from the games. I try to help them, but they just run away because they think that I am going to tease them too. I am 10.

A: As far as I'm concerned, all those "cool" guys are about as "cool" as earwax. Guys that are *really* cool don't try to exclude others.

But apparently these three guys have become convinced that they are as useless as rotten bananas. This is obvious because they don't trust you (or anybody) enough to believe you are sincere in wanting to help them.

I admire you for trying to show them they do have value. Don't be discouraged—remember how the world treated Christ, even though He just wanted to help. It will take a lot of time to build up that trust. Perhaps you could write them a note, explaining how you feel. Or it may take inviting them to your birthday party or helping them with homework or choosing them to be on your ball team. There are many ways to make them change their minds about you. Just don't give up, because it will be well worth it. Let them know that others need them and that they can make a valuable contribution. After all, even "rotten" bananas make fabulous muffins!

Karl Haffner

MASTERS OF THE NIGHT

As twilight settled over the Congress Avenue Bridge, the nightly crowd gathered. They spread blankets and lawn chairs on the grassy riverbank below the bridge. Some brought picnic lunches, while others tossed Frisbees, but they all waited for dark.

On the bridge above the river more people crowded along the railing for a better view. Customers more interested in the coming sight than eating packed the restaurants above the bridge.

As the sun slid behind the buildings of downtown Austin, Texas, shadows enveloped the bridge. Soft rustling noises began to emanate from the underside of the bridge. Frisbee games stopped, and the crowd grew silent.

Then the bats streamed out.

First dozens . . . then hundreds . . . then hundreds of thousands blackened the sky like a living thundercloud. The soft flutter of 3 million membranous wings filled the air as the colony of Mexican free-tailed bats left their roosts under the bridge for their nightly feeding. They would eat 10,000 to 30,000 *pounds* of insects by dawn.

Congress Avenue Bridge is one of about 60 bridges in Texas that house a total of 6 million bats. The citizens of Austin once feared bats, but now they proudly refer to their city as the "Bat Capital of America."

Bats have three important jobs in God's creation. First, they pollinate plants. In addition, they spread seeds when they eat fruit. And finally, they help control the insect population.

Bats play a vital role in the balance of nature, so give bats a break!

Jane Chase

IT ISN'T FAIR

Q: My best friend's family was in an automobile accident, and my friend got hurt really bad. Why does God let stuff like this happen, especially to Christians?

A: It doesn't seem fair, does it? To help us find some answers, let's go back to the Garden of Eden. Remember when Adam and Eve made the choice to sin? Everything went haywire. That's why we have accidents, disasters, and death, and a planet that seems to be about to self-destruct.

Now, God doesn't *cause* these terrible things. Satan does. OK, you're probably thinking, *But why doesn't God stop him?* Well, God is allowing sin to take its course so that we, along with the rest of the universe, can see its awful results. Once we really understand what sin does, we won't want any part of it. Don't misunderstand, though. We're not saying your friend's sins caused the accident. He or she just happens to be living in a world that's affected by sin *and its consequences.*

Sometimes God allows people to suffer because it gives others a chance to respond to their needs. That experience helps to build our characters. We're sure you're already thinking of ways to show kindness and give encouragement to your friend during his time of recovery from the accident.

No one has all the answers about why God allows suffering. But because Jesus suffered and died for us, we can know that one day the suffering will end—*forever.*

Art and Pat Humphrey

BLESSINGS IN DISGUISE

When Hudson Taylor and William Burns went to Swatow in war-torn China as missionaries, Hudson was only 24 years old. The two Christians found lodging in a basement apartment and had to enter their living space through a trapdoor in the floor of the house above.

Soon after they set up a medical clinic, Taylor had to travel to Shanghai for medical supplies. He put his spare clothes in a box and mailed it. It would reduce the baggage he'd have to carry. Reaching Shanghai, he discovered that his promised medical supplies had been destroyed, so he continued on to Ningpo, where he hoped he could find what he needed. On the way his servant robbed him and escaped with all his money.

At Ningpo he found what he needed, but some of the people he was traveling with got sick and he had to wait a month for them to recover. During that time he met a girl by the name of Maria Dyer. They later married.

Friends lent him money for his return trip to Swatow, but before he left, riots broke out there and his partner, William Burns, became a prisoner. Had Taylor been with him, he'd have been in prison too.

While he waited for things to cool down, a missionary friend became ill with smallpox. Taylor took care of him until the person died, then had to burn all of his own clothes because of possible smallpox contamination. That's when the box he packed in Swatow arrived with all his extra clothes.

Hudson Taylor learned that when bad things happen, you've got to give God time to show you how He's still looking out for you.

"YOUR SON WILL LIVE"

There was a certain royal official whose son lay sick at Capernaum. When this man heard that Jesus had arrived in Galilee from Judea, he went to him and begged him to come and heal his son, who was close to death.

"Unless you people see miraculous signs and wonders," Jesus told him, "you will never believe."

The royal official said, "Sir, come down before my child dies."

Jesus replied, "You may go. Your son will live."

The man took Jesus at his word and departed. While he was still on the way, his servants met him with the news that his boy was living. When he inquired as to the time when his son got better, they said to him, "The fever left him yesterday at the seventh hour."

Then the father realized that this was the exact time at which Jesus had said to him, "Your son will live." So he and all his household believed.

John 4:46-53

It's early in His earthly ministry, and already Jesus has learned that many people believe in Him only after they've witnessed a miracle. "Turn water to wine," or "heal my child," or "make me rich" they pleaded. "Then I'll follow You."

Is it so different today? "Hey, what's religion done for me lately?" people ask. So many forget that the greatest miracles of God happen in the heart, where He chases away sin and vanquishes evil thoughts. You want a miracle? See what He can do with your heart right now.

TEAMWORK

Jesus said, "Father, forgive them, for they do not know what they are doing." Luke 23:34.

Have you ever sat and gazed at a picture of thousands and thousands of people milling about a marketplace or attending a sporting event and asked yourself, "How can I tell all those people about Jesus?"

Japan is a crowded country. Cities such as Tokyo, Osaka, and Kobe fairly bulge with humanity. I used to ride my motorcycle along their busy streets and freeways wondering if what we student missionaries were doing was making a difference, whether our presence would ever help save anyone.

But just as quickly as that thought entered my mind, a silent voice would remind me of an often overlooked fact of life. I can't save anyone. Not one person will be in heaven because of me. Only *Jesus* can save people. If my Japanese friends had any hope of living forever with God, they'd need Jesus in their lives!

What about all the people in the picture, the ones who might not ever hear the good news of salvation? Jesus gave the answer to that question from the cross. He said, "Father, forgive them, for they do not know what they are doing."

If you ever decide to become a student missionary, make sure you understand that your job is to show people a healthier, happier way to live. But when it comes to saving anyone, only Jesus can accomplish that. You give hope. He gives life eternal.

Teamwork!

MR. MARTIN'S STORE

Every time I see Mr. Martin, I feel ashamed," Beth sighed as she and her friend Ann watched a man struggle through the snow, his crutches slipping on the ice-covered sidewalk.

Mr. Edward Martin made a meager living selling candies and other small items from his open-air store on the side of the street. He always smiled and was kind to everyone, even though his clothes were old and threadbare.

"He needs an *indoor* store where he can be safe and warm," the girls agreed.

"But that's up to the adults," Beth insisted. "We're just teens."

"True," her friend agreed. Then she grinned. "But we're teens on a *mission!*"

The two put their heads together and formulated a plan. First, they wrote up a petition on Mr. Martin's behalf. They knew that town leaders took note of petitions with many signatures.

Next, they went door-to-door looking for supporters. "We want to help Mr. Martin," the girls announced, holding out their clipboards.

"Great. Wonderful. Sounds good to me" came the quick responses. "We've been buying from Mr. Martin for years," neighbors would say, grabbing the pencil and adding their names to the list. "It's about time someone did something to help him."

It took work, but eventually the two girls had 500 names on their petition. The city council took notice and sent an official letter to Mr. Martin telling him that he could have a space near his home for setting up shop. The town would even help with the modest building project.

Teens on a mission—that's a powerful force for good. Are there any needs in your community?

SNUBBED BY SISTER

Q: I am a 10-year-old boy. My sister never wants to play with me. I ask her to play a game with me, but she never does. If I want to do something, she thinks that her stuff is more important. I don't know if I should go on with this or let God take care of it.

A: I think you should let God take care of it. But what, exactly, does that mean you need to do? From the Bible we know it involves at least these things:

1. Treat your sister as you want to be treated. Are there any things you are doing to her that would make her ignore you? Think about how you wish she would treat you, then work hard on treating her that way.

2. Talk with her one-on-one and share your feelings. Sometime when you are both in a good mood, bring it up and ask why she doesn't want to play games with you. It could be that she doesn't like the games you want to play. In that case you need to find a game you both enjoy. Or it may be she feels embarrassed to have her brother around because she wants her independence. Again, maybe you can work out a compromise in which you can play together some of the time. Just talking about it often brings understanding.

3. Forgive, forgive, forgive. The Bible teaches we are to forgive seven times 70. What Jesus was saying is there should be no end to our forgiveness. Even though your sister has treated you like a canker sore, forgive her for the past and move ahead.

Karl Haffner

FAITHFUL

The story is told of a dog that lived in Luco, a small town in the hills of central Italy. Every morning his master, Carlo, would hurry to the bus stop in the square and catch a ride to the factory in a nearby town. The dog would escort him to the square, see him off with lots of tail wagging and warm licks, and then wait all day for the bus's return.

When evening arrived, the dog would be at the curb to welcome his master and escort him back home again. This went on for two years.

What the dog didn't know was that Italy was involved in a world war. One day enemy planes bombed the factory where Carlo worked. That night the dog met the bus, but no familiar feet appeared. No friendly fingers rubbed his ears, no happy voice called his name. So he spent the night in the square and waited all the next day. But the same thing happened again. Carlo didn't step from the bus, because he had been killed.

Thirteen years later the dog was still in the square meeting the evening bus. At night he'd crawl under the parked vehicle and sleep. People brought him food and water, but no one could lure him away from his post by the curb.

Eventually the town awarded the little dog a medal. "For great faithfulness," the citation read.

God has a reward waiting for His dedicated juniors. Someday He'll say, "Well done, good and faithful servant! You have been faithful with a few things; I will put you in charge of many things" (Matthew 25:23).

OUT OF SIGHT

Q: Are we going to see all the things mentioned in Revelation; or will God take us first?

A: The book of Revelation brims with very vivid images of high-flying angels, thrones, scrolls, a dragon, a lamb, a beast, terrible plagues, strange horses, a lake of fire, and a beautiful city made of gold. Are we going to see all these things?

Revelation is a written account of a dream God gave to John. In order for the apostle to understand what was going to happen in the future, God used symbols to illustrate important points. For instance, the woman in Revelation represents God's church. The beast and dragon are, of course, the devil.

These symbols show what's happening behind the scenes while we struggle to overcome Satan on this earth.

We will witness *some* of the events foretold in Revelation such as the plagues, the Second Coming, and best of all, the New Jerusalem and re-created world. However, Christians have no reason to fear what is to come. Sadness? Yes. Careful preparation to withstand evil forces? Certainly. Fear? Absolutely not.

Remember the story of Noah? God warned of a terrible flood to come. So Noah built an ark. Have you ever noticed that the ark had only one window? When the flood came, the boat rocked, the thunder roared, the earth shook. But Noah remained safely inside, out of reach and out of sight of the terror.

STRANGE CONVERSION

The University of Cambridge, England, boasts many deep thinkers. One of them was named Tom. Also in the community was a priest by the name of Hugh. Both young men were well respected and could have been friends except for one thing. Hugh believed that priests could forgive sins. Tom insisted that the sinner could come boldly before God in prayer and receive forgiveness just by asking.

"That's ridiculous," Hugh would say.

"But it's true," Tom would state firmly.

One day Tom came up with a plan to get his message across. He knew Hugh believed that anyone who had sinned should confess that sin to a priest, so he made his way to his room, knocked softly, and entered. "Please hear my confession," he said.

Hugh blinked. "Well, well," he chuckled. "My preaching has paid off. You're coming over to my side, huh?"

Tom bowed his head. "I confess that it has been a thrill to learn that Jesus forgives sins freely. But I've been tempted to tell a man named Hugh that Jesus loves him too, and wants to save him, and will forgive his sins even if he doesn't burn candles and kiss little statues."

Hugh sat in silence for a long moment, then hung his head as the Holy Spirit spoke to his heart. Perhaps it was true. Maybe God did forgive the sins of anyone who asked.

It was one of the strangest conversions in history. From then on Hugh Latimer and Thomas Bilney were great friends and became effective preachers for God. Eventually both gave their lives as martyrs for their freely forgiving Lord.

THE "BEAUTIFUL ATTITUDES"

Now when he saw the crowds, he went up on a mountainside and sat down. His disciples came to him, and he began to teach them, saying:

"Blessed are the poor in spirit, for theirs is the kingdom of heaven.

"Blessed are those who mourn, for they will be comforted.

"Blessed are the meek, for they will inherit the earth.

"Blessed are those who hunger and thirst for righteousness, for they will be filled.

"Blessed are the merciful, for they will be shown mercy.

"Blessed are the pure in heart, for they will see God.

"Blessed are the peacemakers, for they will be called sons of God.

"Blessed are those who are persecuted because of righteousness, for theirs is the kingdom of heaven.

"Blessed are you when people insult you, persecute you and falsely say all kinds of evil against you because of me. Rejoice and be glad, because great is your reward in heaven, for in the same way they persecuted the prophets who were before you."   Matthew 5:1-12

What beautiful, hopeful words! Can't you just see the sad person in the crowd beginning to smile, maybe for the first time in months? Can't you imagine the mother who has lost a child to sickness stopping her weeping for just a moment? Notice the shy person by the rock beginning to feel he's worth something after all. And that group by the trees who have been especially persecuted by the Romans. Jesus is saying they can look forward to a kingdom of their very own! Not only did Jesus heal people's bodies; He healed their minds as well.

EMPTY TOMBS

Why do you look for the living among the dead? He is not here; he has risen!" Luke 24:5, 6.

Not long ago I stood at the graveside of someone I loved very much—my mother. Cancer had claimed her life, and now I faced a future without her.

Sure, I was sad. My heart was breaking. But I couldn't help remembering another group of people who hurried to a grave to pay their last respects to someone they loved—Jesus Christ.

What they found shocked them from the tops of their heads to the soles of their feet. Jesus was gone! The tomb was empty.

Suddenly two men appeared wearing gleaming clothes. "He's not here," they confirmed. "He's risen."

My mother's tomb isn't empty. No angel has come to awaken her—yet.

But someday it *will* happen. I know this because of the empty tomb that Christ's followers found on that mysterious Sunday morning 2,000 years ago. Jesus proved that God's power is stronger than death and that Satan can't hold people in their graves forever.

When I was a child my mother would wake me from my naps with a soft "Charlie Boy. Wake up, Charlie Boy." If I must sleep the long sleep of death, I know that God won't bother blowing a trumpet to wake me up. No sir. He's going to lift my mother from her resting place in Collegedale, Tennessee, and tell her, "Go wake up your son." Then I'll hear those loving words again and see my mother's face hovering over me. "Wake up, Charlie Boy," she'll say.

Yup. There's going to be a *lot* of empty tombs someday!

REWARD

Sitting at the edge of the garbage dump, Mike let the coins run through his fingers. He'd *never* seen so much money.

Mike Young, a hardworking garbage collector, had stopped at the house of Mrs. Stella Jones earlier that day and carted off boxes of rubbish. The woman had been spring cleaning and was happy to see all the junk disappear into Mike's truck. In the evening, while unloading the boxes and bags he'd collected, he noticed a silver paint can. It was heavy and jingled when shaken. Prying open the lid, Mike had found rolls of bills and piles of coins. *This came from the Jones house*, he remembered.

Jumping into his truck, he hurried back to the old woman's street. She gasped when she saw the can in the collector's outstretched hands. "That's my life savings," she cried. "I'd have suffered terribly if you hadn't returned this."

Years passed. Mike forgot all about the can and the money.

One day an important-looking envelope showed up in his mailbox. The document inside summoned him to appear before a lawyer in town. Mike's hand trembled. What had he done that was so terrible?

"Did you return a can of money to Mrs. Stella Jones?" asked the man behind the big wooden desk.

"Yes," Mike responded, only now remembering the incident. "Is there something wrong?" The lawyer smiled. "Mrs. Jones died recently. Being childless, she left her home"—he passed a signed document across the desk—"to you."

Sometimes people have to wait until Jesus comes to receive a reward for kindness. And sometimes not.

A TIME TO DATE

Q: I am 13. I like a girl. We are already good friends, and I like her a lot. Should I ask her out?

A: The Bible tells us "there is a time for everything . . . a time to embrace and a time to refrain, a time to search and a time to give up, a time to keep and a time to throw away, a time to tear and a time to mend, a time to be silent and a time to speak, a time to love and a time to hate" (Ecclesiastes 3:1-8).

There will be a time when it's right for you to ask girls out. Don't rush into anything. Ask God to show you His timing—and He will!

Karl Haffner

THE COP AND THE CAT

Not long ago in Germany lived a little white kitten hidden away in a Berlin alley. People in the area saw her roaming their backyards, raiding their garbage cans. Many tossed stones in her direction in an attempt to drive her away.

One afternoon people spotted the hungry animal by the main road as it tried to keep out of sight of passing vehicles. A policeman stood nearby, directing traffic through a small construction zone.

All at once, a milk truck turned the corner a little too fast and a container of milk dropped from a rack and splattered on the road. Traffic came to a standstill as white liquid oozed across both lanes.

The policeman ran and retrieved the now empty container and walked to where the truck driver waited, red-faced and full of excuses. After a short conversation in which the officer told the motorist to be more careful and secure his load more tightly, the policeman returned to his post, only to notice the white kitten crouched in the middle of the road lapping up milk as if it hadn't eaten for days.

Instantly the officer held up his hand to keep any traffic from moving. Then he bent near the cat and said softly, "Please, little white kitten, hurry. A lot of people are trying to get home."

Not until the animal had drunk its fill and walked gratefully away did the policeman allow any cars to pass. The man had made an animal's heart glad. He'd done the same for many of the drivers who patiently waited while he treated one of God's creatures with respect and love.

GETTING TO HEAVEN

Q: How do you get to heaven?

A: When I was a little boy, I used to stand in our backyard in Tennessee waiting for Jesus to come. I'd gaze up into the sky, watching the clouds drift by, wondering if *that* one or *that* one was filled with holy angels and Jesus Himself.

One summer afternoon, tired of playing Superman with my friend Roger, I sat down and began watching the sky when suddenly a terrible feeling swept over me. *What if I'm not ready?* I thought. *What if I sinned and didn't even know it? What if Jesus came and refused to take me back to heaven with Him?* I ran and found my mother loading clothes into the washing machine. "Am I going to be saved?" I gasped. "Hurry. I've gotta know."

Mom smiled. "Of course you are," she said.

"How can you be sure?" I asked.

"Because Jesus loves you very much and wants you to be with Him in heaven," Mom said softly, looking at me with eyes that always quieted my fears.

How do you get to heaven? By believing God loves you so much that He's willing to forgive your sins and help you prepare to be a citizen of His new earth. Then you allow Him to lead you, correct you, and finally save you.

I still occasionally scan the sky and wonder. But I'm never afraid. "Now there is in store for me the crown of righteousness, which the Lord, the righteous Judge, will award to me on that day—and not only to me, but also to all who have longed for his appearing" (2 Timothy 4:8).

EXPLODING SNAKE

First, Alice got sick. Then Barry stepped on a huge taipan— one of Australia's deadliest snakes—and almost got bit in the face. But Barry's father killed the serpent and Pastor Turner put it in a bottle to show visitors. Soon thereafter Pastor Turner's tractor slipped off his truck and crushed his chest, knocking him unconscious for a week.

There's more.

While Pastor Turner lay unconscious, the snake in the bottle began to swell. Apparently the pastor hadn't put in enough preserving fluid. People started coming to the mission station to stare at the swelling snake.

"I cast a devil out of Alice," said the witch doctor, "and it went into the snake. It was on its way to find the enemy of our people when Barry stepped on it and his dad killed it. Pastor Turner put it in the bottle and that made the devil angry, so the tractor fell on him. If that snake bursts before Pastor Turner gives it a proper burial to appease the devil, the pastor will die."

Christian missionaries don't believe in such mumbo jumbo. They know that the God of heaven is more powerful than any devil, especially one living in a dead snake. But the people around the mission station didn't know that—yet.

The missionaries prayed and left the swelling snake in the bottle, where it continued to expand. The next day the corpse exploded. But Pastor Turner got better in spite of the dire warning of his impending doom. Weeks later he carried the bottle to church and showed everyone, including the witch doctor, that God is more powerful than demonic powers. The whole village agreed—even the witch doctor!

SALT AND LIGHT

Jesus is standing on a beautiful mountainside in Galilee preaching to a large group of people. Looking down at their upturned faces, He does something strange. He calls them names!

"You are the salt of the earth. But if the salt loses its saltiness, how can it be made salty again? It is no longer good for anything, except to be thrown out and trampled by men.

"You are the light of the world. A city on a hill cannot be hidden. Neither do people light a lamp and put it under a bowl. Instead they put it on its stand, and it gives light to everyone in the house. In the same way, let your light shine before men, that they may see your good deeds and praise your Father in heaven."

Matthew 5:13-16

Has anyone ever called you salt before? How many of your friends say, "Hey, Light, come here"? Of course, Jesus had a much deeper meaning in His words. He was telling us that Christians add flavor and guidance to people's lives. Their kind acts and helpful words make our old world a better place to live and give friends, neighbors, and family members a little joy (light) in their sometimes sad (dark) lives. Neat, huh?

So get out there and spice up someone's life today with a bit of salty kindness. If you see a friend down in the dumps with their face hanging around their knees, shine a little love light on 'em. After all, you're salt and light. You've got work to do!

STRANGERS NO MORE

Therefore go and make disciples of all nations, baptizing them in the name of the Father and of the Son and of the Holy Spirit, and teaching them to obey everything I have commanded you." Matthew 28:19, 20.

All too soon my year in Japan ended. I had to get back to my job at the radio station at Southern Missionary College and continue my studies in communications in preparation for a life of service to the God I loved.

We had a going-away party at the Osaka Center, and many of our students showed up to say goodbye. Singing favorite songs, we retold all the embarrassing stories we could remember about each other. There was a lot of hugging and laughing and even some tears. The next day I boarded the airplane that would carry me away from the land to which I'd dedicated 12 months of my life.

Jesus said that we should "go and make disciples of all nations." Well, we'd done that. All of us student missionaries had traveled far to fulfill God's command. We'd lived in strange houses and eaten new foods. Each day we'd seen unusual sights and listened to the sweet banter of a different language. But you know what? When we got back to America, everything seemed so strange. Japan had become our home, and we hadn't even realized it.

God needs student missionaries to accept the responsibility of introducing people to Jesus. I can tell you from experience that He takes the "strangeness" away and replaces it with a warm, never-fading feeling of home. Why not include "student missionary" in your future plans?

ALMOST DROWNED

Ann Nesmith and her camp counselor, Mrs. Cochran, sat on the dock happily soaking up the sunshine. The day had been perfect with lots of Pathfinder Club activities, hikes in the woods, delicious food, and swims in the lake.

All at once the two friends saw a curious sight. An inner tube, probably cast adrift from a nearby camp, floated by just within reach. Absentmindedly Mrs. Cochran plucked it from the water and placed it beside them. She'd return it to its rightful owner later in the day.

"I'm getting hot," Ann admitted. "How about a cooling dip?"

Mrs. Cochran grinned. "Last one in is a dork!"

With a happy squeal, the pair launched themselves off the dock and landed with a giant splash in the lake. But it suddenly became obvious that they hadn't chosen their target correctly. The bottom was eight feet down, and Ann couldn't swim. Mrs. Cochran disappeared under the water and rose again, sputtering and coughing.

"Help!" Ann gasped as she struggled to stay above the surface. "Help!"

Both were in peril. Both needed saving. That's when the counselor remembered the inner tube.

"Throw the tube!" she shouted to a camper standing nearby. "Hurry!"

The girl on the dock grabbed the large, rubbery tube and tossed it into the air. Her aim was good, and the lifesaving device landed with a *splat* between the two struggling swimmers. Holding on to it, both kicked their way back to shore and spent a long time regaining their composure and thanking God for the curious object that had happened by at just the right moment.

MAYBE I SHOULD JUST . . .

Q: I am a 14-year-old boy. Last year my father left us for a different woman. Now it seems my mom always gives my sister's boyfriend more attention than she gives me. I'm not sure whether or not my mom loves me anymore. Same with my sister. She doesn't really love me as much as she used to. I don't know what is wrong with me. It's like they're sick of me being around. Maybe I should just commit suicide.

A: Let's break down these problems.

Father: Understand that his decision to leave is in no way your fault. Often fathers become confused and make decisions they regret.

Sister: Girls usually go through a "boy-crazy" phase in which they simply get dizzy over guys. This phase will not last forever, but her relationship with you will. Give her time.

Mother: The problem seems to be a lack of communication and love. Even though your mom doesn't adequately express it, that doesn't mean she's stopped loving you. She too struggles with feelings of rejection and failure as she has to adapt to your dad's leaving. Work on communicating better with her and showing her love, and it will be easier for her to show her love to you.

You: First off, God loves and accepts you just as you are. He created you to be you. God finds value in you, or He wouldn't have died for you. As you keep reminding yourself of the worth you have in God's eyes, you will begin to love and accept yourself more.

Yes! You *are* loved. You *are* accepted. You *are* needed. Don't sell yourself short!

Karl Haffner

HEROES

My family met at Fall Creek Falls State Park near our home in Tennessee, and we had a great picnic and enjoyed my cousin's new puppy, Bear.

When the adults started hiking to the falls, we kids decided to take turns carrying the puppy. He was so cute all snuggled up in a backpack.

Eventually Bear got restless, and so I volunteered to carry him. We were way ahead of the adults, who were poking along talking and stuff.

As we crossed a little bridge I slipped on a root. *I must protect little Bear,* I thought as I fell. So I didn't break my fall, and my head hit full force against a jagged rock.

It cut my head deeply, and I was losing a lot of blood. Not only that, Fall Creek Falls is in the middle of nowhere!

But God sent heroes! The first was my 11-year-old cousin, Andrew. Even before the adults got there, he had ripped off his scrubs and tied them tightly around my head, which helped a lot. Then he ran to find a car phone to call 911.

Next, God sent a kind man who helped my dad carry me off the trail. My mom kept telling me, "Pray, Jessie, pray!" and I did.

By the time I got to the ambulance I was losing consciousness, but I remember asking the paramedics to pray. Then came more heroes—nurses, doctors, and a plastic surgeon who prayed with me too. There were many prayers that day. And many heroes!

Jessica Zollinger,
grade 5, Tennessee

MUSIC ON MY MIND

Q: What kind of music is OK for a Christian to listen to?

A: When James White (Ellen's husband) was a young man, he and his father and two of his sisters got caught in a rainstorm one evening while traveling. So they stopped at a little inn to take refuge. Because they had nothing else to do, the White family decided to spend the evening singing hymns.

The innkeeper and his family had also been forced inside by the rain. They enjoyed the music so much that they asked for one song after another. The next morning when James's father went to pay the bill, the innkeeper told him he owed nothing. Why? Because the family had paid him the night before in singing.

Why do you think that innkeeper was so moved? Because music had done its job—to inspire, uplift, and encourage. No, you don't have to go around singing hymns all the time. God has blessed His children with the ability to create a wide variety of acceptable music to please people of every culture and taste. But remembering that music is a gift from God, we should use it wisely.

It's important to keep in mind that just as God employs music to draw us closer to Him, Satan creates music to draw us away from God. Music that stirs up our sexual nature or that has lyrics (words) that don't fit with Christian principles is definitely not for those who want to stay close to God. Just as we are careful with the food we put into our bodies, we should also watch what we choose for our musical diet.

Art and Pat Humphrey

GOD'S DRUMS

Meri had just settled down to sleep in her little African hut when she heard the drums. "They're calling my people to a religious meeting," she said excitedly. "I must go." As she was preparing to leave, she heard someone say, "The White man is going to preach!"

She and her relatives had gone just a little way when they heard the drums again. "Hurry!" Meri urged. But no one responded. As a matter of fact, they weren't on the trail at all. She was in bed. It had all been a dream. *I wonder what it means?* she wondered.

Months passed. Then in October of 1946, as the village rested under a hot midafternoon sun, the sound of beating drums echoed in the humid air. Meri frowned. Where had she heard that sound before? Then she gasped. The dream!

"We must answer the drums," she announced to her family. "They call from my dream!"

When the group arrived at the meetinghouse, Meri looked inside and, sure enough, a White man was standing up to preach. His name, she found out later, was Pastor M. E. Lind.

Meri enjoyed every word of the sermon, but most of her friends and relatives weren't interested. It didn't matter. By now she knew that the drums that had called her were God's drums and she must answer. Soon she gave her heart to Jesus.

Her family evicted her from her home, but that didn't even matter. She was marching to the beat of a new drummer now. In due time she led hundreds of souls to Christ and was always ready to answer the call of her Saviour.

WAYWARD LOVE

You have heard that it was said, 'Do not commit adultery.' But I tell you that anyone who looks at a woman lustfully has already committed adultery with her in his heart. If your right eye causes you to sin, gouge it out and throw it away. It is better for you to lose one part of your body than for your whole body to be thrown into hell [the grave]. And if your right hand causes you to sin, cut it off and throw it away. It is better for you to lose one part of your body than for your whole body to go into hell [the grave].

"It has been said, 'Anyone who divorces his wife must give her a certificate of divorce.' But I tell you that anyone who divorces his wife, except for marital unfaithfulness, causes her to become an adulteress, and anyone who marries the divorced woman commits adultery."

Matthew 5:27-32

First of all, Jesus isn't saying we should chop off body parts if we find ourselves doing things we shouldn't with them. He means that it's better to live without a hand or eye than lose our home in heaven. Sin begins in our brains, but we can't live very long without a brain in our head!

Second, for those of you planning on getting married someday, notice that Jesus said that a couple had only one reason for a divorce. Only one. "Marital unfaithfulness" means sleeping with someone who isn't your husband or wife. So keep all your body parts and stay in your own bed!

Ask Jesus to guide your thoughts and actions today.

ASPEN TREE WORSHIP

For I know the plans I have for you," declares the Lord, "plans to prosper you and not to harm you, plans to give you hope and a future. Then you will call upon me and come and pray to me, and I will listen to you. You will seek me and find me when you seek me with all your heart." Jeremiah 29:11-13.

Under the shade of the aspen tree,
    I think of my love for God
    And His love for me.
As the cool breeze sweeps between the trees,
    A glimpse of love shimmers from the leaves.
    The smell of damp sage hangs low in the air,
    With the love of God the day is so fair.
As the morning mist begins to disappear,
    My picture of Him becomes more and more clear.
    The air seems so crisp and clean,
    As God's love wisps off the trickling stream.
A doe and her fawn nibble freely nearby,
    Where the green grass invites you to carelessly lie,
    For the rest of the afternoon staring up into the sky.
As the day grows older and the sun begins to rise,
    The tree bids me closer,
    Closer to God's side.
Under the shade of the aspen tree,
    God's love makes me feel so free.
Without God's love where would I be?
    Surely not under the shade of the aspen tree.

Tiffany Canther,
12, Arizona

LIGHT IN A FOREST

Chad frowned. Life on a working farm could be a royal pain, especially when a cow decided to wander off. That's exactly what one had done that very afternoon, and it was his job to round up strays.

Something else bothered the teenager as he scoured the open pastures. He suffered from what doctors call "night blindness." Without a flashlight or full moon, he was as good as lost when the sun went down. A cloudy night was fast approaching.

It arrived while he was deep in the forest beyond the south pasture. Suddenly he realized that he couldn't see. He tried desperately to find his way, but in a world gone dark, he knew it was hopeless.

Then he thought of God. His mom had told him many times how God cares for people, even teenagers looking for lost cows. So he prayed.

Far above, the clouds moved silently, herded by evening breezes. Suddenly several parted, allowing the moon's yellow light to tumble from the sky and slip through the trees, illuminating the forest path where a young boy knelt. When Chad opened his eyes, he could just make out the trail leading back to the farm. The teenager was so happy as he stumbled out of the forest that he began singing! When he reached the barnyard, the clouds drifted together, shutting out the light.

Grabbing a flashlight, Chad headed out again and before long found his missing cow.

Miracles are funny things. Sometimes they're as complicated as a stony heart changing into a loving one. Other times they're as simple as the wind pushing aside a cloud.

NEW FRIENDS

Q: I'm 13. Ever since my family has moved to a military base in North Carolina, I haven't found friends my age. All my friends in my neighborhood are in high school. They are all very nice and treat me like one of the family. My parents don't like them very well because they curse and don't really care about school, but I do get good grades in school and care about it. Isn't that all that matters? It's also kind of hard for me because I'm a Christian. What should I do?

A: Schedule a peace conference with your parents. In preparation, read Proverbs 13:1-3, pray about it, then brainstorm by listing all the problems you see associated with this issue and all the solutions you may want to consider. Don't evaluate your list; just write down everything that comes to mind. When you walk in to the peace conference, your parents will see you have thought it through and are prepared to consider lots of options.

Parents are a funny species. Sometimes they do things that make as much sense as a religious grunge album. But remember, even though some of their actions seem irrational to you, they have reasons for behaving the way they do. For example, maybe your parents had too much freedom while they were growing up and it caused them a lot of hurt. Or they may have been irresponsible when they were your age, so they assume you are irresponsible as well. These are the kinds of things that will surface at the peace conference and, hopefully, bring you to some kind of understanding.

Karl Haffner

DOGS HELPING DOGS

The tide was retreating beside a small coastal town in southern England. People gathering to watch the sunset noticed a Labrador retriever swimming toward a nearby pier. When the dog tried to climb out of the water, it discovered that wet seaweed made the wooden dock slippery. Time and time again, the animal tried to scamper onto the pier but failed to the point of exhaustion.

Suddenly another retriever ran the length of the dock, gave a sharp bark to catch the attention of the floundering pooch, leaped into the waves, and climbed back out with ease. The first animal swam to the same spot and was able to escape safely.

Miss Napier of Algiers in northern Africa sent the family dog to the market each morning. The animal would return with her order of 12 warm rolls in a basket and lay them at her feet.

One morning, though, she found only 11 rolls. It happened again and again. The baker said he put 12 in the basket. Then Miss Napier discovered that between her house and town was a mother dog with a litter of puppies. Every morning her pet would leave one roll with the hungry mother. She instructed the baker to put 13 rolls in the basket, which he did until one day all 13 arrived at the Napier home, signaling that the puppies were grown.

Where did those two dogs learn to be so loving and kind to other dogs? From the same Creator-God who taught us to be loving and kind to other people!

LOSING SOMEONE IMPORTANT

Q: Why would God take someone important away from you when you really need them?

A: Has this happened to you recently? I'm so sorry. Losing someone you love is terrible. It makes you feel lonely and hurt deep inside.

But God didn't take that person away from you. Satan did. Before sin entered our world, people did not know death or loneliness. There were only life, joy, and endless love.

Please make sure you place the blame for death where it belongs—squarely on Satan's evil shoulders.

"God could've kept it from happening!" you say with a touch of anger in your voice. That's true, and someday He will. He will erase Satan and sin completely from the universe. Until then, death will continue to be a part of life on this earth.

By the way, God knows how you feel. He watched as human beings nailed His own Son to a Roman cross. God heard Him cry out in pain, and He was there when Jesus took His last breath. Why didn't He stop that horrible scene? Because He knew His Son's death was necessary so you and your family could live again without pain.

You need to read a couple special texts: "I will not leave you comfortless; I will come to you" (John 14:18). "For the Lord comforts his people and will have compassion on his afflicted ones" (Isaiah 49:13).

You have three friends ready to help you through your sorrow. Jesus, who experienced death, and His loving Father, who watched it happen. Ask Them with the Holy Spirit to comfort you right now.

BULLET-CATCHING COW

Titus Afrikaner loved danger. He hunted hippos, chased lions, stalked dangerous prey for fun, and killed men to get what he wanted.

A certain man owned a herd of cattle that Titus coveted. When the man wouldn't give him the herd, the warrior determined to kill him. The cattleman armed himself. He wasn't about to lose his livelihood without a fight.

That afternoon Titus began stalking his quarry, but low bushes and the cattle themselves prevented a clear shot at the owner. He waited patiently. Suddenly the cattle moved apart, and Titus saw the man. Simultaneously the man spotted Titus. Both leveled their guns. Both fired. At that precise instant, while the bullets were in route to their targets, a cow slipped between the shooters and received both charges. The unfortunate animal dropped dead instantly.

Titus Afrikaner stared in disbelief, then turned and ran. For the first time in his life he felt real fear. The bullet from the cattleman's gun would have killed him for sure!

The great missionary to Africa, Robert Moffat, came to Titus's home and heard the story. "My friend," Moffat said, "you've just told me something about Jesus."

"I did?" the African asked.

"Yes. He came to this earth and stepped between us and the devil so that we wouldn't be destroyed. He accepted our deadly anger and hate and died so that we could live on and have a chance to learn about His love."

The vivid illustration struck a responsive chord in Titus's mind. In time, he believed in Jesus and gave his heart to God.

LOVE WHO?

Jesus continues His sermon on the mountainside with this great advice. Listen:

"You have heard that it was said, 'Eye for eye, and tooth for tooth.' But I tell you, Do not resist an evil person. If someone strikes you on the right cheek, turn to him the other also. And if someone wants to sue you and take your tunic [shirt], let him have your cloak [coat] as well. If someone forces you to go one mile, go with him two miles. Give to the one who asks you, and do not turn away from the one who wants to borrow from you.

"You have heard that it was said, 'Love your neighbor and hate your enemy.' But I tell you: Love your enemies and pray for those who persecute you, that you may be sons of your Father in heaven. He causes his sun to rise on the evil and the good, and sends rain on the righteous and the unrighteous. If you love those who love you, what reward will you get? Are not even the tax collectors doing that? And if you greet only your brothers, what are you doing more than others? Do not even pagans do that? Be perfect, therefore, as your heavenly Father is perfect."

Matthew 5:38-48

Love your enemies? If someone hits you on one side of your face, let them slap the other side too? Tough stuff, huh? But that's exactly what Jesus did. His perfection should be a pattern for our lives. We may not be perfect, but we should always try to be.

Ask Him for help today.

REFLECTING JESUS

But what about you?" he asked. "Who do you say I am?"
Matthew 16:15.

The video store brimmed with Saturday-night renters as my wife and I elbowed our way in. We were looking for a little entertainment to add to our evening fun.

My wife enjoys romantic stories in which two deserving people find each other, fall in love, and live happily ever after. I, on the other hand, want car chases, heart-stopping mysteries, and adventures filled with thrills and excitement. She's an Anne-of-Green-Gables type and I'm a good-guy-meets-bad-guy-and-good-guy-wins type. Of course, we're always careful to choose videos with the least amount of bad language and promiscuity. It greatly limits our choices, which means we search longer than most.

When we finally made our selections, we took the little tickets to the counter. After the clerk, who also happened to be the store-owner, found our tapes and accepted our money, he handed the bag to us with these words: "You folks have been in here before, and I just have to say that you have the best taste in videos of any of my customers." Then he made several suggestions for future viewing, each right in line with our personal checklist of what constitutes acceptable Christian entertainment.

Young people, like it or not, the world is watching you. They see what you do, listen to how you speak, and observe your reactions. As a Christian it's your privilege to reflect Jesus to those who don't know Him. What is your answer to Jesus when He asks you, "Who do you say I am?"

TREASURE IN THE ORGAN

Thirteen-year-old Graham Ward positioned his fingers above the old pump organ's keys. He'd been invited to take part in a special Thanksgiving program and wanted to get some practice in before the big event. The organ, a recent gift to the church by old Mrs. Noland, was as ancient as its benefactor.

Placing his feet on the pedals, Graham began to pump. The right pedal went down easily, but the left pedal was stiff. "What's going on?" the young musician asked. "I've got to practice or I'll embarrass myself in front of the whole congregation."

Moving to the back of the instrument, he bent and removed a panel. There, surrounding the workings of the left pump, were several tin cans. "Aha," he announced. "Can't play with garbage in the works."

Graham picked up one of the cans and noticed it was very heavy. Peeking inside, he discovered it was full of money! So were the others.

The boy ran and showed his father what he'd found. "I'm sure Mrs. Noland didn't know the money was in here when she gave us the organ," Graham said. "We should take it back, don't you think?"

When the old woman saw the cans and money stashed inside, tears filled her eyes. "My husband had been saving for our old age but never told me where he was keeping our treasure," she explained. "You found it—and could have kept it. But you brought it back to me. Thank you!"

As Graham played the organ for the Thanksgiving program, he felt joyful. So did a lonely widow in the audience whose thankful heart sang with the music.

I'M A NERD

Q: I am a nerd. Every single person I see looks at me and laughs. I'm 14, five feet two inches tall, weigh 92 pounds, wear thick glasses and braces, am in the ninth grade, and try to make bad grades so everyone won't think I'm a nerd.

All the good-looking girls hate me and get guys to scare me so bad that I cry, and then everyone laughs. Our cafeteria is really crowded, but not a single person has ever sat with me. When my parents ask me how school is going, I just can't let them know what a failure I am.

A: Who determines whether or not you are a nerd? I think of many friends who appear to be "nerds"—complete with glasses and braces and undesirable bodies—and yet some of them are my heroes. At times I find myself wishing I could be them! Or at least I wish I could do what they do, be it singing, writing, playing baseball, or whatever.

What makes the difference? They capitalize on the talents they have. Refusing to listen to what others call them, they rise above their shortcomings and do whatever it is that they do best.

I am sure you have talents that enable you to do some things better than any of your classmates. Even if your talent is being a goofy nerd, do it well and others will admire you. You can be a whiner and complain about your situation, or you can be a winner and make the most of what you have. A winner or a whiner— I say be a winner. It's up to you.

Karl Haffner

TIGER FAMILY

Zoos are fascinating places. Adventist young people love to walk among the animals, imagining what it will be like in heaven when there'll be no cages and they can sit and play with leopards, hop with the kangaroo, stroll with the elephants, or romp with a rhinoceros.

Consider the tiger. Big, strong, fast, and ferocious, it makes the common house cat seem like—well, a kitten.

Tigers can rip a gazelle, ox, or human being to shreds without even breaking a sweat. Razor-sharp claws, bulging muscles, and keen eyesight make the animal a force to respect. But have you ever watched a mother tiger with her cubs? Those little guys jump on her tail, nibble at her ears, pounce on her tummy, or even roar in her face, and she just yawns. She treats them tenderly, licking the dirt off their coats, carrying them to safety if danger approaches, and letting them sleep surrounded by her powerful body.

What makes the difference? Family. They're family to her, not dangerous strangers or creatures to hunt and kill. She could snuff out their life with just a bite, but mother tigers are one of the most loving creatures in the world to their young.

There are privileges to being family, especially when you're a member of *God's* family. "Those who believed in his name, [Jesus] gave the right to become children of God" (John 1:12).

Juniors, don't ever fear the future. Oh, we may not enjoy what happens. Events may even make us uncomfortable for a while. But we've got a heavenly parent watching over us, a Father whose power makes the mother tiger seem like . . . well . . . a kitten.

FAKE BIBLE

Q: Since the Bible has been translated so many times, how do we know that the one we have now isn't a fake?

A: Have you ever played the game in which someone whispers something to someone, then that person whispers to the next person? By the time the message reaches the last player, it has completely changed. Did that happen to the Bible? Did all those writers, rewriters, translators, updaters, and transcribers create such a mixed-up mess that we shouldn't trust it anymore?

Since earliest times, those who collected and copied them considered the books of the Bible as sacred. The individuals who did this work took great pains to make sure every letter, word, paragraph, and chapter was identical to the original. If a new translation was in order, those who did the actual writing worked from preserved manuscripts written in the original Bible languages—Hebrew, Aramaic, and Greek. They wanted to be absolutely certain of maintaining the purity of every single truth and life-enriching doctrine. Our Bibles *can* be trusted.

But here's the greatest test. If when reading the Bible you feel closer to heaven and find comfort in its pages, then God is still at work, changing lives through the power He placed in the Bible long ago. "And we also thank God continually because, when you received the word of God . . . you accepted it not as the word of men, but as it actually is, the word of God, which is at work in you who believe" (1 Thessalonians 2:13).

THE LITTLE FIGHTER

Harry did one thing well. He fought. When an opponent would step into the ring and look over at Harry, he'd snicker. But not for long. What the little fighter lacked in size, he made up for in ferocity.

At the age of 19 Harry lost his edge and began losing fights. Looking back over his life, he decided that he had done nothing worthwhile. The future looked gloomy. "I'm worthless," he said. "I may as well end everything now."

Standing in the stairwell of his apartment building, he pulled a small handgun from his pocket. As he pressed the barrel to his temple, he heard a voice upstairs saying, "I am no longer worthy to be called your son."

Boy, I know that feeling, Harry said to himself. *I wonder who is saying that?* He crept close to the doorway from which the voice was coming. "But the father said to his servants, 'Quick! Bring the best robe and put it on him. Put a ring on his finger and sandals on his feet. . . . Let's . . . celebrate. For this son of mine was dead and is alive again; he was lost and is found'" (Luke 15:21-24).

Harry slipped the pistol back into his pocket and opened the door to discover a religious meeting in progress. He sat down in the last empty chair, listened, and soon began studying the Bible. Before long, Harry became a worker for God. Even when his health failed at age 39, he continued preaching until the day he died.

Yes, Harry Moorhouse was a fighter. But he spent the last half of his life fighting our world's most fearful opponent—the devil.

PRAYER OF
A THANKFUL HEART

And when you pray, do not be like the hypocrites, for they love to pray standing in the synagogues and on the street corners to be seen by men. I tell you the truth, they have received their reward in full. But when you pray, go into your room, close the door and pray to your Father, who is unseen. Then your Father, who sees what is done in secret, will reward you. And when you pray, do not keep on babbling like pagans, for they think they will be heard because of their many words. Do not be like them, for your Father knows what you need before you ask him.

"This, then, is how you should pray:

"'Our Father in heaven, hallowed be your name,
your kingdom come, your will be done on earth as it is in heaven.

"'Give us today our daily bread.
Forgive us our debts, as we also have forgiven our debtors.

"'And lead us not into temptation, but deliver us from the evil one.'

"For if you forgive men when they sin against you, your heavenly Father will also forgive you. But if you do not forgive men their sins, your Father will not forgive your sins."

Matthew 6:5-15

Isn't that a beautiful prayer? Talks a lot about forgiveness, doesn't it? Seemed to be a big issue then. And it's still a big issue now.

Hey, if God knows what we need before we ask, why pray? The answer is simple. Prayer keeps us focused on where our blessings come from.

Take some time today and pray, thanking God for being your heavenly Father.

MY FRIEND

When Jesus entered Jerusalem, the whole city was stirred and asked, "Who is this?" The crowds answered, "This is Jesus, the prophet from Nazareth in Galilee." Matthew 21:10, 11.

I have a friend. Can you guess His name?
　　He's someone I love, and He loves me just the same.
He keeps me company, at home and at school.
　　Some people don't believe in Him, but I think He's really cool.
He knows all my secrets, but He'd never tell a soul.
　　He holds my hand when I'm scared and keeps me warm
　　　　when I'm cold.
He shares my smiles, my laughs, and my sorrows.
　　He shares my dreams and my hopes for tomorrow.
He tries to keep me on the right path. He picks me up and
　　　　puts me back.
　　And when I stray, He doesn't laugh. He helps me in the
　　　　areas in which I lack.
He's made so many promises, and He even keeps them all.
　　He never forgets one, whether it's big or small.
He'd love to be your friend, too. He knows no one is more
　　　　special than you.
　　He'd love to come along, you know. But where uninvited,
　　　　He won't go.
Have you guessed yet who could be my amazing friend?
　　Or has this all passed by you, even though you've read to the end?
I want to thank you for playing along with this game,
　　And if you listen closely, I'll spell out His name—
　　J-E-S-U-S.

Michelle Bernal,
14, Alaska

TAKE THE POINTS BACK!

The University of Chicago had the ball. Their man raced down the field on the outside. The opposition tried to stop him, but each attempt failed. Thirty. Twenty. Ten. Five. *Touchdown!*

Fans roared approval. Team members congratulated each other as the numbers on the scoreboard flipped upward by six.

In the excitement, no one noticed a man on the field engaged in close conversation with one of the referees. Suddenly the newly acquired points vanished from the scoreboard and an angry buzz swept the bleachers. "Stagg's on his honesty kick again," some grumbled; but respect and admiration also lurked in their moans.

Amos Alonzo Stagg was coach of the Chicago team. His man had just scored the touchdown. But something had gone wrong with the play; something that the referees, the players, and the crowd hadn't noticed. The runner, in his all-out attempt to make it to the goal line, had stepped out of bounds and only the coach had noticed.

"We don't deserve them," Stagg said, pointing at the scoreboard. "I'd rather lose every game than win one unfairly." So the points vanished.

Did such an honest man have a chance in the competitive world of professional football? During the years that Stagg coached the team, they won 273 games, a fantastic record. *Time* magazine reported that Stagg "invented just about everything there is to football today." The huddle, forward pass, shift, man in motion, unbalanced line, onside kick, delayed buck, sleeper play—all were his ideas. His teams won seven Big Ten titles, and four teams never lost a game! Amos Stagg died at age 102 in 1965. Does honesty work? Just ask Chicago football fans.

NAG, NAG, NAG

Q: My mom constantly nags me about my messy room. Help me! What can I do? I am 12 years old.

A: Sometime when you and your mom are both in a good mood, talk about it and try to come up with a compromise. On the one hand, remember that your mom wants a clean home and how much it bothers her if your room looks like Martha Steward exploded in it. On the other hand, she needs to understand that you need a place of your own where you can enjoy your privacy.

Ask your mom what specifically bothers her about your room. Then perhaps you can work out a deal in which she grants you privacy so long as your messy room doesn't affect the rest of your family with things such as odors that stun buffalo or noises that pop eardrums. Maybe you can at least clean up the room a little. You may even find friends trapped under those mountains of clothes with whom you'll enjoy getting reacquainted. So if you both give a little, you should be able to work something out that you can each live with.

Karl Haffner

HARK! IT'S A . . . *SHARK!*

A six-foot-long eellike creature glides through the ocean, 400 feet below the surface. Even farther down, a club-shaped fish called a wobbegong skims the ocean floor, searching for food with its antenna-like feelers. Then there's the megamouth that looks like a normal fish but has thousands of teeth and luminous organs in its mouth to attract prey.

What do all these creatures have in common? They are all sharks. Half of the 368 species of shark are less than three feet long. Only about 70 species grow to six feet or more. Just 15 species reach longer than 12 feet, and many of them never come to the surface. Others are harmless to humans.

Great white sharks are one of the ocean's most difficult creatures to kill. But when you capture them, you must handle them with care in order to keep them alive.

The whale shark is the largest shark—50 feet in length. It is harmless to humans. The smallest shark is the dwarf dog shark, less than eight inches long!

Sharks keep the oceans healthy by eating weak fish. That prevents disease from spreading and wiping out whole schools of fish. Sharks' brains are as large as the brains of some mammals, and they can be trained as easily as a house cat.

Among God's most unusual creations, many shark species live such secret lives that scientists know almost nothing about them. Perhaps God has hidden them for a purpose—the predators of the deepest depths are the only ones humans aren't hunting to near extinction.

Jane Chase

I DON'T GET HEAVEN

Q: I can't imagine myself living up there in heaven forever. I just don't get it.

A: It *is* hard to imagine living forever, especially when we are still in a world in which people tell us that "all good things must come to an end." It's like going to a birthday party and having so much fun that you don't want it to end. Well, in heaven the good times will *never* end!

Recently we heard a pastor say that when he was in fifth grade he asked his teacher how long eternity is. She told him to picture a seagull taking a drop out of the ocean once every 1,000 years. By the time the ocean gets dry, she said, that will be the first *second* of eternity.

Maybe you're wondering, *How am I going to keep busy forever? Won't I get bored?* Don't worry. You will find loads of fun things to learn about and discover. The Bible tells us that "eye has not seen, nor ear heard, . . . the things which God has prepared for those who love Him" (1 Corinthians 2:9, NKJV). That's true of heaven—the Bible just gives us an occasional glimpse into what our future home will be like.

Finding out about heaven will be sort of like opening up wrapped presents on Christmas Day—a surprise! But we do know that heaven will have no pain, no sickness, no disappointments, no arguments, no tears—just 100 percent happiness all day, every day. And the best part is we'll get to live forever with Jesus.

Art and Pat Humphrey

THE WOMAN'S GOD

Mary Slessor moved through the night jungle with a prayer on her lips. "Please, God, close the wild beasts' mouths." She was hurrying to stop a war between two angry African tribes.

"A woman? Stopping a war?" the chief at the village had chuckled. "Impossible!"

"You see only a woman," Mary told him. "But don't forget this woman's God."

At midnight she reached the camp of the village warriors. Dancing around a campfire, they shouted and waved their spears, preparing themselves for battle. "Don't do this," she pleaded. "You and the other tribe must sit down and talk about your differences. No one must die."

Some of the men laughed. Others told her to go to get some rest and they'd discuss things calmly in the morning. But while the woman slept, they hurried away to the battlefield.

In the morning she rushed to the other camp and found that tribe's warriors ready for the kill. "Stop," she called. "No one must die!"

One of the men stepped forward from the snickering group and knelt before her. "Do you remember me?" he asked. "You came to my hut when I was young and healed me. You speak wisely. This is a foolish war. We want to stop it too."

Before long, Mary had both sides sitting around a conference campfire at which they solved their problems to everyone's satisfaction. No one died. Peace returned.

Mary Slessor stopped many wars in Africa's jungles. She became known as the White Queen of Okoyong. Many saw only the woman. But thousands came to know and love the woman's God.

TREASURE HUNT

Jesus continues His sermon to the people seated around Him on the mountainside. He has talked about praying, loving, and keeping hope alive. Now He adds treasures and lamps to the list. Listen.

"Do not store up for yourselves treasures on earth, where moth and rust destroy, and where thieves break in and steal. But store up for yourselves treasures in heaven, where moth and rust do not destroy, and where thieves do not break in and steal. For where your treasure is, there your heart will be also.

"The eye is the lamp of the body. If your eyes are good, your whole body will be full of light. But if your eyes are bad, your whole body will be full of darkness. If then the light within you is darkness, how great is that darkness!

"No one can serve two masters. Either he will hate the one and love the other, or he will be devoted to the one and despise the other. You cannot serve both God and Money."

Matthew 6:19-24

I know all about the "moth and rust destroy" part of what Jesus said. Once I wanted a certain car with all my heart. It was truly cool and looked like it was doing a hundred miles an hour even when parked.

Years later I saw that same car in a junkyard, covered with rust. It didn't look so cool then. I decided to start storing my treasures in heaven by keeping my hands, feet, and eyes focused on things that really matter—such as being kind and helpful. Those treasures can't rust.

PROPER ARMOR

Put on the full armor of God so that you can take your stand against the devil's schemes. Ephesians 6:11.

Sonja smiled sweetly. "Of course, I wouldn't recommend that all teens go to the movie I saw last night," she said. "A lot of young people would be tempted to do wrong if they saw it. But I can look at any movie I want to, and the bad parts don't harm me one bit."

Then there's Fort Pulaski.

Engineers spent almost 20 years building this Savannah, Georgia, marvel. It boasted walls 32 feet high and 11 feet thick. A deep moat surrounded it and offered protected pads for 140 cannon. "The enemy may make it very warm for you," Robert E. Lee told his Southern officers at the outbreak of the Civil War, "but they can't breach these walls."

No one mentioned that to the Northern army. Soon they showed up with a brand-new type of cannon that utilized rifled barrels. It increased the accuracy and range, and doubled the damage the shell caused when it slammed into its target. The fort that would not fall surrendered within 30 hours.

That harmless movie with those few scenes of violence or lust may be making more of an impact on you than you think. They may be planting subtle messages in your brain so that, when faced with situations similar to those encountered by the actors, you might react as they did in the movie.

Maybe it's time to put on God's armor, not your own. Fort Pulaski fell. So can you.

BOTTLE OF HARD WORK

Mark my words. You'll fail unless you do it."

Jim shook his head. "I can't. It wouldn't be right."

The meatcutter sighed. "Look, you bought this butcher store. Don't you want it to thrive?"

"Yes."

"Well, the man who owned it before you always gave a bottle of whiskey with each order from the chief cook at the hotel. In return, he bought all his meats here. Stop giving him his weekly bottle, and he'll stop purchasing from us. We'll go out of business."

Jim lifted his chin. "It's against my Christian principles to give away whiskey to stay in business. I'd rather give away a bottle of hard work!"

The meatcutter was right. When the flow of liquor stopped, so did the orders. The shop folded.

Years later, in 1924, Jim opened a dry-goods store in Hamilton, Missouri, the town where he'd grown up. The meatcutter hadn't been *totally* correct, because the store he opened was his five hundredth! Jim had kept his bottles full of hard work and had made it big by giving people an honest deal, not whiskey. You probably sleep on sheets purchased at Jim's store, or wear clothes from one of his retail outlets.

He stayed true to what he believed, never drinking a drop of liquor and providing good service to his customers.

In this day and age of hostile takeovers and corporate under-the-table deal making, actions that sometimes leave customers and employees out in the cold, it seems there's a lot to be learned from the man who wouldn't alter his principles—J. C. Penney.

PLAYING WITH FIRE

Q: I'm a 14-year-old guy, and I have a problem with looking at dirty magazines. How do I handle it?

A: You handle the problem of lust like you handle fire. You don't—it handles you. Your only hope is to trust in God and to stay away from the temptation.

When I was a boy, we spilled a can of gasoline in our garage. We didn't know how to clean it up, so a neighbor kid and I suggested to my youngest brother that he light a match and toss it into the pool of gasoline. None of us realized how serious the consequences could be. When my brother tossed the match, our garage exploded into flames. Needless to say, we didn't roast marshmallows and sing campfire songs. And my dad was not a happy camper.

Dirty magazines have an enticing appeal about them. They approach you as a friend and promise some fun and excitement. But you're dealing with a potential explosion that can destroy you. You're messing with fire.

God does not want you to be scarred. If it continues to be a big problem, share your feelings with a mature Christian. Read 1 Thessalonians 4:3-5 and talk to God about it.

Karl Haffner

SISTER AND THE SNAKES

Australia is known for beautiful beaches, towering rock formations, and something a little less appealing—snakes.

Heather lived in a small town surrounded by wild and beautiful countryside. One day her grandmother had hung clothes out to dry and asked Heather to bring them in from the line.

The girl had just begun working when she heard a soft hiss in the grass nearby. Looking down, she froze. Slipping among the blades was a dreaded brown snake, a highly poisonous breed of viper.

Heather glanced in the direction of her little brother's playpen farther out in the yard. She noticed that he was sticking his chubby arm through the slats, reaching for something. Inches from his hand lay a deadly black snake. "Grandfather!" Heather screamed running toward the porch where she grabbed the only weapon she could find—a broom. "Grandfather! Snakes!"

A man appeared on the porch, took one look at his frantic granddaughter, and then rushed back into the house. By now, Heather was at the playpen, pushing her little brother away from the viper and beating the snake with her broom. The creature coiled in confusion. Grandfather reappeared, rifle in hand. Soon both uninvited visitors were dead, and Heather and her brother were safe.

It takes courage to run in the direction of great danger, armed only with a broom, to save someone's life. But that's what Heather and Jesus did. They both faced a deadly serpent in order to save others. No, Jesus didn't have a broom. He was carrying a cross.

SAVED LITTLE ONES

Q: When babies die, will they be saved?

A: My brother Bob and his wife had a tragic experience many years ago. While serving as missionaries in Ethiopia, they had a baby. But it was born dead.

On that terrible day it was raining hard. Bob carried the tiny, still form out of the hospital and took it to a quiet place on a hillside, where he buried it deep in the ground. The rain brushed the tears of anguish from his cheeks and gently laid them on the grave.

When I heard that story for the first time, it broke my heart. It still does.

Someday that faraway grave will open, and a little baby's heart will start beating. His eyes, so long closed by death's silent sleep, will blink, and he'll see Jesus smiling down at him. And he won't be afraid.

The baby's parents are looking forward to a joyous reunion on that day. This time it won't be raining, and the tears staining their cheeks will spring from unspeakable joy.

Babies can't sin. They don't know right from wrong. But they do know when they're loved. Heaven will be filled with children, like my brother's baby, who'll never know anything but love. "Do not be amazed at this, for a time is coming when all who are in their graves will hear his voice and come out" (John 5:28, 29). I hope today's the day.

HEART HUNTERS

Police found the body of Aribo's brother under his hut. To make an unusual murder even stranger, the corpse didn't have a heart. Someone had removed it.

"Heart hunters!" the village people gasped, remembering that in parts of Africa the people consider a human heart valuable medicine. Some wicked men had even killed people in order to steal their hearts.

About that time two students from an Adventist school arrived to do some fund-raising. "Those two men," the village witch doctor announced, "are the heart hunters. They killed Aribo's brother."

Needless to say, the villagers didn't exactly welcome the visitors to their huts after that. "Get away from us!" the people demanded.

But when the students tried to board the truck that would take them back to school, the passengers threw them off. They couldn't leave nor could they stay.

The next day a kindly truck driver invited them to sit with him in his cab. That seemed to satisfy the passengers. But the truck hadn't gone two miles when it overturned on a steep corner and injured everyone except for the two students.

"They have magic charms in them," the witch doctor announced. "We must welcome them with open arms."

Now the Adventist young men could move freely in the village. Everyone gave generously, hoping that some of those magic charms would rub off on them.

God can use any situation to His glory if we're willing to endure a few lies and taunts. Give Him time, and you, like those students, can become heart hunters of the spiritual kind, stealing souls from the devil and bringing hope to those held hostage by evil.

WORRY WARTS

Some people spend their lives filled with worry. Jesus told the people seated before Him on the mountain to stop wasting brain cells on such a negative emotion. Here's what He said:

"Therefore I tell you, do not worry about your life, what you will eat or drink; or about your body, what you will wear. Is not life more important than food, and the body more important than clothes? Look at the birds of the air; they do not sow or reap or store away in barns, and yet your heavenly Father feeds them. Are you not much more valuable than they? Who of you by worrying can add a single hour to his life?

"And why do you worry about clothes? See how the lilies of the field grow. They do not labor or spin. Yet I tell you that not even Solomon in all his splendor was dressed like one of these. If that is how God clothes the grass of the field, which is here today and tomorrow is thrown into the fire, will he not much more clothe you, O you of little faith? So do not worry, saying, 'What shall we eat?' or 'What shall we drink?' or 'What shall we wear?' For the pagans run after all these things, and your heavenly Father knows that you need them. But seek first his kingdom and his righteousness, and all these things will be given to you as well. Therefore do not worry about tomorrow, for tomorrow will worry about itself. Each day has enough trouble of its own."

Matthew 6:25-34

THE GIFT OF MERCY

Is anything too hard for the Lord?" Genesis 18:14.

A crying woman came before the great French ruler Napoleon. "What is it you want?" he asked.

"It's my son," she said. "He has been convicted of a crime, and I beg his pardon from you."

Napoleon conferred with his councilors, then spoke to the visitor. "This is your son's second offense, and justice demands his death."

"I know," the mother cried. "My son has lived a sinful life. But I don't plead for justice from you. I plead for mercy."

The emperor shook his head. "But he doesn't deserve mercy."

"Sir," the woman urged, "it would not be mercy if he deserved it."

Napoleon smiled. "You speak wisely. Mercy is for the undeserving. He won't be put to death."

Did you catch the meaning in that story? Many juniors refuse to ask God for forgiveness for their sins because they think they're too bad. "I'm terrible, and Jesus won't ever want to be my friend," they say. "My heart is so full of evil thoughts and my hands are so busy doing evil things that God can't have mercy on me."

Want some good news? That's exactly the type of person to whom God offers oceans of mercy. "Let the wicked forsake his way and the evil man his thoughts," pleads Isaiah. "Let him turn to the Lord, and he will have mercy on him, and to our God, for he will freely pardon" (Isaiah 55:7). Go ahead. Ask God for mercy and forgiveness. He'll pardon you today.

LIFEBOAT

Pete Collins loved reading adventure stories, especially those involving heroics on the high seas. Often he'd row his boat beyond the breakers during family vacations and imagine saving lives.

When Pete grew up, he joined a lifeboat crew. Its dedicated men lived in large houses near where ships often floundered in stormy seas. They trained daily, guiding their lifeboats through rolling waves, building their muscles, and preparing for the time when they had to rescue someone.

One night, after the balmy days of summer had passed, a storm roared in from the ocean. Shrieking winds rocked the house. The light beam from the lighthouse vanished into the sweeping rain and icy sleet. In the distance a foghorn moaned, adding a feeling of doom to the scene.

At about 2:00 in the morning the watch stationed above the building saw a flare arch low over the horizon. A ship was in distress! He sounded the alarm. Pete and his team jumped into their gear, gathered their ropes and flotation devices, and raced for the lifeboat.

As they struggled toward the ocean, Pete saw waves as tall as buildings crashing across the sands. The water boiled like a cauldron, and an icy wind sucked the breath from his lungs. For the first time in his life he felt truly frightened.

"Captain," he shouted to the man in charge, "we'll never get back."

The man nodded as he helped push the boat toward the breakers. "We don't have to come back, Pete," he said. "But we do have to go out."

When God calls you to do something, don't let difficulties stop you. Start out! Let Him take care of what happens after that!

MONEY

Q: I want to be rich like Bill Gates. Is that wrong? I'm 12 years old.

A: There's nothing wrong with being rich. If your primary goal in life, however, is simply to get rich, then it's wrong. Think about the scriptural counsel: "You cannot serve two masters: God and money. For you will hate one and love the other, or else the other way around" (Matthew 6:24, TLB).

Money is neither good nor bad. It's only when money takes the place of God and turns into an obsession that it becomes wrong to be rich. Make serving God your primary goal, and the money may or may not come.

Karl Haffner

DUMB AND NOT SO DUMB

A man kept several white-footed mice as pets. One night they escaped from their cage, poked around the kitchen, found a hole in a cupboard, and took up housekeeping in a dark, inaccessible corner.

When the man discovered the empty cage, he worried that his little friends would starve, so he placed hickory nuts on the floor before going to bed.

Around dawn he heard something mysterious. It sounded like someone was throwing rocks at his house. Soon he discovered the source of the commotion. As he watched, one of the escapees scurried across the kitchen floor, grabbed a nut, and headed back to the hole. One problem—the mouse could fit through, but the nut couldn't. *Clunk.*

The rodent tried gripping the nut with its teeth and backing in. *Clunk.* It pushed from behind. *Clunk.* Finally, the little critters discovered that they could enjoy the nuts only if they ate out—in the kitchen. It never occurred to them to spend a few moments enlarging the hole!

Two water hens lived on a farm that raised beautiful pheasants. One day the farmer installed a new drinking station for his prize birds. When a pheasant stood on the handle, the top would spring open, providing a refreshing drink. But when a little water hen tried the same trick, its weight wasn't enough to lift the lid. That's when it asked (in hen language) a friend to join it. When the two stood on the handle, their combined weight lifted the lid.

Facing a challenge? Stop, think, and use your head. Are you a water hen . . . or a mouse?

SAVED ANYWAY

Q: Will those who believe in Christ but not in the seventh-day as the Sabbath go to heaven?

A: Something important happened right before Jesus died as He hung between two criminals, all in terrible agony.

"Hey! Aren't you the Christ?" one demanded with an angry, sarcastic voice. "Why don't you save yourself—and us, too?"

The other thief had been watching Jesus carefully. He'd seen Him give comfort to His weeping mother even while pain racked His bruised and bleeding body. And he'd heard Him ask God to forgive the guards for their cruel actions. Not one curse did Jesus hurl at the crowd. Not one murmur of anger or hate had escaped His parched lips.

"Don't you fear God?" he asked, addressing the other criminal. "We deserve to die. But this man is sinless." At that moment the second thief fully believed what he'd heard about this stranger from Nazareth. As his body trembled in pain, he called out, "Jesus, remember me when you come into your kingdom" (Luke 23:42).

Christ answered him immediately. "I tell you the truth . . . you will be with me in paradise" (verse 43).

The thief didn't have time to accept most of the things Jesus taught, but he was saved anyway—because he believed in Jesus. We, on the other hand, have time. Obeying *all* God's laws keeps us safely within the boundaries of His saving power. With us, belief must be combined with obedience.

MIDNIGHT BATTLE

Pedro Bernardo traveled up and down the Amazon River by canoe selling Christian books to the villagers he passed. At night he'd find a quiet nook by a protected bank, tie his boat to a tree limb, and drift to sleep amid the muffled sounds of the jungle.

Early one morning he discovered that he'd tied his canoe to a very dangerous tree. No, the limbs and leaves weren't the problem. It was what lived in the tree that almost cost him his life.

The sting of the fire ant can burn like a flame. If enough of the large creatures sting you, you die. As Pedro slumbered under that particular tree that night, an army of fire ants began marching down the rope, heading straight for the weary literature evangelist.

At that moment a gentle breeze drifted across the waters, pushing the free end of the canoe around until it came to rest against the limb of another tree. Unknown to the slumbering Christian, this tree contained a colony of black ants—deadly enemies of the fire ants. A new army swarmed down the limb, boarded the canoe, and met the fire ants just a couple feet from Pedro's head.

All night long a fierce, silent war raged, with casualties on both sides. At dawn, when Pedro awakened, he rolled over to discover that his canoe had been a battleground and was littered with dead and dying fire ants. Their black cousins had gained the upper hand and driven the red army out of the canoe, back up the rope, and into their own tree.

From every enemy, God provides a Saviour.

HERE COMES THE JUDGE!

Have you ever had someone judge you? Many times people "pass judgment" or make a decision about us without hearing all the evidence in our favor. That's what Jesus was talking about when He spoke to those assembled on the mountainside with Him. Listen to what He said.

"Do not judge, or you too will be judged. For in the same way you judge others, you will be judged, and with the measure you use, it will be measured to you.

"Why do you look at the speck of sawdust in your brother's eye and pay no attention to the plank in your own eye? How can you say to your brother, 'Let me take the speck out of your eye,' when all the time there is a plank in your own eye? You hypocrite, first take the plank out of your own eye, and then you will see clearly to remove the speck from your brother's eye.

"Do not give dogs what is sacred; do not throw your pearls to pigs. If you do, they may trample them under their feet, and then turn and tear you to pieces."

Matthew 7:1-6

Before we make any judgment, we'd better be sure all is right in our heart. We may be just as guilty as the next guy and end up condemning ourselves!

As for the dogs and pearls, Jesus was saying, "Don't waste your time with people who make fun of God and the Bible."

If they refuse to listen to you when you talk about Jesus, move on. But never stop asking God to show you ways to help them.

THE GRACE TO FORGIVE

In him we have redemption through his blood, the forgiveness of sins, in accordance with the riches of God's grace that he lavished on us with all wisdom and understanding. Ephesians 1:7, 8.

Night settled over the smoldering battlefield, hiding the terrible carnage from view. In the darkness the moans of dying soldiers filled the humid air, reminding all of the violent battle that had taken place that afternoon at Gettysburg, Pennsylvania.

Guns had crackled, cannons had roared, swords had slashed. In the end the Southern army had fled.

Suddenly the survivors of the battle saw a curious sight. In the darkness a tiny light cast by a lantern moved among the dead and dying, stopping now and then as though its owner was searching for something. "John Hartman?" a voice echoed from behind the glow. "John Hartman, your father calls for you."

Again and again the heartbreaking words drifted across the carnage.

The glow of the lantern outlined the desperate face of an older man as he searched in the darkness. Then another voice, weak and faltering, called, "Over here, Father."

Mr. Hartman hurried to his fallen son, carefully picked him up, and carried him home. The man had tried to teach his son that it was wrong to kill, even in battle. But the boy, headstrong and longing for adventure, had run away and joined the army. Even though his son had disobeyed him, the father still loved his wayward child.

Today Jesus is calling out to you. How will you answer?

BLAME THE TEENAGERS

The midnight blast shook the ground. In the morning all that remained of the beautiful sundial in Denver's Cranmer Park were bits and pieces.

It had been no ordinary sundial. Six feet across and carved out of red Colorado sandstone, it had been an exact copy of an ancient Chinese time-telling device. Now it lay in ruins, victim of an unknown bomber.

"Probably some teenager trying to show off," adults in the city grumbled.

"Yeah. They're nothing but trouble," others agreed.

"Hey, we didn't do anything," high school students throughout the metropolis responded with growing frustration. "Every time something happens, we get blamed. Makes us mad! Let's go out and really blow something up. They say everything's our fault anyway, so why not?"

"Wait," other teens advised, "that would just prove the adults right. Why don't we do something that will show them how wrong they are to blame us for the bad stuff that happens."

One by one, school by school, the teenagers of Denver began to go from door-to-door, business-to-business, raising money to replace the destroyed sundial. "Hey," adults began to say, "we'd better get in on this before the teens do it all!"

When public officials unveiled the beautiful new sundial later that year, the glory belonged to the very teens the city had blamed earlier. One junior high school alone raised a large chunk of the money.

If that new sundial ever gets blown up, one group in Denver won't be under suspicion. The teens! They've proved themselves above the rumors and nasty accusations and have shown once and for all that all teens aren't bad. Most, in fact, are very, very good.

UNKIND FRIEND

Q: I'm 12 and have a question. My friend is always cutting me down around other friends. He especially says mean things about me when we are around girls. What can I do to make him stop?

A: I had a friend in school who was much like the person you describe. To give you an idea of what he was like, notice how he signed my yearbook: "Dear Karl. You are a stupid schmuck. A real dorkface idiot. Nothing personal! Your friend, Loren."

I remember being afraid to be around other people (especially girls!) when my "friend" was near because I never knew how he might publicly embarrass me. I realize now he never was a friend, but rather someone who used me to feel better about himself. Usually kids who are always ragging on friends don't like themselves, so they have to dog others.

In your case, I would suggest you talk firmly with your friend and let him know you won't tolerate the cutting comments any longer. If you don't see any change, stick with your promise and hang out with other friends. You won't be losing a friend—you'll be gaining self-confidence.

Karl Haffner

A FALL AND A FIRE

Playing in my backyard one day, I threw a ball over what I thought was a finished brick wall. When I tried to jump the wall, I caught my toe and landed flat on my back on gravel and stickers. I was in great pain.

Suddenly I felt a tremendous pressure turning my head to look at the sky. Just then a cement brick fell right on my forehead. It hurt! But if I hadn't turned, I would have died. That brick would have landed on my temple, injuring my brain. Even though I ended up with a broken nose and wrenched back, I believe an angel was trying to protect me. So thank You, Lord!

Tucker Burnett,
10, Arizona

When I was only 4 years old we went to my grandmother's house for Mother's Day. Before going to bed, I played with my racing-car set and had fun watching them zoom around the track.

At about 4:43 a.m. my dad smelled smoke but thought that it was the burned rubber on my racing car tires. Then he looked out the window and saw flames raging under the apartment building!

He quickly called the fire station and got everyone out of the apartment. By the time the firefighters got there, nearly the entire bottom section of the building was engulfed in fire. The good news is that they put out the fire and no one was really hurt. My grandmother lived on the bottom part of the building, but her apartment wasn't burned down.

I'm glad God was able to wake my dad up in time.

Rodney Brown,
14, California

LAUGHED AT

Q: How are teens supposed to tell others about Jesus without being laughed at?

A: We are so excited that you want to witness for Jesus! Here's a little story that we hope will help.

Jorge was a young Christian who had never witnessed for his faith. One day at church the minister preached a sermon about sharing Jesus, quoting Romans 1:16.

The next Monday at school Jorge made up his mind to tell others about how to get to heaven. He prayed, "Lord, the first person who comes into the classroom, I'll tell him or her about You." Just then David ambled in. *Oh, no!* he thought. *Not David! Please, Lord!*

Jorge froze. For the next 10 minutes he and David sat in silence. Then the bell rang and class began. Jorge felt horrible. He had let God down.

So he prayed. Then God gave him an idea. He decided to find his classmate and just talk to him. He said, "David, I've known you a long time, but I've never told you about the most important thing in my life. Can I share it with you?" There it was. A plain and simple witness. Do you think David laughed? No way. Instead, David said, "Jorge, I've always known there was something different about you. I've just been waiting for you to tell me."

Get the picture? *Ask God to show you opportunities to share what Jesus has done for you.*

Become friends with a wide range of individuals, and you'll certainly have opportunities to share Christ. When others know that you truly care about them, they won't laugh. They'll listen.

Art and Pat Humphrey

HIDDEN BY RAGE

Where's Wanda?" the angry woman with the knife shouted. She peered over the assembled Sabbath school members and growled. "I'm not about to have my daughter join this church. I'll kill her first!"

The woman paced up and down the aisles, searching for her child, knife waving menacingly in front of her. "She says she wants to be baptized and follow some strange God. I won't allow it. Tell me where she is!"

No one spoke. Everyone sat motionless with fear.

At the front row the woman stopped and stared. "If you see her, tell her this is waiting for her." She thrust the knife into the air and then plunged it downward. The warning was quite clear.

As quickly as she'd arrived, the woman stalked out, mumbling curses under her breath.

What's amazing about this story that took place in Indonesia some years ago was that Wanda, the girl for whom the woman was searching, was there that morning. She wasn't trying to hide but was sitting, trembling with fear, on the front row, inches from where her mother stood. She and her friend were in plain sight, but the woman hadn't seen her.

Rage does strange things to the human mind. But thankfully, God is more powerful than rage. He can take that violent emotion and use it to His benefit, allowing its poison to cloud the senses. That same power later transformed the woman's heart. Months later it was her turn to sit on the front row, preparing for baptism.

KNOCK, KNOCK

Jesus began wrapping up His mountainside talk with a startling announcement—we can have anything we want! All we have to do is ask. Right? Listen:

"Ask and it will be given to you; seek and you will find; knock and the door will be opened to you. For everyone who asks receives; he who seeks finds; and to him who knocks, the door will be opened.

"Which of you, if his son asks for bread, will give him a stone? Or if he asks for a fish, will give him a snake? If you, then, though you are evil, know how to give good gifts to your children, how much more will your Father in heaven give good gifts to those who ask him!"

Matthew 7:7-11

I know what you're thinking. "Hey, I'd like to have a new computer or that cool leather jacket I saw at Penney's." But before you toss your allowance and head for the mall, you might want to remember what Jesus had been talking about just before the "Knock, knock" portion of His speech.

He'd been telling everyone not to concern themselves with material stuff such as clothes and food. Furthermore, He'd instructed His hearers to stop judging others and to lay up treasures "in heaven" instead of on earth. The focus of His talk was people's minds, not their wallets.

Jesus tells us to ask for *spiritual* gifts, which He gladly provides. When we beg for wisdom, He's there with a trunkful. You see, it's the door to *understanding* that opens when we knock.

SHARED GRACE

Don't be afraid," David said to him, "for I will surely show you kindness for the sake of your father Jonathan." 2 Samuel 9:7.

Great rejoicing spread through the Union camp. The Northern forces had captured two sons of General Robert E. Lee, commander of the Southern army.

"Hang 'em," shouted Mr. Stanton, the secretary of war.

"The Southern army has several of our officers," replied his assistant. "They're planning to hang them, so it's only right that we do the same."

While the North rejoiced, the South cried out in anguish, especially the families of General Lee. When Confederate president Jefferson Davis heard the news, he sent an immediate message to President Lincoln, begging mercy for his general's sons.

Lincoln received the message at midnight. "What's the meaning of this?" the president asked a sleepy Stanton.

"Those boys deserve to die," the official responded. "Besides, the South's about to hang two of ours."

Lincoln shook his head. "I can't stop the enemy from killing our men. But for us to hang their men in this manner would stamp 'murder' on my heart. It can't be done!" After scribbling some words on a scrap of paper, the president ordered, "Send this message to the officer in charge of the fort where the boys are held." The message read: "Immediately release both of the sons of Robert E. Lee and send them back to their father."

Like David of old, Abraham Lincoln was showing mercy for the sake of the boys' father, General Lee. Why not carry on that beautiful tradition today by showing mercy for God's sake?

GUIDED ARROW

Ross watched the arrow zoom upward, silently piercing the hot desert air. It sure beat sitting at home on a Sabbath afternoon. Besides, the air seemed just a little cooler out here, away from the hum of machinery and traffic.

The arrow slowed as it reached its highest altitude. Ross could barely make out the slender shaft as it arched over and began its long drop earthward.

Sabbaths could be boring when there wasn't anything going on at church. He'd spent the last hour shooting arrows into cactuses, fallen logs, and anything else that presented itself as a target. But his new game of firing arrows high into the sky was fun. Ross grinned as the shaft picked up speed. He'd lost all track of time and wasn't exactly sure where he was. Mom and Dad had stayed back in the car to nap.

The boy glanced down at where he knew the arrow would fall just to see what he might hit. He blinked. There, in direct line with the rapidly descending object were Mom and Dad standing beside the family automobile.

He didn't have time to pray, to ask God to forgive his recklessness. All he could do was draw in a quick breath and shout, "Look out!"

At that moment the arrow embedded itself with a soft *thwang* into the ground just feet from where his parents were standing.

The boy dropped to his knees. "O God," he prayed, "forgive me. Forgive me!"

Ross has a new prayer now. It starts like this: "Dear God, help me to be more careful."

MORE FRIENDS

Q: I'm wondering how I can have more friends. I'm not popular in my school. I'm 13.

A: I once heard it said: "Friendship is heaven, and lack of friendship is hell." We all need friends. Here are a few suggestions as to how to have more of them.

Be friendly to everyone. You've probably heard the cliché "To have a friend, you have to be a friend." It has a lot of truth to it.

Focus on them. You'll never hurt for friends if you ask people questions about themselves. Ask just about anything: "What's your favorite ice cream? What's your favorite TV show? How can I get better grades, like you?" Everyone loves to share their opinion. Let them give it to you.

Be yourself. Too many kids try to be someone they admire. If you're a nerd, be a nerd. It doesn't matter who you are—just be genuine.

Karl Haffner

BRIGHTER LIGHTS

Lawrence Maxwell, former editor of *Guide* magazine, wrote a beautiful illustration highlighting our life with Jesus in the February 14, 1962, issue. Here's what he said:

"One day I toured a battleship with my dad and twin brother. What an exciting trip! We saw gun turrets and mighty guns, torpedo tubes and engine rooms. Then we stood in line to look into the ship's searchlight. The sailors gave us heavily tinted glass to protect our eyes, but what a tremendous light that was!

"From then on, when I used a flashlight, no matter how bright that flashlight may have been, it seemed dim and dull in comparison. The experience reminded me of the beautiful song by Helen H. Lemmel that juniors like to sing. 'Turn your eyes upon Jesus, look full in His wonderful face; and the things of earth will grow strangely dim in the light of His glory and grace.'*

"At one time I was an organ student and thought I was doing just fine. Then a famous organist visited our college and played on the auditorium organ. His fingers tripped effortlessly up and down the keys as his feet danced over the pedals with unfailing grace and accuracy. Suddenly my own playing seemed dreadfully poor.

"Now I know what it means when the Bible says our goodness is as filthy rags compared to the purity and goodness of Jesus.

"Once we catch a glimpse of Christ and hear the music of His love played in our hearts, nothing can compare. Nothing."

---

*© 1980 by John M. Moore. Assigned to Singspiration (ASCAP), Division of Zondervan Corp.

WAGES OF LOVE

Q: If the wages of sin is death, why isn't Satan dead by now?

A: For the same reason we aren't. We've all sinned, but we're still kickin'.

Let's travel back in time for a moment until we're in the Garden of Eden and God the Creator (Jesus) is talking to Adam. "You are free to eat from any tree in the garden; but you must not eat from the tree of the knowledge of good and evil, for when you eat of it you will surely die" (Genesis 2:16, 17).

But when Eve, and then Adam, ate from the tree, they didn't drop over dead on the spot. You see, what the sin of disobedience to God's law does is separate us from the life-sustaining power of Heaven. When earth's first inhabitants allowed sin to enter their lives, they began the dying *process*. Years later they did die, and every generation since Eden has fallen victim to that deadly pattern.

When Jesus died on the cross, He became a painful example to the universe of what that terrible separation can do. But when He rose from the dead, He showed what can happen when men and women choose to end their separation from God by accepting His forgiveness and saving grace.

As you invite God into your heart, you close the gap, allowing Jesus to save you from that endless separation brought on by sin. You may die an earthly death (as Jesus did), but you'll live again in heaven. Those who remain separated, such as Satan, will experience a death that has no resurrection.

THROUGH THE MOB

Bring out the Methodist! Where is the Methodist?" The mob's angry voices rang with bitterness and hate. Their town had a visitor whom they'd grown to despise, a man who preached a much different message than the church to which they belonged, a man who said that Jesus wanted to be their friend and would forgive their sins if they just asked. It was blasphemy!

John Wesley had come to town to visit a sick friend but suddenly found himself the center of a riot. Heavy footsteps sounded outside his friend's bedroom and then, with a crash, the door separated from its hinges and slammed to the floor.

Wesley stood to face his attackers. "Here I am," he said calmly. "Did one of you want to talk to me?"

The mob fell silent. Here was no monster such as the church leaders had reported. Wesley was no evil being breathing fire and spitting poisonous words. He was a man—a simple man with kind eyes and a gentle voice.

As the mob parted, their screams and shouts silenced, Wesley walked across the room. He descended the steps and walked through the large gathering outside, smiling as he passed. Through the town he went until he reached the docks and boarded the ship that would take him away.

Did his confrontation with the mob deter him from visiting other towns where he wasn't welcome? No. This Reformer, who founded the Methodist Church, traveled to cities and towns throughout England and the American colonies, continuing his work for God.

Our world needs men and women like John Wesley, people unafraid to demonstrate Christ's love even to angry mobs.

WORDS

When Jesus had entered Capernaum, a centurion came to him, asking for help. "Lord," he said, "my servant lies at home paralyzed and in terrible suffering."

Jesus said to him, "I will go and heal him."

The centurion replied, "Lord, I do not deserve to have you come under my roof. But just say the word, and my servant will be healed. For I myself am a man under authority, with soldiers under me. I tell this one, 'Go,' and he goes; and that one, 'Come,' and he comes. I say to my servant, 'do this,' and he does it."

When Jesus heard this, he was astonished and said to those following him, "I tell you the truth, I have not found anyone in Israel with such great faith. I say to you that many will come from the east and the west, and will take their places at the feast with Abraham, Isaac and Jacob in the kingdom of heaven. But the subjects of the kingdom will be thrown outside, into the darkness, where there will be weeping and gnashing of teeth."

Then Jesus said to the centurion, "Go! It will be done just as you believed it would." And his servant was healed at that very hour.

Matthew 8:5-13

The centurion understood something important. Jesus doesn't have to be physically present to change lives. His words are enough.

"If only Jesus were here," some juniors moan. "Then He'd tell me what to do." Relax. Jesus may not be walking around your town, but His words are available 24 hours a day, 365 days a year! Where? In your good ol' Bible!

WAITING FOR GOD

We do not make requests of you because we are righteous, but because of your great mercy. O Lord, listen! O Lord, forgive!" Daniel 9:18, 19.

Before Daniel uttered those words in prayer, he'd confessed that God's people, now exiled in Babylon, had "sinned and done wrong. . . . [They had] been wicked and . . . rebelled" (verse 5). Not exactly a pretty picture. But God forgave and eventually restored the captives to their homeland.

Listen to a modern-day Daniel share her feelings about grace and our uncertain future:

A wandering thought in my head as time unwinds,
    A steady but quick pace down to Your grave,
    I kneel in prayer and imagine the golden stair.
I pray for Your forgiveness and hope You will soon be here.
I adore You and can't wait to see You,
    God my Saviour and my knight in shining armor.
We await Your second coming and are ready to face You
          without shame,
    For God is not a game.
We should never give shame to the name of God on most high,
    For no married man should have a wandering eye,
    A man is to his wife as the Bible is to God.
We should keep the law, not one thing should flaw.
I tell you the truth, youth and beauty will soon go poof.
    But no matter what, God will always be there for you,
    For you are not alone.
Give me your hand, and we'll walk to the throne.

Sara L. Sherron,
14, California

THE BABY
OF ROARING CAMP

It was a sound never before heard in Roaring Camp. The wind seemed to stop rustling the pine trees, the river paused in its headlong rush for the sea, and the flames ceased their crackling and hissing in the fireplace.

Roaring Camp was used to lots of swearing, cursing, and angry talk. But the new sound made every rough, dirty gold miner sit up and take notice. It was the plaintive cry of a newborn baby.

The mother died two hours after her child was born, so the miners appointed Stumpy, a man wanted by the police, to care for the baby. When they peeked in to see the new arrival, they removed their hats. "Just don't seem proper to be looking at a pure, innocent little baby with our hats on," Stumpy insisted.

The child needed a cradle, so the men ordered one from a catalog. The new cradle made the cabin look old and dingy, so they built a new cabin. The new cabin made the other cabins look old and dingy, so they constructed more new cabins. Can't have new cabins without a new grocery store. And look at the streets! Yup, they gotta be fixed.

The miners themselves began bathing, combing their hair, and brushing their teeth. "Roaring Camp has changed," one man said a few months later. "It's—why, it's like heaven!"

All because of a little baby.

Can you think of another child who came into a rough, dingy, and dark world and changed it with His presence? Here's a hint. Think Christmas.

TOUGH COMPETITION

Q: I'm almost 13. There is this girl I really like, but I have tough competition. Our landlord's son has known her longer, plus his sister is her best friend. At times when he and I are alone he is OK, but when she is around he is a show-off. Sometimes I just want to punch his face in. I just moved and hardly have any friends here. He tells her the secrets that I tell him. I would really appreciate your help!

A: Sounds to me like your landlord's son is insecure. He displays his insecurity by showing off when the girl is around. That is not unusual, as even popular kids can be unsure about themselves.

Don't allow his behavior to control you. It's easy to react in anger when someone is treating you like rotten milk. But anger benefits nobody. If it gets hold of you, it eats at you until you become a hateful, bitter bulldog. Take control of yourself and act—don't react.

Decide how Christ would act toward him and this girl, and try to do the same. Whether or not this will help you win over the girl remains to be seen. Keep in mind, however, that girls tend to be much more perceptive than guys. (We don't realize that, because we're not that skilled in social things.) Girls sense that a guy guided by God is more likely to be conscientious, kind, and loving—qualities that attract many girls.

Karl Haffner

BROTHER AND THE BULL

Y ou're about to meet a hero who is short, can't run very well, and hasn't spent a day in school. And he's only 5.

Parts of Australia are great for raising cows. To make more cows, you gotta have bulls, and that's exactly what Justin's father had purchased. "He's a mean one," the man warned his family. "Stay away."

Justin took one look at the huge animal and decided that was *very* good advice.

A few days later the boy was watching the cows come in for milking when he saw the new bull lower his head and start toward something near the barn. That something was his little sister Emily! Dad was too far away to help. If Emily was to be saved, he'd have to do it himself.

The boy raced to his sister's side and tried to lift her. He wasn't strong enough. The bull, now in a full gallop, thundered closer and closer.

Justin grabbed his sister under her arms and tried to drag her. It worked. He dug his heels in and pulled until his teeth ached. Emily didn't like being disturbed from her play and protested. She hadn't seen the bull now charging with incredible speed, horns lowered.

With a final mighty effort the lad pulled the girl through the barn's side door and slammed it shut just as the bull galloped by, shaking the earth.

God asks us to be big brother to the world. Satan attacks, and people aren't aware of the danger. They need us, no matter how old, tall, educated, or frightened we may be. Become a hero to someone today.

"COME, LORD JESUS"

Q: Do you think Jesus will come in our lifetime?

A: I must be careful how I answer your question. If I say yes, I'm suggesting I know as much as God, which I certainly don't. "No one knows about that day or hour, not even the angels in heaven, nor the Son, but only the Father" (Mark 13:32).

Be very wary of anyone who says they've figured out the month or year of Christ's return. They're trying to play God.

If you'll rephrase your question and ask, "Do you *want* Jesus to come?" or "Are you *preparing* for Jesus to come in our lifetime?" my answer is a resounding yes! Why? Because all the biblical signs are pointing to a soon return. All the prophecies concerning the Second Coming have been or are being fulfilled. The conditions for His return are just like Jesus said they'd be. Besides, I'm sick and tired of living in a world rotting away because of sin and selfishness, aren't you?

When Jesus comes is His business. Getting *ready* to meet Him—that's ours. Let's prepare together!

"Behold," Christ announces in Revelation 22:12, "I am coming soon! My reward is with me, and I will give to everyone according to what he has done."

With John I shout, "Amen. Come, Lord Jesus" (verse 20).

PRISON OR THE POT

At one time in New Guinea people ate people. Yeah, I know. *Gross!*

But Jesus tells His followers to go into all the world. *All* of it. That includes places where cannibals live.

Kalapi and Alia met Jesus and gave their hearts to Him. When they heard that famous command from the Bible, Kalapi told his friend, "We've got to go up into the mountains."

"But if the cannibals don't put us in cooking pots, the government will throw us in jail," Alia responded. "It's against the law to preach religion in cannibal villages." But the two men set out anyway, traveling for days through snake-infested jungles. When they reached a village, they hung their Picture Roll on a tree limb and began telling everyone who'd listen about a Saviour who forgives sins and makes lives clean of evil thoughts and actions. People listened and believed.

One day two police officers appeared in the village and ordered the young missionaries out. "But this isn't a cannibal village anymore," Kalapi protested. "Most of these people are Christians now." His words fell on deaf ears as they sent him and Alia back to the city. Luckily, they didn't end up in jail but were told to *stay out of the mountains!* To make sure they obeyed, a police officer went to guard the village against further "disruption."

Here's the really neat part. The police officer the government sent was a Seventh-day Adventist! The spark Kalapi and Alia ignited continued to burn. When God says "Go into all the world," He goes with us.

DON'T CRY

Soon afterward, Jesus went to a town called Nain, and his disciples and a large crowd went along with him. As he approached the town gate, a dead person was being carried out—the only son of his mother, and she was a widow. And a large crowd from the town was with her. When the Lord saw her, his heart went out to her and he said, "Don't cry."

Then he went up and touched the coffin, and those carrying it stood still. He said, "Young man, I say to you, get up!" The dead man sat up and began to talk, and Jesus gave him back to his mother.

They were all filled with awe and praised God. "A great prophet has appeared among us," they said. "God has come to help his people." This news about Jesus spread throughout Judea and the surrounding country.

Luke 7:11-17

Have you ever stood at the graveside of someone you loved? You remember all the wonderful things you and that person used to do, such as play games or attend class or go for bicycle rides in the country. Perhaps it was a grandparent, brother, or sister, or even a mom or dad.

In times like that we need to remember what Jesus said to the widow as she followed the casket of her son. Two simple words: "Don't cry."

Jesus wasn't saying, "Don't cry because you're sad." That's normal in a sinful world. No, He was saying, "Don't cry because you think you'll never see your son again." He knew better. And so do we.

BLESSINGS IN DISGUISE

Soon after my parents' marriage ended, my mother, who'd been raised an Adventist, decided to go back to church.

After a few weeks my mom met a really nice, caring Christian man. They started to date and a year later got married. Mom had a new husband, and although I never thought I would feel that way, I was really happy to have a wonderful stepdad. I now live in an Adventist home, something I don't think would have happened if my parents had stayed together.

Many times I wondered, "Why would God let us go through all that hurt and unhappiness?"

Then one day during school worship we read Romans 8:28: "All things work together for good to those who love God" (NKJV). This text really made a difference in my life.

Now, I don't think divorce is God's plan. In fact, I'm sure it isn't. But now I realize that even though divorce isn't God's ideal plan, even a bad situation can work out for good.

I appreciate the blessings I enjoy being raised in an Adventist home, being able to go to an Adventist school, and having Christian friends. It is something good that God brought out of something bad. I have learned to look for the bright side of things and to wait for God to work things out for good.

I believe God brings blessings in disguise. What has come out of this has definitely shown evidence of God working in my life. It has helped me to realize how much He loves me. I'm so glad He does.

Lindsay June Moore,
grade 7, Tennessee

OTHERS' FEELINGS FIRST

Rod slammed the door, trying to keep the rain and wind from following him into the cozy gas station. Huddled around the heater in the center of the room sat several other truck drivers who'd found refuge from the storm.

"Heavy rains and high winds over most of the area tonight," the announcer on the radio said. "Motorists should be on the alert for hazardous driving conditions and slippery roads."

"Whooeee!" Rod said as he seated himself by the counter. "This weather ain't fit for man nor beast." Just then he noticed a small beagle puppy huddled on a crumpled towel in a corner of the room. "Got yourself a dog, huh?" he called over to his friend Ci.

"No," the man answered. "I think someone left him here earlier today when they stopped for gas. He just kinda appeared. Looks scared."

Reaching over, Rod picked up the trembling pup. "Must be the runt of the litter."

"This just in," the radio announcer called from the speaker mounted overhead. "A little girl named Kathy who lives on Route 58, 10 miles east of the grade school, said she lost her puppy today. It's a beagle, 3 months old."

Rod grinned. "Well, that mystery is solved." He headed for the door. "Gotta get this little fellow back home where he belongs."

"In this weather?" Ci retorted. "Besides, it's 50 miles out of your way."

"One thing I can't stand to see is a scared puppy or a lonely little girl," the burly truck driver responded. "'Bye."

That night a girl and her puppy were reunited because someone put their feelings first.

MEAN STEPDAD

Q: I'm 12. I have a stepdad who is real mean. Every time he gets mad about something he gets mad at everyone, especially me. My mom says to pray for him. I've tried, but nothing happens. I just need some advice because I don't know what to do.

A: Trying to change people is like trying to change an opossum into a toad—it doesn't happen. Only God can transform your stepdad.

Understand that your parents have struggles and pressures similar to the hard things you go through. You may be the target they dump their frustrations on. It's not fair to you, but it does help you not to take some of the anger and criticism so personally.

You can help your dad see how his behavior is affecting you. Gently approach him and tell him how you feel when he gets angry. Don't accuse him, but let him know your viewpoint.

Karl Haffner

EAT YOUR WEEDIES

Your mom and dad probably aren't crazy about the things. They pace the lawn, deadly spray bottle in hand, shooting each bright-yellow spot in the carpet of green. Others simply mow down the little weedy pests, chopping off their golden heads before they can spread seed. Still others dig in a vain effort to remove the entire root so the pesky plant won't grow again.

Dandelions are the "curse" of the urban landscape. City officials complain about them, and homeowners go to great lengths to get rid of them. Most people see them as nothing more than a common, worthless weed. But not everyone.

Dandelions are a multimillion-dollar crop industry in Texas, Florida, Arizona, California, and New Jersey. Most get used in the restaurant business.

A serving of dandelion leaves has almost 300 percent of the daily requirement of vitamin A, more than half the requirement of vitamin C, protein, phosphorus, iron, potassium, thiamine, riboflavin, calcium, and magnesium.

The dandelion's botanical name (*Taraxacum officinale*) means "official remedy for disorders." It improves liver function and lowers cholesterol and blood pressure. Also it stimulates urine production. Health food stores sell dandelion juice for making tea (one teaspoon to one cup of warm water).

As early as 1200 B.C. people were eating dandelions. The inhabitants of Europe and Asia have had them on the menu for at least 1,000 years.

God doesn't put anything on earth without a purpose. Every part of the dandelion can be eaten, from leaves and flowers to roots. Explore the possibilities of dandelions. Then eat your weedies!

JEWELS IN OUR CROWN

Q: How come so many Seventh-day Adventists don't wear makeup or jewelry?

A: Here's a question for *you*. When you really love someone, what is the main thing you want to do? Make them happy, of course! We show our love for our parents by doing our best to please them. And in the same way, we show our love for God by our loyalty and by making Him happy.

The Bible often associates wearing jewelry and makeup with disloyalty to God. When Jacob presented his family at the altar of the Lord at Bethel, they got rid of their earrings (Genesis 35:1-5). And in Exodus 33:1-6 God told Moses that the people would need to strip their ornaments before they could enter the Promised Land. Why? Because wearing jewelry represented a turning away from the true God to the idols and customs of the people around them. Painting the face is also a pagan custom, as the example of Jezebel so "colorfully" illustrates (see 2 Kings 9:30).

It's not that God dislikes jewelry. Read Ezekiel 28:12, 13, and you'll find that Lucifer once wore every precious stone.

When God puts jewelry on us in heaven, it will signify His adorning us with His character. Right now God wants to adorn us inwardly with a character fit for heaven. And one day He will give us a gorgeous crown decked with jewels that represent the lovely character God has developed in us.

Art and Pat Humphrey

WHEN TEXTS STOPPED BULLETS

I'm not a criminal," Marco insisted as the officer in charge of the firing squad motioned for him to start digging. "I'm a Seventh-day Adventist, and we don't get mixed up in such activity."

The officer shook his head. "You're lying. You were found with the gang of robbers, and that means you're a criminal. Now dig!"

Marco thrust his shovel into the ground as his mind raced. The Guatemalan dictator of that time was a man of action—usually violent action. The authorities ordered criminals to march out into a field carrying shovels. The officer in charge would tell each to dig a hole. Then the firing squad would line up, aim their rifles at the heart of each felon, and shoot. The bodies would tumble into the freshly dug graves.

"I *am* a member of the Adventist Church, and I was only trying to witness to those men," Marco insisted, knowing it would be his last chance to save himself. "See, I've got a New Testament right here in my pocket."

"You don't know anything about the Bible," the officer snarled.

"I can recite the verses I've underlined. Test me. I'll prove I'm a Christian, not a crook."

The officer shrugged. "OK. Recite this one." He let Marco see the first couple words. The prisoner cleared his throat and repeated the text word for word, complete with the reference. "And this one," the officer commanded. Marco quoted the next text. "And this one." The same thing happened.

When Marco finished, the soldier handed back the Bible. "I'm convinced. You're not a thief. You may go."

FAITH HEALING

A few days later, when Jesus again entered Capernaum, the people heard that he had come home. So many gathered that there was no room left, not even outside the door, and he preached the word to them. Some men came, bringing to him a paralytic, carried by four of them. Since they could not get him to Jesus because of the crowd, they made an opening in the roof above Jesus and, after digging through it, lowered the mat the paralyzed man was lying on. When Jesus saw their faith, he said to the paralytic, "Son, your sins are forgiven."

Now some teachers of the law were sitting there, thinking to themselves, "Why does this fellow talk like that? He's blaspheming! Who can forgive sins but God alone?"

Immediately Jesus knew in his spirit that this was what they were thinking in their hearts, and he said to them, "Why are you thinking these things? Which is easier: to say to the paralytic, 'Your sins are forgiven,' or to say, 'Get up, take your mat and walk'? But that you may know that the Son of Man has authority on earth to forgive sins. . . ." He said to the paralytic, "I tell you, get up, take your mat and go home." He got up, took his mat and walked out in full view of them all. This amazed everyone and they praised God, saying, "We have never seen anything like this!"

Mark 2:1-12

FAMILY OF GOD

Joash was seven years old when he began to reign. 2 Kings 11:21.

Family. For many, even the word brings to mind scenes of happiness and contentment. It always has for me.

By today's standards, my family was large. I had one sister and two brothers. With Mom and Dad, that made six of us. Whenever we traveled together, we had plenty of luggage to haul around. Except once.

When I was a baby, before my little sister was born, my parents were missionaries in Korea. In June of 1950 Communist forces from the north invaded their neighbors to the south. The city of Seoul, where we lived, was in an uproar with everyone trying to flee at the same time.

The American military forces in South Korea made arrangements for all U.S. women and children to get out of harm's way by hopping aboard a fertilizer ship bound for Japan. Because of space restrictions, passengers could take only one suitcase each.

Guess what my mom packed in her suitcase? Diapers. Lots of diapers. For me! She left behind her pretty dresses and warm coats. She didn't pack any extra shoes or socks but simply stuffed her suitcase with diapers. Like Joash of old, I was hidden from harm by someone who cared about me. My mother sacrificed her own wants so that I could stay dry and healthy.

A Christian family is the best reflection of God's love on earth. Its members care about, make sacrifices for, and constantly support each other. Aren't you glad you're a part of the family of God?

DUMPSTER DAN

Distinguished people drink. Dan wanted to be distinguished. Famous people drink. Dan wanted to be famous. Sociable people drink. Dan wanted to be sociable. So why was Dan standing up to his neck in garbage yelling at the top of his lungs?

The story began the night before when Dan, a professional businessman, went out for a few beers at a local bar. After about an hour he began staggering home but on the way grew extremely sleepy. Crawling into what he believed to be a safe place, he drifted into a dazed stupor.

Unknown to the snoring businessman, he'd chosen a trash dumpster in which to spend the night. At dawn a truck came, picked up the receptacle, emptied its contents into its cavernous bed, and hurried on to the next collection site. The first thing Dan knew, he was wedged in tightly between some company's outdated correspondence and a restaurant's discarded boiled pasta.

When the truck reached the city's dump site, Dan and the rest of the garbage landed on top of a smoldering, smelly heap of refuse. That's when sanitation workers saw a head sticking out of the pile, its eyes wide in horror, mouth screaming for help.

Dan got his wish. He became very famous when newspaper and television reporters arrived along with an ambulance. Sociable? You betcha. Everyone wanted a look at the fool who spent the night in a dumpster. Distinguished? Well, that may be a bit difficult with a cityful of garbage on your head. But two out of three isn't bad.

RATS!

Q: I'm a 10-year-old boy and I really like my cousin's neighbor. She likes me too, I guess, because she always asks me to ride around on my bike with her. What should I do?

PS: She even laughs at my stupid jokes!

A: Sounds like the beginning of the love bug gnawing at your gut like a rat on cheese. Those tingling feelings will be with you for a long time, pal—for different girls and at different times. But the feeling of wanting to be with girls is normal and healthy.

As far as your cousin's neighbor is concerned, I'd go on bike rides and fly kites and paint animal cookies and go puddle jumping in a rainstorm. Have fun with her—and lots of other friends. Do fun stuff with groups of guys and girls.

Since you are 10, my guess is you won't want to get married for at least a year (or probably more like 15 years). So don't get too serious about one girl at this point. That's my advice.

PS: There are a zillion girls out there who will laugh at your stupid jokes. I know, because a few of them even laugh at mine! The rat will be nibbling for a long time. Don't get too eager.

Karl Haffner

BOY SAVES DOG

Martin Nicholson couldn't believe his eyes. On a tiny ledge above the roaring, foaming rapids, surrounded by towering cliffs, lay a dog—cold, hungry, alone.

The boy's heart went out to the frightened animal. Sympathy is one thing. Action is quite another. Martin was a boy of both!

As he ran home to get some food for the trapped creature, he had no way of knowing that the dog had been on that ledge, unable to escape, for four days.

Inch by inch, Martin lowered himself down the cliff, digging his toes into whatever tiny cracks in the rocks he could find, hoping that the plants he clung to wouldn't release their grip on mother earth.

At last he reached the frightened pooch, who gratefully accepted the food Martin had brought. The boy couldn't climb out of the canyon with the dog so, after a tender pat on the animal's head, he left the poor creature to face another lonely night.

Early the next morning Martin returned, this time with several strong men and long lengths of rope. Soon all were safe and sound.

A meeting in Toronto, Canada, invited Martin as guest of honor. "Why did you risk your life to help that animal?" people asked.

The boy shrugged. "I have a puppy at home. She gets hungry. When I saw the dog on the ledge, I figured he'd be hungry too. So I fed him."

A simple act of kindness? The people of Canada thought it was much more and awarded Martin a medal for his outstanding affection for a helpless creature!

DOUBTS ABOUT GOING

Q: If you want to go to heaven, and you don't think you're going to make it, what will happen?

A: Doubts about heaven can come from two sources. First, it may be Jesus gently reminding you of the high standards you're supposed to be shooting for. When He comes, He wants to find you actively involved in fighting sin and temptation, not just sitting back with an I-give-up attitude.

Second, Satan loves to make us believe we're totally unworthy of being saved. He does that by constantly throwing temptations in our path, making the world of sin seem so inviting, leading us into body- and mind-destroying habits, and keeping us so busy we don't have time for spiritual activities such as Bible study, worship, and prayer.

The journey to heaven isn't a joyride. It doesn't just happen. It takes work—real work—on your part. But you don't make the trip alone. Jesus walks beside you, whispering encouragement and help in your ear. Listen to what Paul said about his highway to heaven. "I know what it is to be in need, and I know what it is to have plenty. I have learned the secret of being content in any and every situation, whether well fed or hungry, whether living in plenty or in want. I can do everything through him who gives me strength" (Philippians 4:12, 13).

When feelings of doubt creep up on you, ask God to give you strength, and tell Satan to bug off!

FACE IN THE CLOUDS

Thunder rumbled and lightning flashed as the island of New Guinea trembled under the storm. A native to the island watched as the clouds boiled in the sky, driven by fierce winds over the mountains.

Suddenly the clouds seemed to form the outline of a face. It lasted for only a few seconds, but the image appeared so kind and loving, so peaceful even in the midst of the storm, that the man stood transfixed by its beauty. Then the face dissolved as other clouds swallowed up the mists that formed it.

Months passed. One day a stranger arrived in the village and hung a Picture Roll on a branch. "Come listen to me," he called. "I want to tell you a story and show you some paintings of Someone who lives beyond the clouds but once walked here on earth."

The villagers saw a baby in a manger, then a young man working in a carpenter shop. "He was always kind to others," the visitor said. "See Him healing sick people and raising the dead? Oh, how He loved people!"

Heads nodded as the villagers whispered, "That is a wonderful man. But are these stories really true?"

All at once, one in their group rose to his feet. "The stories are true, because I've seen that face before. It looked down on me from the sky."

That was proof enough. "Tell us more," the villagers urged. "Tell us everything about the Man who watches us from the clouds."

The face in the storm had shone light into the hearts of the islanders and changed their lives forever.

SABBATHKEEPING

Have you ever wondered what you can and can't do on Sabbath? During Jesus' ministry, He provided a very clear answer.

On a Sabbath Jesus was teaching in one of the synagogues, and a woman was there who had been crippled by a spirit for eighteen years. She was bent over and could not straighten up at all. When Jesus saw her, he called her forward and said to her, "Woman, you are set free from your infirmity." Then he put his hands on her, and immediately she straightened up and praised God.

Indignant because Jesus had healed on the Sabbath, the synagogue ruler said to the people, "There are six days for work. So come and be healed on those days, not on the Sabbath."

The Lord answered him, "You hypocrites! Doesn't each of you on the Sabbath untie his ox or donkey from the stall and lead it out to give it water? Then should not this woman, a daughter of Abraham, whom Satan has kept bound for eighteen long years, be set free on the Sabbath day from what bound her?"

When he said this, all his opponents were humiliated, but the people were delighted with all the wonderful things he was doing.

Luke 13:10-17

What does Jesus say we can do on Sabbath? Set people free from the bondage of sin, that's what! How are we supposed to do this? That's up to us. God gave us perfectly good brains for figuring out how to do what He says. Let's get busy and use them!

FAMILIAR HONESTY

The money brought into the temple . . . was paid to the workmen, who used it to repair the temple. They did not require an accounting from those to whom they gave the money to pay the workers, because they acted with complete honesty. 2 Kings 12:13-15.

Every junior has heard the story of how the boy king Joash raised money for repairing the Temple in Jerusalem. He instructed Jehoiada the priest to take a big chest, bore a hole in its lid, and place it by the altar where everyone would see it.

Especially interesting was the fact that the king and officials asked for no record of how the workers used that money, because everyone involved "acted with complete honesty."

I remember watching my father count money—lots of money. He was secretary-treasurer of the New York Conference and during camp meeting each year made sure all collected offerings arrived safely at the local bank. Even today, in my mind I can still see him surrounded by piles of cash in his little cabin office, counting, counting, counting.

Some people might be tempted to pocket a few bucks for themselves. I mean, who would know? But my dad considered every penny, dime, quarter, and dollar sacred money, just like the coins found in Joash's Temple chest.

Dad knew that stealing money from the church was just like stealing from your own family. To be more exact, it would be like robbing yourself.

How many of you would consider sneaking up to your room, tiptoeing across the floor, slipping open your dresser drawer, and, after looking one way and then another, make off with $5 of your own money? Ridiculous! Family doesn't steal from family.

"GRAB THE TUBE!"

Carlos Lopez heard a familiar voice saying something unfamiliar. "Help!" The call echoed from downriver. "Help!"

It was Mother. She was in big trouble. Ten-year-old Carlos summed up the situation quickly. He and his family had been tubing down the broad, deep American River west of Sacramento, California. The sun was warm, and the water felt cool and inviting. Carlos and younger sister Lydia enjoyed the sparkling tickles of the ripples against their skin, always being careful not to float too far from shore where the water ran faster. But apparently Mother had swum out by mistake, and the swift current now carried her straight toward the dangerous rapids farther downstream. Father was too far away to hear his wife's frantic calls.

"Lydia, throw me the big inner tube!" Carlos ordered. Then he began swimming out in the river. He'd learned to swim at an early age, but had never been in such dangerous waters before. When Mother saw him coming, she screamed, "No. Go back. Don't drown with me." But the boy kept moving toward her. Seeing how determined he was to save her, the woman took courage, found new strength from somewhere deep inside her aching body, and kicked against the swirling, tumbling rapids.

"Grab the tube, Mother!" Carlos shouted. She reached out and took hold. Together, exhausted mother and trembling son made their way back to shore.

Love is a very powerful motivator. "My son is and always will remain a hero in my heart," Mrs. Lopez tells friends and family.

If you ever find yourself in spiritual trouble, remember you've got a hero racing to your rescue. His name is Jesus.

ALKA SELTZER AND GARLIC

Q: I'm 13 years old and really like a girl at my church. She smiles at me a lot. I don't know if she likes me, but now she really acts like a jerk. Does that mean she doesn't like me anymore? I don't do anything wrong.

A: Because she acts like a jerk may mean she doesn't like you anymore. Or it may mean that her Alka Seltzer tablets were laced with garlic. There's no way to really know why a person acts like a jerk.

Seriously, often people act different because of circumstances nobody knows about. Her parents may be getting a divorce. She may be a victim of abuse. Or she may be struggling to get good grades. The point is, you never know what is going on in a person's private life. Keep treating her in such a way that you can honestly continue to say, "I know I don't do anything wrong." That's all you can do.

Karl Haffner

MITZI

That one?" the woman gasped.

"Yes!" her son nodded.

The dog pound brimmed with beautiful, healthy canines. But Alex had chosen the most flea-bitten, skinniest, pathetic-looking mongrel of the bunch.

Mom sighed. Ever since her husband had left, Alex had begged for a dog. The woman knew that her son's heart was breaking and needed a friend. But this one?

So it was that Mitzi, an abandoned little black dog, moved to the comfortable surroundings of Alex's room.

Something remarkable happened. The little animal began to fill out. Her eyes began to shine, and her coat grew in thick and healthy. Alex and Mitzi became inseparable.

"You've got to be kidding!" friend Jarad laughed when he heard Alex mention that he was going to enter Mitzi in the local pet show. "You'll be competing against Bruce, my pure-blooded Collie. You're going to lose!"

That didn't stop Alex from combing Mitzi's coat until it shone. Nor did it prevent him from teaching his furry companion to follow him after a simple command. And it *certainly* didn't halt him from spending hours playing with his dog, showering her with love and kindness.

At the show's conclusion, the judge stood and cleared his throat. "As you know," he said, "we award blue ribbons for the very best dog in the show. There are many lovely animals here. But one has caught our attention. Her eyes sparkle. Her coat shines as if brushed many times, and she never takes her eyes off her master. Such a relationship between boy and dog is a joy to behold. That's why this year's ribbon goes to—Alex and Mitzi."

In life, love wins the greatest awards.

PROOF POSITIVE

Q: Can you prove that God is God?

A: This young woman has asked an important question. How do I know that the God I'm trying to tell you about really exists? How can I be sure He does what He says He does, and will do what He promises to do?

Perhaps someone has asked you the same question, only they'd say, "Why do you go to church on Saturday? God doesn't care on which day you worship." Or they might ask, "Why do you believe the Bible? It's just a bunch of old stories, right?"

Here's the only answer I can offer. I know God is God because of what He has done and is doing for me. When Jesus lives in my heart, I find greater joy and satisfaction in life. I treat people better. I love my wife more. I look forward to the future.

But when I chase Jesus away by being stubborn or selfish, I quickly become depressed, frustrated, angry, impatient, and grow resentful of life and the things that happen to me.

I know God is God because He changes me from sad to glad again and again. Nothing on earth can do that. No person has that kind of power. Only a loving, forgiving God can make such a difference in me.

"Delight yourself in the Lord and he will give you the desires of your heart. Commit your way to the Lord; trust in him and he will do this: He will make your righteousness shine like the dawn, the justice of your cause like the noonday sun" (Psalm 37:4-6). God proves Himself to *me* every day.

COAT FOR COAT

Evangelist George Whitefield reined in his horse as he and his friend came face-to-face with a masked bandit. "Your money or your life," the outlaw demanded.

The two travelers emptied their wallets into the highwayman's hands. The bandit waved his gun menacingly, then spurred his horse and hurried away.

"Whew, that was close," said the friend. "I thought we were goners for sure."

George nodded. "Yeah. The guy looked desperate. Let's hurry on to town before he changes his mind and comes back to kill us."

They'd gone only about a mile when the bandit returned at full gallop. "Stop," he shouted. The two travelers obeyed. "I want the coat you have on," he said, pointing at George. "It's better than mine."

"Friend," said the evangelist, "you can have anything you want. I'm a Christian, and God tells us to love our enemies. Here's my coat."

"Well," the bandit sneered, "I'm not a Christian, but I'll give you my old coat for your trouble." With that he rode away in a cloud of dust and laughter.

George and his friend had ridden only another mile when they heard the now familiar thunder of hooves behind them. But before he could catch them they reached the safety of the town.

That evening they found out why the robber was trying to catch them the third time. When Whitefield examined the coat the thief had "traded" for his new one, in the pocket he found the money the man had stolen during their first encounter.

"The Lord works in mysterious ways," the evangelist chuckled.

EYE OF A NEEDLE

A certain ruler asked him, "Good teacher, what must I do to inherit eternal life?"

"Why do you call me good?" Jesus answered. "No one is good—except God alone. You know the commandments: 'Do not commit adultery, do not murder, do not steal, do not give false testimony, honor your father and mother.'"

"All these I have kept since I was a boy," he said.

When Jesus heard this, he said to him, "You still lack one thing. Sell everything you have and give to the poor, and you will have treasure in heaven. Then come, follow me."

When he heard this, he became very sad, because he was a man of great wealth. Jesus looked at him and said, "How hard it is for the rich to enter the kingdom of God! Indeed, it is easier for a camel to go through the eye of a needle [a very small gate in the Jerusalem wall] than for a rich man to enter the kingdom of God."

Those who heard this asked, "Who then can be saved?"

Jesus replied, "What is impossible with men is possible with God."

Peter said to him, "We have left all we had to follow you!"

"I tell you the truth," Jesus said to them, "no one who has left home or wife or brothers or parents or children for the sake of the kingdom of God will fail to receive many times as much in this age and, in the age to come, eternal life."

Luke 18:18-30

SHARING EVERYTHING

Hezekiah] did what was right in the eyes of the Lord, just as his father David had done. 2 Chronicles 29:2.

I grew up with a great role model in my house—my dad. No, he wasn't perfect, but he provided a beautiful reflection of God's love to our growing family in so many ways.

Take Thin Mints, for instance. Thin Mints were chocolate-covered peppermint candies we both liked *very* much. But with four kids in Christian schools all at the same time, Dad seldom had money to buy such luxuries. This left a lot of Thin Mint boxes on grocery store shelves and very few in our refrigerator.

Occasionally Dad would buy a small carton of the wonderful stuff and bring it home. As far as I can remember, no one else in the family liked them. They were our own special treat.

Here's the neat part. After a meal my dad and I would head for the fridge, where he'd remove one Thin Mint from its box. Then I'd watch as he took a knife and cut the little round candy right down the middle—half for him, half for me. Then we'd stand there and eat our treat, rolling our eyes in ecstasy.

Dad loved Thin Mints as much as I did, but he always shared them with his young son. He wouldn't think of enjoying one without me!

Family is more than ancestral trees and strange squiggles on DNA charts. It's more than birth certificates and marriage licenses. Family means sharing everything. Even Thin Mints.

SEA WALK

Seventh-day Adventists keep far away from alcohol for many reasons. Here's one of them.

Reid was a sailor with the United States Navy, and his ship was on maneuvers somewhere in the middle of the Pacific Ocean. Like many seamen, Reid liked to drink. His habit became so bad that his friends on board shut him in an empty room in order to "dry out." Alcohol does more than make a heavy drinker walk funny and smell like sewage. It can affect the mind as well.

After a few hours' rest, Reid woke up and glanced out the porthole. "Hey," he said, "we're at port, and there's the little boat down there that will take me to the city, where I can get something to drink." At least he wasn't seeing all of those snakes and spiders he'd been complaining about recently.

Quickly he packed his bag and rushed up on deck. "Lower the rope ladder," he told his shipmates. "I'm going on leave, and you can't stop me!"

The men thought their friend was joking, so they lowered the ladder. By now a crowd had gathered, and everyone watched Reid wave goodbye, descend the swaying ladder, and step into the ocean.

"Man overboard!" someone shouted as the rest of the sailors doubled over with laughter. Bells rang and sirens blared as the ship came about.

If you want to drink, be prepared to make an absolute fool out of yourself. Alcohol does weird things to the human brain. It makes it see things that aren't there. Unfortunately, it also keeps it from seeing something that is there, a Saviour longing to help take away the habit.

I'VE GOT YOU, BABE

Q: I am 13 and really like this girl in my Sabbath school class. Actually, I think I'm in love with her! I don't think she likes me, but I'm pretty sure she likes my best friend. Sometimes she says "Hi," but usually she just walks away. I don't know what to do. How can I get her to like me?

PS: Since she doesn't like me, or probably doesn't like me, I've been thinking about leaving church. Although I really don't want to.

A: Unfortunately, you can't make anybody like you. If you could, I would have married Cher, the woman I was in love with when I was 13. No matter how hard I tried to force her to like me, the black-haired singer from Hollywood never returned my love or knew that Karl Haffner breathed. (I used to sing Cher's greatest hit, "I've Got You, Babe," all alone to the mirror with my hairbrush microphone.)

What is important is that you be yourself and don't allow others to control you. Be the person God made you to be and don't change in order to get a girl to like you. Girls who like guys who pretend to be something they aren't are as shallow as a frosted flake.

In sum, act—don't react. To try to make her like you is reacting to her. To leave church is reacting to her. You say you don't really want to leave church, then act on that, because that is who you really are. Determine what you want to do and act on it—regardless of what others say or do or think. Act—don't react!

Karl Haffner

FIRE ON THE HILL

Here's a story from a junior who gave up smoking the hard way!

My friend Matt and I decided to go to our grass hut in the sandpit off Jade Park to smoke a cigarette. After lighting up, we threw our matches onto the ground.

Later, as we were walking down the hill, Matt smelled burning grass. Turning around, we saw that the hillside had caught fire. We raced back up and tried jumping on the flames to put them out and received first-degree burns on our arms and legs.

Others began arriving as we stripped off our shirts, put them in a mud puddle, and raced back to the fire. By the time the fire truck arrived, we'd already taken out half of the fire, but it was still spreading quickly with plenty of dry grass and dead trees to feed it.

More than half of the sandpit burned, but no one was seriously injured. When a policeman interviewed us, we told him the truth. Then our parents had a very long talk with us.

Three weeks later Matt and I went back to the fire zone and saw beautiful new growth. Because the dry grass had been burned up, fresh grass and trees could take root. God brought something good out of something bad.

As for Matt and me, we're thankful that the Lord took pity on us and helped us to quit smoking, because it was a bad habit.

Jake Weaver,
14, Alaska

God can bring something good out of anything and anyone.

BAPTIZED-READY

Q: How do you know if you are ready to get baptized?

A: You've asked an important question. It shows that you're doing the right thing—thinking about baptism before taking that big step.

One of the most touching stories we've heard about baptism happened during some recent evangelistic meetings. A Cuban refugee who had as a judge formerly hated and imprisoned many Seventh-day Adventists gave his heart to the Lord. He was baptized by one of the very men, a pastor, whom he had once imprisoned!

That story shows us exactly what baptism means. It is a desire to give up your old ways and live a new life with Jesus! And it's a public announcement that you really, really love Jesus and that you want to follow Him all the way.

How do you know you're ready for baptism? If you accept and understand the basic teachings of the Bible, want more than anything to live by those principles, and love Jesus with all your heart, then you are ready for baptism.

We suggest that you talk with your parents, your pastor, and with Jesus as you get ready for this important step! As you study, pray, and counsel with others, Jesus will let you know when the time is right. And He will be with you all the way.

Art and Pat Humphrey

SAHAN STOLE THE TRUTH

Sahan dropped to his knees. He must not be caught now!

It was midnight, and the most dangerous part of his plan still lay ahead. He'd come to his uncle's house to steal a book on black magic. His uncle had said that he'd been reading about the devil lately. Well, Sahan wanted that information, but he knew his uncle would think him much too young to be involved in the occult.

The intruder crept silently across his uncle's office and paused by the desk. *He said it was a big book*, the boy mused. As he reached into the top drawer, his fingers brushed a large volume. *Here it is. Now I can find out more about the devil.*

The midnight visitor didn't stop running until he was back in his own house. For the first time he held the book to the light and read the title: *The Great Controversy Between Christ and Satan.* "This ought to be good," Sahan said excitedly.

He started reading and soon discovered that black magic wasn't the theme of the volume at all. "This is a *Christian* book!" he declared angrily. "But as long as I went to all that trouble getting it, I may as well read it."

He did—all the next day and all the next night. By the time he finished, he'd found a new power for his life, a power that comes from God, not the devil.

Today, when anyone asks him how he became a Seventh-day Adventist, Sahan says, "It all began when I crawled into my uncle's house at midnight and stole the truth."

CHILD OF THE KINGDOM

Here's a short event in the life of Christ that should bring a smile to the face of every junior.

People were also bringing babies to Jesus to have him touch them. When the disciples saw this, they rebuked them. But Jesus called the children to him and said, "Let the little children come to me, and do not hinder them, for the kingdom of God belongs to such as these. I tell you the truth, anyone who will not receive the kingdom of God like a little child will never enter it."

Luke 18:15-17

Jesus once said, "If you've seen Me, you've seen the Father" (see John 14:9). So when we imagine that wonderful scene with Christ inviting the little children to His knee, we're looking at a mirror image of what would happen if it were God the Father seated there. Kinda shoots a great big hole in the *God-is-a-power-to-be-feared* concept, doesn't it?

Children are pretty good judges of character. If kids found themselves attracted to Jesus, it was because they knew at first glance that here was a kind, gentle man whom they could trust. He had tons of stories to tell and always made people, young or old, feel good about themselves.

Would you like to sit on Jesus' knee today? Then close your eyes, imagine the kindest, noblest man you can imagine, and then plunk yourself down. Tell Him your troubles. Tell Him your dreams. Tell Him a joke! He loves to listen to you. Why not take a few moments and talk to Him right now!

COMMUNITY

There was great joy in Jerusalem, for since the days of Solomon son of David king of Israel there had been nothing like this in Jerusalem. 2 Chronicles 30:26.

When King Hezekiah called the people of Israel and Judah to come to Jerusalem for a special Passover celebration, he had a good reason. Many Israelites had turned their backs on God, choosing to worship idols, or nothing at all.

Sound familiar?

What is it that most Americans worship nowadays? We as a nation aren't exactly filling our churches each week. Millions would rather watch the ball game on cable than attend religious services.

But God isn't worried about numbers. He's concerned about hearts.

While traveling through Germany, my mother, sister, and I spent the Sabbath with some Adventist acquaintances. When church time rolled around, we suddenly found ourselves surrounded by soldiers—American soldiers from a nearby Army base. They'd come to worship with us. We weren't in a church with a big pipe organ and we had no pews—just some folding chairs. No famous preacher stood to preach—unless you consider my mom famous.

What we did have was *community*—Christian community. Our church, our community, consisted of a handful of hearts joined by a common love for God.

After our church service we ate a meal together and then waved goodbye as our military friends headed back to base. As far as I know, I've never seen them again. But it didn't matter. For a few hours, in a foreign land, we'd been a community built around a shared love for God.

THE QUEEN IS COMING!

Mr. Dezbor was a nervous wreck. After all, it isn't every day that the queen of England visits your store.

Queen Elizabeth and Prince Philip had come to America on royal business. As their stay drew to a close, the queen made a request. She'd like to visit a large supermarket in the city. That's when officials contacted Mr. Dezbor, manager of just such an establishment.

The man sprung into action, tidying up the aisles, making sure his check-out servers were in place, the counters scrubbed, and the bakery displaying its best-smelling products.

Rows of police officers took up positions around the market as the limousine arrived. Out stepped the royal couple. They had a marvelous time going up and down the aisles, seeing how Americans did their shopping and what types of products lined the shelves. The queen even chatted with a few surprised shoppers.

When the visit ended, Mr. Dezbor and his crew breathed a happy sigh of relief. All had gone well. However, one person wasn't happy with the visit. No sir! The store's supervisor should have been there, welcoming the queen and prince, showing them around. But when called with the news of the upcoming royal visit, he didn't believe it. "Quit kidding around," he grumbled. "I'm far too busy to play your silly games." Then he hung up. Only later did he discover his mistake.

Today voices shout, "The King of heaven is coming!"

"Nah. You're joking," some respond.

"No, He's really coming!"

"Yeah, right. That's a good one."

Juniors, it's true. It's really true!

THE MEANING OF LOVE

Q: How can I tell if I'm in love? What does it feel like? Is love at first sight possible? I'm 14.

A: When people talk about love, they often mean very different things. To some people, love involves physical attraction (liking someone a lot because they look good). Others think of love as the feeling you get when your heart thumps, or when you giggle a lot when you see a certain person.

But true love isn't based on feelings alone. Love is a relationship. It involves getting to know and appreciate another person for who they are. Now, it's *possible* to love someone at first sight . . . but it's not likely.

Remember, feelings change, but true love lasts. How do you know if you're really in love? Only time will tell. And at age 14 you've got plenty of that ahead of you.

Our advice? During your teens focus on making lots of casual friends instead of concentrating on one special relationship. When the time is right and true love comes, *you'll know.*

Art and Pat Humphrey

FAITHFUL FRANK

Mother bit her lip and twisted the handkerchief between her fingers. In the distance she could hear the shouts and see the beams of the flashlights sweeping the fields and forests.

Midnight had come and gone, but still no word of Dillon, her 4-year-old son. He'd been missing since suppertime. "If only Frank were here," the woman said to her husband as he ran in for a sip of water. "We'd put him on the trail, and he'd lead the searchers straight to our little boy."

"Frank?" the man responded angrily." That good-for-nothing mutt couldn't find his own tail." He sighed. "Put that down as our next purchase—a dog with a pedigree, one with good blood in its veins. We need an animal we can rely on!"

The hours dragged by. "Dear God," Mother prayed, "please look after Dillon. Please!"

At 3:00 a.m. she heard people talking—excited voices coming toward the house! Grabbing a sweater, she ran outside.

Hundreds of searchers were walking up the street. The man in the lead was carrying a wriggling bundle, and running along-side him, barking and yipping with joy, was Frank the mutt.

"We were searching the tall grasses by the river when we heard the dog howling," the man said as he lowered a grinning child into his mother's arms.

"And," the little boy continued, "Frank kept me warm. He sat beside me all night!"

The local radio station awarded Frank a medal, and Father said, "Get another dog? I should say *not!* Where would we ever find a more faithful friend than Frank!"

SHOWING THE WORLD

Q: Why is baptism important?

A: First of all, we must believe that it *is* important because Jesus was baptized. If it didn't matter, He would've found something better to do on that sunny afternoon by the Jordan River.

What does our friend Ellen White say? "Baptism is a most sacred and important ordinance, and there should be a thorough understanding as to its meaning. It means repentance for sin, and the entrance upon a new life in Christ Jesus" (*Child Guidance,* p. 499).

Baptism is important because it's a symbol of something deep inside your heart. It's a way of saying to your whole church family, "I love Jesus so much I'm willing to do what He did. I'm publicly showing I'm a Bible-believing, Bible-obeying Christian."

You're also reminding those who attend your service what the apostle Paul said: "We were therefore buried with him through baptism into death in order that, just as Christ was raised from the dead through the glory of the Father, we too may live a new life" (Romans 6:4).

When you come up out of the water, you're telling everyone, "This is what Jesus can do for you. He can wash away your sins and let you begin a brand-new life with Him by your side."

Can you get to heaven without being baptized? Yes. But the Saviour hopes you'll share what you've learned with others. Through this simple act, your friends can witness a demonstration of God's saving grace in action.

CANNIBALS TO CHRISTIANS

An Air Force bomber had been forced down at sea. For two and a half days Mac, the flight engineer, and six other crewmen had drifted on a life raft before arriving at an island in the South Pacific known to contain cannibals.

After they had set up camp, a single native appeared during the night and then vanished as quickly as he'd come. "It's only a matter of time now," the airplane captain had warned. "He'll be back with others, and we'll end up as supper."

The copilot shook his head. "Maybe not," he said. "I've been told that missionaries have been coming to these remote islands for years. Maybe he was a Christian native."

The next night a flickering light appeared on the shore followed by a line of very dark, very large men. The tail gunner unlatched his pistol as the others aimed whatever weapon they had at the approaching group. "Hold your fire," the captain called. "They're not armed."

As the man in the lead reached camp, he held up his hand. In it was a Bible. Then, to the relief of the airmen, he read a passage from it in broken English.

Mac shook his head. What were the odds? They'd crash-landed on the open sea, sailed in a life raft for two and a half days, and then bumped into an island where missionaries had turned cannibals into Christians. Later, safe and sound in a military hospital, the soldier said, "You can tell the world that I'm now a devout Christian. Those islanders showed us how Jesus can change lives. Thank God for missionaries!"

SHORT SERMON

Jesus entered Jericho and was passing through. A man was there by the name of Zacchaeus; he was a chief tax collector and was wealthy. He wanted to see who Jesus was, but being a short man he could not, because of the crowd. So he ran ahead and climbed a sycamore-fig tree to see him, since Jesus was coming that way.

When Jesus reached the spot, he looked up and said to him, "Zacchaeus, come down immediately. I must stay at your house today." So he came down at once and welcomed him gladly.

All the people saw this and began to mutter, "He has gone to be the guest of a 'sinner.'"

But Zacchaeus stood up and said to the Lord, "Look, Lord! Here and now I give half of my possessions to the poor, and if I have cheated anybody out of anything, I will pay back four times the amount."

Jesus said to him, "Today salvation has come to this house, because this man, too, is a son of Abraham. For the Son of Man came to seek and to save what was lost."

Luke 19:1-10

Why did the people call Zacchaeus a sinner? Because even though a Jew (son of Abraham), he collected taxes for the Roman occupiers of the land. Not only that, most tax collectors skimmed money off the top of their collections, filling their own purses with cash while their neighbors went without. In this way they cheated their own people and those for whom they worked. But things changed quickly once the little man met the kind Saviour.

THE PENKNIFE

And Jesus grew in wisdom and stature, and in favor with God and men. Luke 2:52.

"Mother, what are you doing here?" George glanced about, hoping no one was watching.

"You're not going!" the woman said, feet planted firmly at the base of the steps leading up to the ship. George loved his mother. But he loved the sea, too, and wanted to be a sailor.

"You must obey your superiors," the woman continued. "You're far too young for this."

The boy sighed. Mother was right. "OK," he said softly. "I'll stay."

A few days later a package arrived for George containing a skillfully crafted penknife with a sharp blade and ivory handle. "Every time you use this gift," his mother said, "remember my words, 'Always obey your superiors.'"

Years later George sat at a desk writing a letter. A terrible winter had stalled the American Revolution, leaving his Army stuck in blizzard conditions. Hundreds of soldiers, tired of the cold, the starvation diet, and seeming hopelessness of their plight, had deserted. He'd written to Congress pleading for reinforcements and supplies, but few arrived.

"What are you doing?" General Knox asked as he entered George's cabin.

"Resigning!" the man growled.

Knox picked up something from the desk. "Tell me again the story behind this beautiful penknife," he said.

George understood. With a sigh, he tore up the letter. From that moment on, he led his Army with renewed determination, won the war, and became the first president of the country he helped form.

DECEIVER DECEIVED

Darrak ran back to his motel room and burst through the door. "You won't believe the deal I just got," he said, holding out his open hand to his travel companion while grinning broadly. "Paid only $100 for it."

Zack's eyelids rose. "Hey. Great-looking ring! Is that a ruby?"

"You bet," his friend breathed. "The joker who sold it to me wanted five times what I paid. I haggled like crazy, and he caved in. When I get back to the States, I'll resell this baby for a tidy profit, enough to pay for our entire trip."

"But what about customs? They'll soak you for taxes."

"Not if they don't know I have it. I won't declare it and will keep it out of sight." Darrak admired the ring and shook his head. "Imagine buying such a ring for only $100."

When the two travelers returned to the United States, Darrak was able to smuggle the ring successfully past customs and then hurried immediately to a jeweler in town. "How much will you give me for this?" he asked, shoving the ring under the nose of the proprietor.

The jeweler studied the stone under a magnifying glass and then turned to his eager customer. "We don't handle items like this in my store."

"Too valuable, huh?" Darrak said with growing excitement.

"Valuable? Not exactly." The jeweler handed back the ring. "You can buy one just like it at Wal-Mart for $10. The stone is only cut glass. Good day, sir."

Those who try to deceive usually succeed in deceiving themselves.

PUZZLING ACTIONS

Q: I'm 11 and have only a few friends. Now two of them won't even speak to me. I ask them why, but they just walk away. How can I get people to like me?

A: Your friends' actions must be very puzzling. Since they won't talk, try writing each one a little note. Say that you want to be friends. Ask if you've done anything to offend them. *Express your feelings clearly.* Say, "It really bothers me when you walk away and won't talk to me." Suggest that the three of you get together so you can work things out. Or better yet, invite them over to your house for pizza and games.

Try not to show anger or have an accusing or blaming attitude. That would only make things worse. And remember that no matter how nice we are, not everyone will like us. But if you are kind and friendly, have a pleasant attitude, look for opportunities to help others, show an interest in people, and love and accept them for who they are, others will be drawn toward you. That's a promise!

Art and Pat Humphrey

IMMOVABLE ELEPHANT

Two armies from opposing provinces in India faced each other for battle. The peshwa (chief officer) of one of the armies had given the flag of their province to his most trusted elephant driver. "Keep it flying!" he'd ordered.

In the ensuing battle both sides gained and lost ground. Then things went bad for the peshwa and his men. Many of his soldiers were about to turn and run when, through the blowing smoke, they saw their flag flying above the elephant and its driver lying dead at its feet. The last command uttered by the dying driver had been, "Stay. Do not move!" Until it heard otherwise, the elephant wasn't going anywhere.

Seeing the flag electrified the soldiers. With renewed determination, they swept down the hill, forcing their enemy out of the valley. The faithful elephant stood its ground, surrounded by the carnage of war.

The victorious soldiers gathered about their elephant and showered it with praise. As they were preparing to leave, they discovered that the animal wouldn't budge. Other drivers tried to get it to move, but it remained at its post.

Three days went by, and still the elephant stood, flag fluttering above it.

The men remembered that the dead driver had a son, a young boy who'd taken part in the elephant's training. Even though he lived 100 miles away, they sent for him. When he arrived, the elephant recognized the boy's voice and followed him obediently from the battlefield.

You may find yourselves among friends being swept into various kinds of sin. If this happens, remember the elephant. Stay true to the voice of God, and His Son—always.

WHY SIN?

Q: Why is there sin?

A: One beautiful Sabbath morning my dad and I were on our way to a church where he was to speak. My 11-year-old mind was full of its usual questions, and my father was doing his best to answer them.

Suddenly, without warning, a barn swallow flew into the path of the car. There was nothing we could do. The little bird hit the front bumper with a soft thud.

Quickly stopping the car on the side of the country road, we jumped out to see if maybe—just maybe—we'd only stunned the bird. But the little swallow was dead, feathers bent and broken. Overhead, her mate circled, waiting for his partner to fly up to meet him. He was still circling when we drove away.

"Why is there sin?" I asked my dad through angry tears.

He thought for a long moment, then said, "I don't know. No one knows. But one thing is for certain—Jesus is going to put an end to it when He returns the second time."

Some questions have no answers—for now. But someday we'll understand. Someday we'll look into the eyes of the God who has watched a million birds die, who has heard the cry of generations of people, and who hid His face in agonizing sorrow while His only Son hung on a cruel cross.

"'God made him who had no sin to be sin for us, so that in him we might become the righteousness of God'" (2 Corinthians 5:21), Dad quoted. "When we get to heaven, let's ask Jesus your question. I believe He'll have the answer we need to hear."

SAGO FOR THE TEACHER

Pandiki had worked hard all day cutting sago palms and extracting the starch that people would use for thickening soups and making puddings. His mouth watered as he imagined the wonderful meals his wife would prepare using the results of his labors.

He'd planned to spend two weeks on the job before paddling back down the Turama River to his Papua New Guinea village.

"I think I've done enough for today," he told himself as he sat down on a log. "Perhaps I'll rest for a while before setting up camp." No sooner had he closed his eyes than a bright light pierced the shadows of the jungle and a wondrous being stood before him.

"Go back to your village," the visitor said.

Pandiki frowned. "But I've got work to do. I must gather sago."

The being shook its head. "A teacher is coming. You must take with you one tenth of the food you've gathered to give to the teacher." Then, as suddenly as it had appeared, the stranger vanished.

Pandiki sat up with a start. What had just happened? Was it a dream? Without further thought, he packed up his belongings and headed home. When he approached his village, he noticed a large gathering with a stranger standing among them holding up some pictures. Pandiki gasped. That must be the teacher the being had spoken about.

The man gathered up his sago and headed for the crowd. He had food to deliver!

In time, Pandiki and the entire village became baptized members of the Seventh-day Adventist Church.

LEGION

J esus and His disciples] sailed to the region of the Gerasenes, which is across the lake from Galilee. When Jesus stepped ashore, he was met by a demon-possessed man from the town. For a long time this man had not worn clothes or lived in a house, but had lived in the tombs. When he saw Jesus, he cried out and fell at his feet, shouting at the top of his voice, "What do you want with me, Jesus, Son of the Most High God? I beg you, don't torture me!" For Jesus had commanded the evil spirit to come out of the man. Many times it had seized him, and though he was chained hand and foot and kept under guard, he had broken his chains and had been driven by the demon into solitary places.

Jesus asked him, "What is your name?"

"Legion," he replied, because many demons had gone into him. And they begged him repeatedly not to order them to go into the Abyss [place of isolation].

A large herd of pigs was feeding there on the hillside. The demons begged Jesus to let them go into them, and he gave them permission. When the demons came out of the man, they went into the pigs, and the herd rushed down the steep bank into the lake and was drowned. . . .

The man from whom the demons had gone out begged to go with him, but Jesus sent him away, saying, "Return home and tell how much God has done for you." So the man went away and told all over town how much Jesus had done for him.

Luke 8:26-39

"I AM WILLING"

Filled with compassion, Jesus reached out his hand and touched the man. "I am willing," he said. "Be clean!" Mark 1:41.

The man with leprosy requested healing in a rather strange way. He said to Jesus, "If you are willing, you can make me clean" (verse 40). He didn't say, "If you are *able.*" Jesus could do anything. The diseased man knew that. What he wanted to know was Do you *want* to heal me?

I recently worked on a video for the General Conference Youth Department. It showed groups of teens from around the world working on mission projects far from their native lands. On my monitor I saw hardworking young people lugging cement blocks across a fast-flowing river, mixing mortar by hand, whitewashing a newly built school, helping a dentist extract an infected tooth, cutting down trees, and laying brick.

Then I watched as those same teenagers led the singing in Sabbath schools, delivered sermons in churches, told Bible stories through puppets and skits, and harmonized their voices together accompanied by strumming guitars.

Never once did I see a teen sitting off in a corner saying, "I can't do this. I can't do this." They knew, as I know, that young people can do anything. So the question isn't "Can I?" It's "Will I?" People of the world aren't asking you, "Can you help me?" They're pleading, *"Will* you help me?"

Today, as you set out to show God's love to those around you, never doubt your abilities. Instead, work to develop a strong willingness to be of service to God and others.

MIKE'S BIKE

Mike Carey was feeling pretty satisfied with himself. He'd just bought a great-looking bike at the police lost-and-found auction for $5. It wasn't new, but at that price, who cared! It drove like a dream.

Mike's joy was short-lived. The next day as he was wheeling around the neighborhood, a boy named Russell yelled, "Hey, you. You've got my bike."

"No, I don't," responded Mike. "I bought it at the police auction."

"Then I know it's mine," Russell pressed. "It got stolen about a year ago!"

Poor Mike. He pedaled home not sure what to do. When he explained what happened to his mother, she called the police station and was assured that, by law, the bike now belonged to Mike. "Hurray!" the boy shouted.

Then Mother placed her arm on her son's shoulder. "But what if you'd lost your bike and a year later saw someone riding it?" she asked. "How would that make you feel?"

Her son's smile faded. "Yeah. I see what you mean," he said. Mike went out to the garage and pedaled away to find Russell.

Most stories would end here, and so they should. Good deeds don't need to be rewarded. But this particular one was. The police said they couldn't refund the money, and referred the problem to the city council. Impressed by Mike's kind heart, they personally raised the cash to buy him a replacement bike. It's easy for us to imagine that Mike and Russell spent a lot of time together after that, riding their bikes all over the neighborhood, enjoying a new friendship built on a foundation of one boy's good deed.

STRIKING RELATIONSHIP

Q: A kid at school picks on me. I've told him to quit, but he keeps bothering me. How can I get him to stop?

A: We know of a boy who had a similar problem with a girl who teased and hit him constantly. This went on for weeks. The boy told the girl to stop, but she kept on. The girl figured she could get away with it because her victim was a boy, and of course, boys aren't supposed to hit girls! But one day the boy decided he had had enough, so he punched her.

Now, we're not suggesting that you punch the kid. In fact, that's probably the *worst* thing you could do. But this story illustrates that if people ignore or fail to express their feelings, they will eventually explode.

Have you tried talking with this kid, really sharing how it feels to be picked on? Make it known in a kind but firm way that you don't like being mistreated and that you're not going to tolerate it. If it continues, talk to a teacher or parent who can help solve the problem. Maybe you could have one of your parents speak with the kid's parents. They probably have no idea what's going on.

One last thing: pray for this young person. He or she may be dealing with family troubles, lack of love, insecurity, jealousy, anger, or some other problem. Your prayers could make a big difference.

Art and Pat Humphrey

RIDE WITH THE TIDE

Did you know that the days are getting longer? If you haven't noticed, don't feel bad. Each day lengthens by *one five hundredth of a second every century*. Which means that 500 centuries from now each day will be a full second longer.

The earth's rotation is slowing down because of the drag of the tides. When the moon pulls the ocean into bulges, the earth keeps rotating under them. The moon tries to hold the water in one spot, while the earth tries to pull the water around with it. This friction of the water against the earth slows the earth down like brakes on a spinning wheel.

To compensate, scientists adjust time every few years. They add "leap seconds" at the end of June or December to keep our clocks on schedule. By the year 51997 we'll have an extra second every day.

Tides in Canada's Bay of Fundy are the highest in the world, rising more than 50 feet!

If the moon causes tides in the ocean, why doesn't it create tides in lakes and ponds? And why doesn't it make a bowl of soup rise on one side and flood over?

In small bodies of liquid, such as lakes and soup bowls, other forces outweigh the effect of the moon. Wind, weather, and barometric pressure keep the water in place.

God created a complex system of balances to keep the tides in the oceans. There they stimulate the feeding cycles of mussels and barnacles, provide food for the birds and worms, and give life to an abundance of creatures in the tidal pools.

Jane Chase

PROBLEM SOLVER

Q: Do you always know how to solve a problem in *your* family?

A: We wish we could say that we know all the answers whenever a problem arises in our own family, but we don't. However, there is Someone who *does* know the answers, and that's why we spend a lot of time talking to Him. Actually God is much better at solving problems than we are.

We have found that when we do have a misunderstanding or problem, one of the most helpful things is a family meeting. We come together and let everyone calmly share their views or feelings, and then we work together on a solution. We try to make it a situation in which everybody comes away with some degree of satisfaction. But each family member must be willing to compromise, or give, as well. And of course, prayer is always an important part of the problem-solving process.

Whenever people live or work together, some conflict will arise, no matter how much they love or care about one another. Everybody is different and has his or her own unique views and personality. And because we are growing Christians, we all still have a few "rough edges" on our characters that can cause snags in our relationships. The important thing is knowing how to deal with conflict when it arises. An old saying goes, "It's OK to disagree, but not to be disagreeable." In other words, by following biblical principles, we can work out family differences in a loving and peaceful manner, even if everybody doesn't see eye-to-eye.

Art and Pat Humphrey

THE DEACON'S ADVICE

Charles enjoyed a good sermon when he heard one. That's why he was eager to get to services one snowy Sunday morning because a famous preacher was scheduled to appear. (Charles didn't know about the seventh-day Sabbath doctrine.)

Finally he arrived, only to find a handful of people there. "Where's the guest preacher?" he asked.

"He's not coming," a member responded. "Got snowbound."

Charles sighed and made his way to his favorite seat in the balcony. He may as well stick around, seeing as he had dressed up, polished his shoes, and lugged his Bible halfway across town. *Maybe I can learn something helpful from whoever speaks*, he told himself. *Besides, I've been feeling kinda guilty lately. As a matter of fact, I feel lost.*

That's when he saw the deacon step to the pulpit. *Oh no*, the boy moaned. *He's as boring as watching grass grow.*

The deacon opened his big Bible, cleared his throat, and read one verse. "Turn to me and be saved, all you ends of the earth; for I am God, and there is no other" (Isaiah 45:22). He spoke for 10 minutes and was about to sit down when he suddenly pointed up at the balcony. "Charles," he called out, "you're in trouble, aren't you? Turn to Jesus. Turn, turn, turn."

The surprised youth nodded. "I will turn to Jesus," he responded.

From that day forward, Charles had a new determination in his heart. He grew up to be one of the world's most successful evangelists. Not only had he learned to turn to Jesus; he spent his life teaching others to do the same.

ONE CAME BACK

Now on his way to Jerusalem, Jesus traveled along the border between Samaria and Galilee. As he was going into a village, ten men who had leprosy met him. They stood at a distance and called out in a loud voice, "Jesus, Master, have pity on us!"

When he saw them, he said, "Go, show yourselves to the priests." And as they went, they were cleansed.

One of them, when he saw he was healed, came back, praising God in a loud voice. He threw himself at Jesus' feet and thanked him—and he was a Samaritan.

Jesus asked, "Were not all ten cleansed? Where are the other nine? Was no one found to return and give praise to God except this foreigner?" Then he said to him, "Rise and go; your faith has made you well."

Luke 17:11-17

Christ healed 10. One came back and said "thank You." Amazing!

God continues to do miraculous things in people's lives today. He may heal a life-threatening disease using the skilled hands of modern physicians, turn an addict from drugs through programs such as Alcoholics Anonymous, or mend a failing relationship using the whispered guidance of the Holy Spirit. Often people thank their doctor, their pastor, or even themselves, which is fine. But they forget to thank God. They believe that the power to overcome these obstacles came from their own mental or physical abilities when, in fact, it was from God.

Remember, juniors, when something good happens in your life, turn your face heavenward and thank the true Source of all good things.

BEING YOU

"I must preach the good news of the kingdom of God to the other towns also, because that is why I was sent." Luke 4:43.

Do you know why you were born?

"Well," you say, "my mom and dad wanted a kid, and here I am!" Good answer. But there's more.

My dad has home movies of me when I was just a week old. My mom, young and beautiful, is carrying me out of the Adventist hospital in Seoul, Korea, wrapped in white baby blankets. I look really, really ugly with a wrinkled face and squinty eyes. My hair is going every which way, and when I yawn, you won't see a tooth in sight! Strange baby.

Now, 50 years later, I can say without reservation that I know exactly why I was born—so I could write and edit this book for you. It was so I could write other books, such as the Shadow Creek Ranch series and *Echoing God's Love*. Oh yes, it was also so I could marry my wife, Dorinda, live in West Virginia, and watch the birds munching sunflower seeds at our backyard feeder. In other words, I was born in order to do what I do.

"Hey," you say, "I thought we were born to follow some secret plan that God has for our lives." Well, it's not all that secret. God's plan is that we be saved. As long as what you do doesn't interfere with that goal, you're following God's plan perfectly. Simple, huh?

So spend today being what God meant you to be. Enjoy!

KIND TRUCK DRIVER

Mrs. Kimmel kicked at the tire in frustration. Here she was alone on a back road without the know-how to fix a flat—a dangerous situation.

Suddenly a large truck bore down on her. It swept past, shaking the ground, almost blowing her over. "That stupid truck driver thinks he owns the whole road," she said through clenched teeth. "If I were a cop, I'd throw him in jail and swallow the key."

That's when she saw the truck lurch to a stop and begin backing up in her direction—just as fast. A lump of fear rose in Mrs. Kimmel's throat.

"Evenin', ma'am," the driver said with a smile as he jumped down from the cab. "Gotta flat? That's not good. If you'll give me the keys to the trunk, I'll unload the spare and have you back on the road in no time."

True to his word, the stranger jacked up the car, removed the flat, and replaced it with the spare. "There you go," he said after putting the jack away. "No charge. Glad to help."

For the first time Mrs. Kimmel noticed the man's arms. They were blistered, as if he'd been terribly sunburned. "Your arms," she said.

The truck driver smiled. "Oh, this is nothin'. Part of my load exploded just before I drove by. Scared me to death. Kinda burned my arms. I was headed for the hospital when I saw your situation. Guess I'd better get myself to a doctor. See ya!"

We should never be too quick to judge others, because we may not know all the facts behind their actions. But we can always be kind.

PLEASING PARENTS

Q: It seems as if no matter what I do, my parents never appreciate me. They yell if something I did really wasn't so great, and when I do a good job they just grunt. What can I do?

A: We know how you must feel. All of us—young and old—need to feel appreciated by those closest to us.

We have a hunch that your parents don't even realize how they are responding. If your family is like most families—ours included—you probably live a locomotive lifestyle: fast and busy! With all the stress of making a living and day-to-day responsibilities, parents sometimes unintentionally fail to pay enough attention to what's really most important—their kids.

Here's a suggestion: Find a time your parents can give you their undivided attention. Tell them how you feel, and let them know you really want their approval when you do something great. Explain that it really hurts when they yell at you, and then discuss some ways in which the whole family can learn to communicate in a more positive way. Beforehand you might find a book at the library or a Christian bookstore that deals with family communication. As you talk together as a family, encourage everyone to make a commitment to begin using positive communication techniques. Do this, and we suspect it won't be long before you see a big difference in your relationship with your parents!

Art and Pat Humphrey

GOALS

Luther Burbank seemed quite normal except for one rather unusual pastime. For hours each day he sniffed marigolds. He'd go up one row, then down another. *Sniff, sniff, sniff.*

If this particular blossom smelled sweet, you might excuse this behavior. But when Luther and his associates spent their days in farmers' fields sniffing like puppies in a pantry, you'd have to wonder at their sanity, because marigolds smelled terrible.

Here's the interesting part. Luther's sniffing had a purpose. He'd set a goal to find a marigold that didn't stink. Why? Because people liked the look and color of the flower but couldn't get them past their noses. If someone could find a blossom with no odor, discover why, and then start growing nonsmelly marigolds, they'd make it possible for people to enjoy the color without the stench.

"Mr. Burbank, Mr. Burbank," an associate gasped one day, "we've found one that doesn't smell!" Luther studied the plant under a microscope, did some tests, and eventually unlocked the secrets for growing marigolds that pleased both the eye and the nose.

William lived in a comfortable home and felt impressed that God wanted him to do something with his future. So he set a goal and got to work. Many people felt uncomfortable with what he was doing and made his life miserable, even threatening to kill him, which they finally did! What goal had he set? To translate the Bible from Greek into English.

Goals. Do you have one? Luther Burbank and William Tyndale touched lives because they set goals and stuck to them no matter what.

HARPLESS

Q: When we go to heaven, do we necessarily need to play an instrument?

A: Not into harps, huh? Me neither. Guitar, maybe. Perhaps a piano. But I couldn't play a harp if my eternal life depended on it.

I'm not sure who came up with the idea that when we get to heaven we'll all sit around on clouds strumming a stringed instrument. Probably someone who liked doing it on earth—except for the cloud part, of course.

The Bible records a whole orchestraful of instruments being used for praise. "Sing for joy to God our strength; shout aloud to the God of Jacob! Begin the music, strike the tambourine, play the melodious harp and lyre. Sound the ram's horn at the New Moon" (Psalm 81:1-3). "Praise him with the sounding of the trumpet . . . praise him with the strings and flute, praise him with the clash of cymbals. . . . Let everything that has breath praise the Lord" (Psalm 150:3-6).

No, the ability to play an instrument isn't a requirement for going to heaven. And there'll be plenty else to do besides making music while sitting on your cumulonimbus.

But when you've finished exploring the universe, when you've studied all the mysteries of life, when your love for God overflows from your thankful heart, you might try *humming* a few praise songs for Jesus. He'll understand.

GOD SENT THE BREAD

Mr. Müller looked across the tables in the dining room, watching the 85 children in his care eat hungrily. The orphanage had always provided for homeless boys and girls in Bristol, England. But tomorrow would be different. Tomorrow there'd be no food left.

"Food and clothing cost money," he'd told his staff that morning. "I know God is powerful enough to supply all we need. We'll pray hard. This orphanage must never go into debt!"

The man's heart was heavy with concern as he left the modest building for some exercise before returning home that chilly November afternoon. Would God honor their faith? And would they recognize the opportunities their heavenly Father provided? Faith requires action. God doesn't work alone!

When he reached the path leading to his humble residence, Mr. Müller noticed a church member walking toward him. They greeted each other warmly. "I've been to your house twice today," the gentleman stated. "Now, I almost missed you again." The visitor fumbled in his pocket. "There's something I want to give you. I don't know if you need it." He handed Müller £20— then worth more that $100 and able to buy a lot more! Then, with a wave, he was gone.

The orphanage director smiled. That type of thing had happened before. He and his staff would see a need. They'd gather and pray, asking for Heaven's help. Then they'd get busy preparing to discover, recognize, and receive God's blessings.

The next day the dining room rang with the happy voices of children who enjoyed the results of their director's undying faith in a God who provides just enough just in time—when we're tuned in to His leading.

FORGIVENESS FORMULA

At dawn [Jesus] appeared again in the temple courts, where all the people gathered around him, and he sat down to teach them. The teachers of the law and the Pharisees brought in a woman caught in adultery. They made her stand before the group and said to Jesus, "Teacher, this woman was caught in the act of adultery. In the Law Moses commanded us to stone such women. Now what do you say?" They were using this question as a trap, in order to have a basis for accusing him.

But Jesus bent down and started to write on the ground with his finger. When they kept on questioning him, he straightened up and said to them, "If any one of you is without sin, let him be the first to throw a stone at her." Again he stooped down and wrote on the ground.

At this, those who heard began to go away one at a time, the older ones first, until only Jesus was left, with the woman still standing there. Jesus straightened up and asked her, "Woman, where are they? Has no one condemned you?"

"No one, sir," she said.

"Then neither do I condemn you," Jesus declared. "Go now and leave your life of sin."

John 8:2-11

This story illustrates one of our Saviour's most wonderful traits—His unrelenting willingness to forgive and forget.

The woman was guilty of sin. Others had caught her in a sinful act. But Jesus (a) didn't condemn her, and (b) told her to stop sinning.

Today, if you find yourself in the middle of a sin, remember A and do B.

BULLY TIME

Love your enemies, do good to those who hate you, bless those who curse you, pray for those who mistreat you." Luke 6:27, 28.

Would you like to know the secret of loving your enemies? One word—*forgive.*

God's forgiveness seems to know no bounds. He forgave Adam and Eve for nibbling on forbidden fruit, Moses for smacking the rock in anger, King David for arranging the death of the husband of the woman he was lusting after, the prostitute Mary for . . . well . . . you know, and Paul for making life miserable for the early Christians. Jesus even forgave the soldiers who were crucifying Him *while they were doing it!*

The reason Jesus and our heavenly Father can forgive so much is that They love us infinitely more than They hate what we do. They're also providing a clear, powerful example of how *we're* supposed to forgive others. That's right! They expect us to be as forgiving as They are—especially to our enemies.

Let's say there's a guy (or girl) at school that's making your life miserable. He's on your case constantly, spreading false rumors, getting you into trouble with the teachers, and basically being a bully. The problem you face is not what the person is doing, but how you're reacting to it. If you decide, "Hey, I'm going to forgive this person in spite of his actions," your reactions will become different, and thus his effect on you will be different as well. Get it?

When you love your enemies, you're really making life easier on yourself. Try it today.

WINNING LOSERS

The place? Los Angeles, California. The event? The Olympic Games. Contestants line up for the starting gun and then race down the track at full speed. Around and around they go, the lead changing hands several times. Then the fastest runner breaks the tape, and the crowd roars. The second-, third-, and fourth-place runners speed by as well.

Back in the pack, other runners break ranks and head for the showers. The race is over.

But who is that man on the back course, struggling along, running on tired and trembling legs? It's the contestant from the Philippines, thousands of miles from home. He'd come to race and wasn't going to quit until he'd completed the course. When he crossed the finish line, a tumultuous roar of respect and admiration rose from the bleachers.

The place? Indianapolis, Indiana. The event? The 1912 Indianapolis 500 motor race. DePalma has the lead and is holding it steadily. One car jumps the track. Another breaks a piston ring. Yet another burns a crankshaft, while others blow tires. It looks like DePalma's got the race sewn up in two laps.

But what's this? His car is slowing. Dawson flashes past. Then Tetzlaff. Then Merz. DePalma's car has stopped on the track less than a mile from the finish. That's when the spectators see something most unusual. DePalma gets behind his car and with the aid of his mechanic pushes it toward the line. When he inches across, the crowd explodes in uproarious acclaim.

Neither DePalma nor the Filipino runner won his race. But they won hearts by their dogged determination to finish what they started. They truly became winning losers.

BARNYARD DUCK

Q: I'm an 11-year-old boy and attend public school. I behave a lot different there than I do at church. I tend to act like the group I'm with at the time, except I don't do drugs or smoke. People at church wouldn't approve of the way I dress and what I do at school. I can't decide which way to go!

A: Wally was a wild duck heading south with his companions. One day he looked down and spotted a group of tame ducks on a farm. He liked the way they were quacking merrily and eating corn. *It sure would be nice to have some of that corn,* Wally thought.

So Wally flew down, joined the ducks, and began eating corn. The formation continued south, but Wally didn't care. *I'll rejoin them when they come back in a few months.*

By the time the ducks came back a few months later, he had gained some weight from all his corn-eating. His wings were flabby from too little exercise. He tried to get off the ground, but he flew too low and only slammed into the side of the barn. Wally decided to wait until the birds headed back south. But when his friends returned and called to him, he just didn't have the strength to join them.

As the seasons passed, Wally eventually lost interest in rejoining the flock. When they flew by he didn't even notice, for Wally had become a barnyard duck.

Get the connection? (Hint: The wild ducks represent Jesus' followers, and the barnyard ducks represent the non-Christians.) Would you rather be a wild duck or a barnyard duck?

Art and Pat Humphrey

BRIDGE OF PAIN

The man at the window turned from his telescope, made some notations on a piece of paper, and handed it to his wife. She hurried out as he fell back against the pillows, racked with pain.

Beyond his open window rose the towers of the longest suspension bridge of his time—an iron, wood, and concrete link between New York City and Brooklyn. The man on the bed was Washington Augustus Roebling, son of the bridge's deceased designer. After his father died, Roebling determined to finish the project. He had helped his dad create the blueprints and was the only one alive who understood the intricate strength hidden in the detailed drawings.

An accident at the foundation of one of the towers had left the 36-year-old builder an invalid, unable to stand or speak more than a few words at a time. But Washington was a determined man, and nothing was going to stop the construction of the great Brooklyn Bridge.

Eleven years after his accident—in 1883—Washington saw the night sky light up with fireworks. He heard bands playing and politicians making speeches. Then a long line of men and women, horses and carts, began moving across the bridge. His bridge. He'd completed the job despite unrelenting pain.

After the accident he could've said, "My head hurts," or "My stomach aches," or "I just don't feel like working today." Instead, he rented a room where he could watch the construction, installed a telescope, and from his sickbed directed the project.

Whenever you don't feel up to some important task, take a moment and imagine a man lying in a sickbed. Then check out a picture of the Brooklyn Bridge.

LOST!

Q:
What will happen if I don't go to heaven?

A:
The day has arrived. You notice a dark cloud coming closer and closer. Then you see Jesus sitting on His throne surrounded by millions of angels. You hate Him. In fact, you hate the very sight of Him. So you run and hide with a bunch of other people who despise the Lord.

Suddenly, it's a thousand years later. You watch Satan call great crowds of people together, urging them to join his battle against God. In the distance you spot a city made of gold, and you laugh. "We can take that city for ourselves," you shout.

Just as you and the others rush forward, weapons in hand, you hear a voice speaking to you. It's reminding you of all the times you refused to listen to Jesus. You see images of yourself turning your back on God again and again and again until you didn't care what He wanted you to do.

"Yes," you finally agree, "I don't deserve to be in the city with God. I don't want to be there anyway. I hate Him."

With those words on your lips, fire flashes all around and you die, this time forever.

But that's not you. You love Jesus and accept His forgiveness for your mistakes. When He comes, you'll be so glad to see Him that you'll jump up and down and shout, "Here I am, here I am!" And He'll shout back, "Well, come on! I want to take you to your new home, where you won't be bothered by the devil anymore." And away you'll go, your hand safely in His.

KNIFE FOR A BIBLE

PART 1

I don't need religion," Mr. Grimez told his wife. "I've got guns and dogs for protection. Besides, I've captured everyone but the leader without getting hurt."

Mrs. Grimez nodded. Her husband's job was to guard a section of forest in Germany where robbers hid from the law. "But God can protect you in ways that guns and dogs can't," she insisted. Her words fell on deaf ears.

That night Mr. Grimez didn't return home at the usual hour. Growing worried, his wife and mother-in-law knelt and prayed for his safe return. Then they did something else. They prayed for the leader of the robbers, asking God to help him turn away from his life of crime and wickedness. "Please, Lord," Mrs. Grimez said softly, "may he learn of the love, kindness, and forgiveness You offer. This we pray in Jesus' holy name, amen."

At that moment Grimez walked in, and when he saw the two women on their knees, he scoffed at their concern. "I've got my guns and dogs," he reminded them. Then he latched the front door, and everyone went to bed.

The next morning the man gasped when he looked at where his wife usually placed their Bible at night. In its place, he saw a huge, dangerous-looking knife. The Bible was gone.

The window closest to the bed was wide open. Someone had entered the house while they slept and traded the knife for the Bible. But who? And why did he take the book?

Think how wonderful this world would be if enemies prayed for each other instead of fought! We'll read more of this later.

THE RICH FOOL

Many times while Jesus walked the dusty paths of this earth, He'd gather His followers and admirers about Him and do what every junior enjoys—tell stories! The Bible calls them *parables*. For the next few weeks, let's enjoy some of those wonderful illustrations and try to learn the lessons Jesus had in mind. Listen:

Someone in the crowd said to him, "Teacher, tell my brother to divide the inheritance with me."

Jesus replied, "Man, who appointed me a judge or an arbiter [coach] between you?" Then he said to them, "Watch out! Be on your guard against all kinds of greed; a man's life does not consist in the abundance of his possessions."

And he told them this parable: "The ground of a certain rich man produced a good crop. He thought to himself, 'What shall I do? I have no place to store my crops.'

"Then he said, 'This is what I'll do. I will tear down my barns and build bigger ones, and there I will store all my grain and my goods. And I'll say to myself, "You have plenty of good things laid up for many years. Take life easy; eat, drink and be merry."'

"But God said to him, 'You fool! This very night your life will be demanded from you. Then who will get what you have prepared for yourself?'

"This is how it will be with anyone who stores up things for himself but is not rich toward God." Luke 12:13-21

Juniors, it's better to have a rich relationship with God than well-stocked barns, wouldn't you say?

GOOD GUILT

Jacob said, "Please tell me your name." But [the being he'd wrestled with all night] replied, "Why do you ask my name?" Genesis 32:29.

Have you ever wrestled with an unknown force? Think about it. Have you ever stayed awake most of a night because something you did troubled you so much you couldn't sleep?

If that has ever happened to you, I've got good news. You weren't wrestling with Satan—you were wrestling with God! And all He wanted to do was help you turn that guilt into constructive action.

Let's say you're at school and a girl says something unkind to you. Before you know it, you've picked up a milk carton and dumped its contents all over her new leather jacket. Then, realizing that the punishment was *way* more severe than the crime, you say, "Oh, I'm sorry. You made me mad, so I soiled your jacket. I feel like a real heel. You might want to get that dry-cleaned."

That's bad guilt.

Or, you jump up, grab some napkins, and hand them to your wet friend. "Oh, I'm so sorry. I shouldn't have done that. Here, let's get as much off as we can, and then I'll have my mom or dad take us to the dry cleaner after school. I'll pay for whatever has to be done. Please forgive me. Please."

That's good guilt. Good guilt creates action. It forces you to face the problem and motivates you to make things right, no matter what it takes.

TRUE COURAGE

People have been going over Niagara Falls in barrels for years. During the past century a Frenchman named Blondin decided that he'd show the world real courage. "I'm going to *walk* across the falls," he announced.

True to his word, he strung a wire over the gorge, picked up a balance bar, and ambled over the falls. He bounced, ran, danced a jig, turned a few somersaults, and returned to thunderous applause.

The next year Blondin decided to be a little more "show biz," so he walked out to the middle of his line, sat down, and cooked himself a lunch on a small stove. Then he held his hat out at arm's length while someone below shot a hole through it. It all greatly impressed the crowd.

"Who will allow me to carry them across the falls?" he asked when he reached the bank. When no one responded, he turned to Colcord, his publicity man. The man smiled weakly. How would it look if the one who wrote all of those glowing press releases refused to take part in the stunt? So the two started out. Soon Blondin began to falter. This idea wasn't as good as he thought. Poor Colcord had to slip down onto the wire and stand trembling while Blondin rested. They finally reached the other side safely.

Blondin proved he was courageous. But did his bravado make the world a better place in which to live? No. True courage is a young person saying no to drugs or sticking by a friend in need. It is refusing to bend to peer pressure and holding firm to your beliefs. The rest is just "show biz."

SHUT OUT

Q: My best friend doesn't talk to me or do things with me. I feel that she is trying to shut me out. What should I do?

A: It must really hurt to be ignored by your best friend. You're also probably very puzzled to have your friend suddenly stop talking to you for no apparent reason.

Have you had a talk with your friend? It would be a good idea to take her aside and find out if you've done or said anything to offend her that might cause her to back off. Let her know how important your friendship is to you and that you want to continue talking and doing things with her. Apologize if she feels you've hurt her in some way. Tell her in a caring way that if something is bothering her, you'd like to help. This could be an avenue to rebuilding your friendship. It could be that she doesn't even realize how she's treating you or how you're feeling.

Friendships require lots of effort to keep going and growing. Communication, spending time together, trust, and being honest with each other are important ingredients of a true friendship. Both people must give to the relationship, or it just won't work. So if she still doesn't respond after you talk frankly with her about your relationship, then maybe she wasn't a true friend after all.

If she really does have a problem, then what she needs is your prayers and your friendship. The right thing for you to do is to be a friend no matter how she acts. That's what Jesus would do!

Art and Pat Humphrey

THE FLYING CAR

Automobiles provide transportation and convenience. But they also can become deadly weapons in the hands of those who selfishly drink alcohol and then slip behind the wheel. Listen to this amazing story from a girl named Jamie.

When my mom was just a kid she'd been ice-skating with her friend Jo-Ellen. After Jo-Ellen left with her parents, Mom was riding home in my grandpa's Ranchero when a drunk driver sped through a red light, hit another car, and then went flying through the air right at my mom's car. When Grandpa saw it coming, he opened his door and pulled my mom by the arm to get her out, but he wasn't fast enough. The car smashed into the roof, splitting my mom's head almost in half.

When she arrived at the hospital the doctors shaved her head so they could perform surgery. They told my grandparents that she had also injured her spine and neck. The disks in her neck had been pressed together.

From then on, life was very painful for her. She went to a chiropractor, but that didn't help much. The worst for her was knowing that she'd never be able to participate in the activities she enjoyed most: ice-skating, horseback riding, and taking part in rodeos.

My mom thanks God every day that the accident wasn't fatal and that her friend Jo-Ellen wasn't in the car, because the drunk driver's car completely smashed in where she would have been sitting.

Jamie Saenz,
13, California

BURYING THE PAST

Q: How do I bury the past?

A: Have you ever known somebody who just keeps on harping about something you did wrong to them, or that they did wrong to themselves or others? Maybe you've known people who had a bad experience so devastating that they were never quite able to get over it. Somehow they just can't forget or stop talking about it, no matter how many years ago it happened.

How does a person bury the past once and for all? It begins with making a commitment to start a new life, with new thoughts, new feelings, and a new determination to give our problems to God.

Ellen White once told her husband that he needed to bury the past. Telling him that he spent too much time dwelling on the wrongs that people had done to him, she counseled him to let God heal his wounded spirit and to refuse to talk or write about the past wrongs. We think that's good counsel for us today.

Is something from the past bothering you? Take it to the Lord in prayer. He will forgive every sin and heal every wound. All you have to do is ask.

Art and Pat Humphrey

KNIFE FOR A BIBLE
PART 2

When Mr. Grimez found the knife on the table, he knew someone had been in the house with the intention of murdering him. Was it the robber leader? And why did he take the Bible instead?

But he did not hear from the thief again.

A year or so later Germany and France went to war. Grimez fell badly wounded on a battlefield and was left for dead. But a lowly fisherman heard him groan and took him in his boat across the lake to a village.

The kind rescuer sent for Mrs. Grimez, and then he and his wife moved out of their house so the couple could have it all to themselves.

When he felt better and was about to leave, Mr. Grimez asked the fisherman how much he owed him. "You've already paid me more than enough," the man said.

"When?"

The fisherman went to his closet and returned with a Bible. Mrs. Grimez gasped. "It used to belong to us!"

That's when the fisherman told them of the night when he, a bandit leader, had entered their house to kill Mr. Grimez. As he hid he'd heard Mrs. Grimez and her mother read a beautiful passage and then pray for him. He was so moved that he didn't spring from the closet to kill Mr. Grimez when he returned, but waited until everyone was asleep before leaving his knife on the table and taking the Bible. "I wanted to find more beautiful texts," he told them. "Thank you for your prayer. I found God, and He changed my life forever."

Always pray for others. You never know who might be listening.

THE GOOD SAMARITAN

On one occasion an expert in the law stood up to test Jesus. . . . He asked Jesus, "And who is my neighbor?"

In reply Jesus said: "A man was going down from Jerusalem to Jericho, when he fell into the hands of robbers. They stripped him of his clothes, beat him and went away, leaving him half dead. A priest happened to be going down the same road, and when he saw the man, he passed by on the other side. So too, a Levite, when he came to the place and saw him, passed by on the other side. But a Samaritan, as he traveled, came where the man was; and when he saw him, he took pity on him. He went to him and bandaged his wounds, pouring on oil and wine. Then he put the man on his own donkey, took him to an inn and took care of him. The next day he took out two silver coins and gave them to the innkeeper. 'Look after him,' he said, 'and when I return, I will reimburse you for any extra expense you may have.'

"Which of these three do you think was a neighbor to the man who fell into the hands of robbers?"

The expert in the law replied, "The one who had mercy on him."

Jesus told him, "Go and do likewise."

Luke 10:25-37

The Samaritans weren't exactly loved in Jesus' day. The people in Judea considered them scum, lowlifes, undesirables. But Jesus cast a lowly Samaritan in the leading role of His story. Social class doesn't matter to Jesus. Kindness does.

WITNESSES

Then Joshua said [to the people], "You are witnesses against yourselves that you have chosen to serve the Lord." "Yes, we are witnesses," they replied. Joshua 24:22.

Joshua was about to die. He had called all the tribes of Israel together at Shechem and passed on some God-given advice. When he finished, he asked the people if they were going to stay true to what they knew to be right. You just read their response.

It's said that people reveal their true character when no one is looking.

Let's imagine that you've got your driver's license and you're tooling home from work late at night. You pass through a small town with one stoplight. The streets are dark, and not a person is around anywhere. As you approach the light, it turns red. Do you stop and wait for it to turn green again even though every other driver in the county, including the town's only police officer, is home asleep in their beds?

You find a wallet in the ditch with money in it. Do you turn it in to the police?

You happen to know an unkind thing about someone else. Do you share that juicy tidbit with friends?

The true Christian does right simply because it's the right thing to do. Yes, you wait for the green light in the deserted town. Yes, you turn the wallet in. Yes, you keep your mouth shut. Why? Because you are a "witness against yourself" that you're a Christian, and nothing will change that.

I've waited for green lights in deserted towns in the middle of the night. It's boring, exasperating, and character building.

CAREFUL WHAT YOU THINK

J udge Roberts shook his head. "I know Bruce. He'd never steal."

"He did," argued the prosecuting attorney. "He's an employee of the company, handles all the money, and was the only one in the office when the cash disappeared."

"You're trying to send a boy to jail on circumstantial evidence. Bruce is a good, honest person who has lived in this town for years!"

The jury agreed with Judge Roberts and proclaimed the defendant, "Not guilty."

Weeks later Bruce walked into the judge's chambers, threw down a sack of money, and waved a handgun before the astonished man. "I did take the cash," he announced. "If you don't believe me, I'll shoot myself."

"Why did you do it?" Roberts gasped.

Bruce sat down heavily on a chair. "I worked in the treasurer's office. One day the thought came to me that it wouldn't be hard to take some money for myself. A day or two later the thought returned. I had no intentions of acting on those thoughts, but I couldn't stop thinking about it. I even planned the robbery in my mind. Finally, one day I saw I was alone and stole it. Now I'm so embarrassed, I must shoot myself."

"Wait," the judge ordered. "Give me the money and leave town for good. I'll return the cash to the company, and no one will know what really happened."

Months later Bruce returned. "Everyone thinks I'm innocent, and I'm not. I must confess." He did, and went to jail.

Be careful what you think, because thoughts lead to actions. "Above all else, guard your heart, for it is the wellspring of life" (Proverbs 4:23).

JEALOUSY

Q: I have a problem with jealousy. I enjoy gymnastics a lot, but two of my friends seem better at it than I am. I always feel as if I have to try to do better than they. What can I do?

A: Your problem is one that probably all of us have had to deal with at some time in our lives. It's natural to want to excel at whatever we do. And it's also natural—though not right—to feel jealous when somebody else can do something better than we can. But it helps to remember that God has given all of us special talents to use for His glory. And when we truly care about someone, we should be happy when they succeed, even if it means watching them outshine us.

An old saying declares that "no matter how good you are at something, there's always someone who's better at it."

A good remedy for jealousy is to turn (with God's help) those jealous feelings into respect and encouragement. Praise your friends when you see them doing well.

We're glad that you've already taken the first step in overcoming jealousy by admitting that you have the problem. The next step is to pray and ask God to help you deal with your feelings. The third step is to accept yourself for who you are and thank God for the talents He has given you. Ask Him to help you to be not *the* best, but *your* best. Finally, be content with whatever gifts God chooses to bless you with.

Art and Pat Humphrey

THE WEALTHY WOMAN'S TOMB

A rich German woman knew she was about to die . . . and she shuddered.

No, she wasn't afraid of dying. As far as she knew, she'd been a good, kind person, so she had no sense of guilt in her heart. But she was worried about her bones.

Cemeteries where she lived were extremely crowded. As a matter of fact, poor people could rent a grave spot, place their departed relatives in it, and 20 years later someone would remove the casket and rent the grave to others.

"I don't want my bones disturbed," the woman announced. So she gave clear instructions as to what would happen to her body after she died.

Everything was done exactly as she ordered. She had a gravesite purchased, not rented. Her casket was laid deep in the ground and, with large slabs of heavy marble placed over the spot, bound together by iron bands. "This grave has been purchased for all time and is not to be opened," said a plaque on the site.

Time passed. One spring a little seed from a birch tree fell beside the grave. Rains came, and the seed sprouted. Before long, a root found its way along the imperceptibly small space between the two blocks of marble. Seasons came and went. The root grew and grew until one day the caretaker stopped by to examine the grave and noticed that the iron bands were broken and every block moved out of its place—pushed by the power of the little seed.

Jesus once said, "The seed is the word of God" (Luke 8:11). Get it?

THE REAL THING

Q: How will we know who is the real Jesus and not an image of Satan?

A: You hear a knock at your front door and when you peek through the little peephole, you see a woman standing in the entry with a big smile on her face.

"What do you want?" you shout.

"Whadda ya mean, what do I want?" she calls back as if her feelings are hurt. "Don't you know me? I'm your mother."

"My mother?" you gasp. Then you notice she has the same hair color and style as your mom. She's wearing a dress just like your mother wears—white collar, little green stripes. And she's carrying an identical purse to the one you gave your mother on her last birthday.

"Open up," the woman pleads with a warm giggle. "I forgot my keys. Silly me. I've got to start fixing supper. You know how your father hates it when supper's not ready, and your brother Timothy will be home from his football practice soon."

You don't open the door. Why? Because that's not your mother. No matter how much she knows about your family or how much she looks like the woman of the house, it's not her. How can you tell? Because you know your real mom like you know yourself. You're familiar with every detail of her face, the sound of her voice, the way she moves her head and hands.

The only way to recognize an impostor is to know, beyond the shadow of a doubt, the real thing.

BOTTLED BLESSING

Mr. Davy sighed heavily and watched the waves wash over the sand. "Why didn't God answer our prayer?" he asked himself again and again. "We needed a good crop. Although we prayed, our harvest failed." He thought of his children kneeling by their beds asking God to save their potato fields, but the weather had proved too much for the growing plants.

"Daddy," his children had said, "we prayed for a good crop, and you said God would answer. Has He forgotten us?"

Farmers around Grahamstown, South Africa, were facing harsh financial times because of crop failures. What could he say to his children?

Something caught his eye as it tumbled in the breakers. A glass bottle sealed with a cork bobbed in the backwash of the waves. Mr. Davy wasn't interested. He'd seen these "if you find this, write me a letter" messages before. But this bottle rode the next wave and landed right at his toes. Absentmindedly he picked it up, removed the cork, and read the message. Then he smiled broadly.

"Children!" he called as he rushed into their simple house. "Listen to this message I found by the ocean. 'If the person who finds this paper is in need, write to this address and I'll send help.'"

Mr. Davy wrote immediately. Soon a letter appeared in their mailbox with a small amount of cash, just enough to buy groceries for the week. It happened week after week until the next potato harvest put the family back on their feet.

It's amazing what God and a creative, kindhearted friend can do to lift the worries of this world.

SEEDS

While a large crowd was gathering and people were coming to Jesus from town after town, he told this parable: "A farmer went out to sow his seed. As he was scattering the seed, some fell along the path; it was trampled on, and the birds of the air ate it up. Some fell on rock, and when it came up, the plants withered because they had no moisture. Other seed fell among thorns, which grew up with it and choked the plants. Still other seed fell on good soil. It came up and yielded a crop, a hundred times more than was sown."

When he said this, he called out, "He who has ears to hear, let him hear.". . . "This is the meaning of the parable: The seed is the word of God. Those along the path are the ones who hear, and then the devil comes and takes away the word from their hearts, so that they may not believe and be saved. Those on the rock are the ones who receive the word with joy when they hear it, but they have no root. They believe for a while, but in the time of testing they fall away. The seed that fell among thorns stands for those who hear, but as they go on their way they are choked by life's worries, riches and pleasures, and they do not mature. But the seed on good soil stands for those with a noble and good heart, who hear the word, retain it, and by persevering produce a crop."

Luke 8:4-15

What kind of soil will you be today?

JESUS IN MY HEART

The ark of the Lord remained in the house of Obed-Edom the Gittite for three months, and the Lord blessed him and his entire household. 2 Samuel 6:11.

Life changes when God enters the heart. When Obed-Edom allowed David to store the ark of God in his house for a little while, the Bible reports that "the Lord blessed him and his entire household."

Listen how a modern-day Obed-Edom encourages others:

Jesus' love is so deep and wide and long,
　　It will surely reach your heart and give it a song.
Jesus' love gives the sunshine its light,
　　So every day will seem ever so bright.
Jesus' love gives the butterfly her colorful wings,
　　So whenever she flutters around she brings a warming to
　　　　every heart.
And when it seems Jesus' love can't get to you,
　　Just remember to pray, and He'll be right there next to you.
Jesus' love keeps a smile on my face,
　　So the smile will show others His loving grace.
Jesus' love has forever changed my life.
　　In this day and age I don't have to worry,
　　For He has taken all my strife.
Let Jesus into your heart,
　　So Jesus' love can nourish and grow.

Tiffany Canther,
12, Arizona

IRRITATING

Those in line at the cafeteria stood watching a woman arguing with the servers. "I didn't ask if it's tomato. I asked if there's pepper in it."

"There's no pepper in it," the server said.

"Probably full of pepper," the customer snarled. Then she grabbed the soup bowl being handed to the man in front of her and plopped it on her own tray. When the gentleman asked for another order of soup, the woman slammed his bowl back on his tray. "Oh, take it," she growled.

"Is that spinach?" she asked the next server. "Well, I don't want any." Moving to the next server, she blurted, "What flavor is that dessert?"

"It's lime," the server replied.

"I hate lime. I want mint, not lime. Can't you do anything right? If I wanted lime I would have asked for it. How 'bout that applesauce?"

"What about it?"

"Do I have to spell everything out for you? I want some applesauce, but only if it doesn't have cinnamon in it. But it probably does, so forget it!"

Stupid woman, huh? Very irritating. The problem with this customer was that she really didn't know what she wanted. Because of this, she made life miserable for the poor servers behind the counter as well as the others waiting in line.

Sometimes juniors get confused. They aren't quite sure what they want, so they argue and fume, concluding that their parents and teachers are real dorks. They think the world is against them. It's not, and the confusion won't last. If you're not sure what you want, don't insist that everyone try to figure it out for you. Be patient, not irritating.

HE BUGS US

Q: There's this guy who is always bugging me and my best friend (we're girls), even though we don't want him around. What can we do?

A: Your problem sounds similar to that of a young woman we know who attends college. A certain guy would follow her around everywhere. When she came out of class or went to the cafeteria, he'd pop up out of nowhere. Even when she went to her dorm at night, he'd stand at the window and call out to her!

She was so upset that she was ready to drop out of school. But one day she decided to have a talk with him. She let him know that he seemed like a nice enough guy, but she didn't want to be his girlfriend. It bugged her to have him follow her around. And guess what? The guy apologized and said he didn't realize he was getting on her nerves. Since then she hasn't had a problem with him.

It could be that the young man who's "bugging" you just wants to be your friend. Why don't you and your friend sit down and have a talk with him? Tell him in a nice way that you're willing to be friends, but that you and your friend want time to talk about girl stuff without guys hanging around. Also, remember that the more attention you give him by harshly telling him to get lost, the more he'll bug you. If he still keeps bothering you, just ignore him. After a while he'll probably stop and go disturb somebody else.

Art and Pat Humphrey

BONE STRATEGY

Wolf was a dog that looked like a wolf. Friskie was a much smaller animal with an attitude problem. He loved to pick on bigger dogs. When they'd become angry, he'd run away and hide.

The bigger dog loved to chew on bones. What dog doesn't? When Wolf would find one, he'd bury it in the yard. But just as soon as he was out of sight, along would come Friskie, who'd dig it up and steal it.

This went on for weeks. Wolf could have knocked the smaller dog's lights out, but instead he devised a plan. One day he went on his usual hunt and returned with two bones. Where had he gotten them? Some things are better left unknown.

Wolf dug a deep hole in the yard and quickly deposited the big, juicy bone with lots of meat on it. He pushed a few inches of dirt over his prize and then dropped the smaller, less tasty bone on top of the partially filled-in hole. Then he scooped the remainder of the dirt over the depression and went to take his usual afternoon nap.

When Friskie saw the freshly turned earth, he knew immediately that a nice bone hid underneath, just waiting to be stolen. Dig, dig, dig. Scratch, scratch, scratch. Soon he had the small bone in his mouth, and he hurried away. He never knew that just below the first bone waited a bigger, meatier treat.

Wolf had outsmarted the pest.

Sometimes the best way to deal with bullies is to fight with your brain instead of your fists. No bones about it!

WHO'S TO BLAME?

Q: Why does God allow bad things to happen to people you love?

A: This is a common question not only for juniors, but for adults as well.

Whenever something bad happens, we look for someone to blame. Most of the time we accuse God. After all, He's Creator of the universe. He could've stopped it, right?

Then we remember Calvary. In our mind's eye we see Jesus, God's own Son, dying in agony on a Roman cross. "Wait a minute!" we gasp. "Why doesn't He stop *that* from happening? Doesn't He love Jesus?"

Listen. The sinless Man on the cross is speaking. Luke 23:46 tells us that with His last breath He whispers, "Father, into your hands I commend my spirit." Then He dies as lightning flashes across the sky.

Here was Someone who had every reason to be angry at God, to blame Him for the suffering He had to endure. But even at the moment of death Jesus spoke His Father's name with reverence and love, handing over His spirit—or breath—willingly. Why?

Jesus knew what caused suffering and pain. He understood its source. And it wasn't His Father. It was sin.

Don't think of the bad things that happen as individual events allowed by God. Rather, think of them as terrible results of the sinful *condition* of our world. Fire will burn your fingers, not because God allows it, but because that's what fire does. Same with sin. Blame Satan. Trust God.

SEVEN VERSUS 500

Joshua Gianavello knew he had to act fast. An army of 500 soldiers marched to the village of Rora with one goal in mind—to kill all the Waldenses in the valley.

The April 24, 1655, command left no doubt as to the medieval church leader's intentions. "Kill the heretics," he told his military leaders. "Leave not one alive when the sun sets on that day."

By now the soldiers were beginning their climb up the hill called Rumer. Joshua had to act fast. Leaving his home, he made his way up the hill by a different route and on the way gathered six of his friends who were as determined as he to stop the scheduled massacre. All were excellent marksmen as well as devoted Bible students.

The men hid behind large boulders, and when the troops rounded a corner on a narrow path seven shots rang out, and seven soldiers fell dead. The guns spoke again, and seven more fell. Those in the lead looked around bewildered. How large was the attacking army? Who would die next?

"Get out of here!" the soldiers shouted to one another. When those in the rear saw their leaders racing back toward them, fear flashed in their faces. Gianavello and his six friends hurried from boulder to boulder, keeping up their deadly fire. Panic gripped the entire army and, without firing a shot, what remained of the 500 men turned and raced back down the valley. They never knew that only seven men and their brave determination to worship God as they saw fit had driven them away.

KINGDOM COME

The people of Jesus' time expected that the "kingdom of heaven," ruled over by the promised Messiah, would destroy the hated Romans and end everyone's troubles. They were wrong, and Jesus tried hard to explain what that kingdom really was all about. Listen:

He told them another parable: "The kingdom of heaven is like a mustard seed, which a man took and planted in his field. Though it is the smallest of all your seeds, yet when it grows, it is the largest of garden plants and becomes a tree, so that the birds of the air come and perch in its branches."

He told them still another parable: "The kingdom of heaven is like yeast that a woman took and mixed into a large amount of flour until it worked all through the dough."

Jesus spoke all these things to the crowd in parables; he did not say anything to them without using a parable. So was fulfilled what was spoken through the prophet: "I will open my mouth in parables, I will utter things hidden since the creation of the world."

Matthew 13:31-35

Mustard seed? Yeast? What do they have to do with overthrowing the Romans? Jesus understood how disappointed everyone would be if He came right out and said, "Listen up, people. There's not going to be a rebellion here. No driving the enemy out of the land. As a matter of fact, you've gotta learn to get along with the Romans because they're your brothers and sisters in God."

Instead, Jesus spoke in parables, trying to reveal hard truth through simple stories.

SONGS OF LOVE

I will praise you, O Lord, with all my heart; before the "gods" I will sing your praise. Psalm 138:1.

Blondel wasn't rich or powerful or a member of nobility. He had only one talent, but that was enough to save a king.

Richard the Lion-Hearted, king of England, was returning from a crusade to save Jerusalem from the Muslims. On the way the king's boat wrecked in a storm. "I'm *walking* the rest of the way," he announced, and started off across Europe dressed as a poor man so his enemies wouldn't recognize and capture him.

When he failed to arrive in England, people got worried. "He's dead," some lamented. Others moaned that he had been kidnapped. That's when Blondel decided to take action. He crept across the English Channel and began going from castle to castle, fortress to fortress, doing the one thing he did best—sing. After positioning himself near an open window, he sang all the songs he knew the king liked, hoping that if the monarch heard, he'd respond.

One day, from behind the prison walls of a distant fortress, he heard a man begin to hum along with him. Then happy singing broke forth. Returning to England, Blondel joyfully announced, "I've found our king!"

The people raised the necessary ransom and, with joy and celebration, bought back their monarch from his kidnappers.

Jesus left heaven to find you. Today He sings at the walls of your heart because He wants to buy you back from the devil. Why not sing your answer right now?

WHAT THE SERGEANT HEARD

Pathfinders," Pastor Smith called. All eyes turned to the camp leader as evening shadows played tag with the warm glow radiating from the campfire.

"I've been told by the sergeant at the nearby army base that tonight's war game has been canceled." An audible groan rose from the group. What junior wouldn't enjoy camping next to an active war zone, even if the guns and bombs were only simulated? "However, we do have a concern. Two soldiers are missing and may be injured." The man cleared his throat. "I think we should take a moment and pray that God will send His angels to be with the missing men and help guide the searchers."

The Pathfinders reverently stood, removed their caps, bowed their heads, and prayed aloud for the missing men.

Early the next morning the sergeant arrived with the good news that they had found the soldiers unharmed. Then he asked to speak to the group. "What I really wanted to tell you is that last night I was listening to what you said around the campfire. You didn't see me. I was standing behind a tree. But I heard you pray for my missing men. I told the soldiers about it, and they want to come and thank you personally.

"At our base we're training to fight and someday may have to give our lives for our country. After hearing your beautiful prayers, we have a reason to go anywhere in the world because we'll be defending boys and girls like you. Thank you."

We never know when someone may be listening to our words. What a wonderful opportunity we have to encourage and motivate.

STORY SPREADER

Q: What do you do when a guy likes you but spreads stories about you all over the school! (I don't even like this guy!)

A: Wow! What a strange way for a guy to show that he likes you! It's never nice to spread rumors, even if they happen to be true. Usually by the time the rumor gets around it's all blown out of proportion because somebody has changed some of the information. Rumors hurt people and damage relationships.

You probably need to ask this guy why he's telling tales about you. Explain to him that you don't appreciate it and that you'd like him to stop. If he doesn't, take the matter to a teacher he or she should know how to put a stop to the problem. You might also ask your teacher to lead a class discussion on the harmful effects of rumors. (Actually, your tormentor is only part of the problem. The other kids need to know that it's wrong to circulate rumors and that by passing along the gossip, they contribute to the problem.)

Meanwhile, if somebody comes to you with information they heard about you, ask them where they got it. Let them know that it's not true, and request they not repeat it. If someone tries to gossip with you about somebody else, refuse to listen, or change the subject. Tell the person you don't want to participate in hurting other people. Finally, when the time is right, share this text with others: "A gossip separates close friends" (Proverbs 16:28).

Art and Pat Humphrey

MIDNIGHT MUSICIANS

Some people take violin lessons for years, perfecting runs, slides, and fingering. Other people pay big money to see violinists in concert. But you can enjoy a *free* outdoor concert by listening to nature's foremost violinist—the cricket.

These intriguing creatures' wings vibrate 5,000 times per *second,* creating sound waves that humans hear as chirps. Scientists have analyzed recordings of cricket songs and discovered that the notes are one octave above piano range. They are actually a series of slurs like those produced by an expert violinist.

You can hear cricket songs up to a mile away. But the little beasts fall silent when anyone gets too near. In Japan and other Asian countries people keep crickets in tiny cages to act as burglar alarms. They are living motion detectors that stop chirping when a prowler approaches.

Crickets' ears are on their knees. A small swelling on each front leg has a membrane that catches sound as a human eardrum does. They can leap 100 times the length of their bodies. That's like a person six feet in height jumping the length of two football fields in a single bound.

Crickets are one of God's most inoffensive creatures. They don't sting or bite and aren't poisonous. They eat anything, including paper and clothing, but are so small they do very little damage. Since they also eat fly larvae, they are good to have around.

The next time you're out in your yard on a late summer evening, take time to listen to God's violinists. Enjoy the soothing sound before winter wraps the landscape in silence.

Jane Chase

RELATIONSHIP BUILDING

Q: How do you have a close relationship with Jesus?

A: Becoming friends with Jesus means spending time with Him. There are lots of ways to do this, but two ways we'd suggest are (1) talk to Him every day (pray), and (2) read His "love letter" to us (the Bible) daily.

Try this: Start a devotional journal in which you keep track of your talks with Jesus. Divide a notebook into three sections and label them as follows: "Prayer Requests," "Meaningful Texts," and "Praise and Thanks." In the Prayer Requests section jot down specific spiritual needs you are praying for, as well as names of people you want to remember in prayer. Make a note of how and when you believe God answered your prayer.

In the Meaningful Texts section write out Bible texts and promises that seem to have a special message for you. Then make a note next to the text about what you think God is trying to say to you personally through the passage.

And in the Praise and Thanks section list things that you are especially thankful for: how God has blessed you lately, a prayer He has answered in a surprising way, etc.

As you nurture your relationship daily with the Lord through prayer and Bible study, you'll find yourself wanting to spend more and more time with Him. And as you do, Jesus will become your special friend.

Art and Pat Humphrey

JOSHUA WINS AGAIN

T he day after Joshua Gianavello and six fellow Waldenses chased 500 soldiers out of the mountains, the army returned. This time Joshua was ready with 18 men, each armed with either a musket or sling.

Once again the invading army passed through the narrow path. Again missiles of death filed the air. And once again the army turned and ran for its life.

When the officer who'd ordered the two attacks learned of the newest failure, he was furious. "We'll trick them," he said, slapping his fist into his palm. He sent a message to the village saying that all had been a mistake. "Sorry for the attacks," he stated. "We'll be going now." But the Waldenses knew that the officials of the established church and its leader—the one who'd decreed that all Waldenses must be killed—had not changed their minds.

The next day, April 27, 1655, a whole regiment of armed men made another attempt. Because of their numbers, many got by Joshua and reached the now-empty village, where all they could do was plunder anything of value and burn abandoned homes.

Joshua and his men met them as they were returning with their spoils and rained bullets, stones, and large boulders down on them as they tried to negotiate the narrow mountain passes.

After the last shot rang out, Gianavello gathered his faithful band and knelt to thank God for their deliverance. The officer in charge of the attack was frantic when he heard of the new defeat. He'd try again, and this time he'd win.

But Joshua would stand for what he believed, no matter what size the enemy.

WEEDS

J esus told them another parable: "The kingdom of heaven is like a man who sowed good seed in his field. But while everyone was sleeping, his enemy came and sowed weeds among the wheat. . . . When the wheat sprouted and formed heads, then the weeds also appeared.

"The owner's servants came to him and said, 'sir, didn't you sow good seed in your field? Where then did the weeds come from?'

" 'An enemy did this,' he replied.

"The servants asked him, 'do you want us to go and pull them up?'

" 'No,' he answered, 'because while you are pulling the weeds, you may root up the wheat with them. Let both grow together until the harvest. At that time I will tell the harvesters: First collect the weeds and tie them in bundles to be burned; then gather the wheat and bring it into my barn.' . . .

"The one who sowed the good seed is the Son of Man. The field is the world, and the good seed stands for the sons of the kingdom. The weeds are the sons of the evil one, and the enemy who sows them is the devil. The harvest is the end of the age, and the harvesters are angels.

"As the weeds are pulled up and burned in the fire, so it will be at the end of the age. The Son of Man will send out his angels, and they will weed out of his kingdom everything that causes sin and all who do evil. They will throw them into the fiery furnace, where there will be weeping and gnashing of teeth. Then the righteous will shine like the sun in the kingdom of their Father."

Matthew 13:24-43

A THANKFUL PRAYER

The Lord is my light and my salvation—whom shall I fear? The Lord is the stronghold of my life—of whom shall I be afraid? Psalm 27:1.

Thank You, Jesus, for the rain,

That washes away all my pain.

Thank You, Jesus, for the sun,

That reminds me to ask You to come

Into my heart forever.

Thank You, Jesus, for the wind,

That brings me comfort when I have sinned.

Thank You, Jesus, for the sky so vast,

For when I am tired I can cast

A gaze upon the stars that will always last.

Thank You, Jesus, for the tiny flower,

That makes life seem not so sour.

Thank You, Jesus, for Your love,

That is so lavishly poured down from above.

Thank You, Jesus, for dying on the cross,

So I know I will never be lost.

And also, thank You, Jesus, for Your grace,

Without it, I would never be able to see Your face.

Tiffany Canther,
12, Arizona

DEPUTY MICHAEL

May I speak to your parents?" the voice on the phone asked."

"Only my grandparents live here," Michael Zinn responded, "and they're asleep."

A pause; then the man on the phone spoke again. "This is the sheriff's office. We're on the trail of a criminal and need your help."

Michael's eyebrows rose. "What do you want me to do?"

"A store was robbed in Sacramento yesterday. We think the robber is staying at the house across the road from yours. We don't want to attract attention, so we need someone to watch the house and let us know what's going on—lights on or off, cars coming or going, that sort of stuff. Will you help us?"

Michael nodded. "Sure. I'll be your lookout."

The sheriff called for updates that the boy provided, giving details of everything he saw from his front window. It continued until 2:00 the next morning when a car drove up to the house across the street and a man entered. When the sheriff heard the news, he immediately dispatched squad cars to the scene. Then he created a command post in Michael's living room and, when all was ready, ordered his men to move in. They arrested the criminal as he tried to escape.

The next day Michael found himself featured on the front page of the town newspaper. He received a star from the sheriff's office and was named Special Junior Deputy Sheriff.

Michael's classmates at the Chino Seventh-day Adventist school grinned broadly all the next week. A criminal had been caught, and they now had a genuine hero attending their school.

OBEYING PARENTS

Q: My mom lets me do things my dad doesn't let me do, such as wearing makeup and watching certain movies. What should I do? (My parents are divorced.)

A: It must be tough to have two parents who don't see eye-to-eye on important issues, especially when you want to please both of them. It's also especially difficult to have this happen at a time in your life when you're making decisions about what's right and wrong.

When deciding what to do, you should, of course, consider your parents' wishes, but above all, you should consider the wishes of your heavenly Father. The Bible says, "Children, obey your parents in the Lord: for this is right" (Ephesians 6:1, KJV). Sometimes we forget those three little words in the middle of that text that tell us to obey our parents "in the Lord." And remember, even though your mom may *allow* you to do certain things, that doesn't mean you *must* do them, especially if they go against God's standards.

We suggest that you take some time to talk with each of your parents individually regarding your feelings about this. Let your mom know, especially, that you love her and want to obey her, but that you want to follow your convictions to do what is right. Ask God, through prayer and Bible study, to help you decide for yourself what is right and wrong. And then, by God's grace, live up to what you know to be right.

Art and Pat Humphrey

COUGHING COW

I f it weren't for Nathan Straus, you might be dead."

One evening Mr. Straus, a wealthy department store owner in New York, was watching his cow being milked. Suddenly it made a strange noise.

"Just a cough, sir," the hired hand stated. "This cow's got tuberculosis."

"Tuberculosis?" Straus gasped. "My children drink its milk!"

"Not to worry," said the worker. "Cows don't pass the deadly disease on to those who drink their milk. All the doctors say so."

But Straus wasn't convinced. One in three children died before the age of 5 in New York, usually of tuberculosis. He'd heard of a Frenchman named Louis Pasteur who advocated heating milk to 150° F for about a half hour. Pasteur claimed it would kill all germs in any liquid. "I'm going to run a test using my own money," announced Mr. Straus. "I'll give 2,000 children heat-treated milk and see if they stay healthier than those who don't drink treated milk."

Many opposed his test. "It's bad for business," wailed the milk producers. "He's playing doctor with our children," complained the medical profession. One physician even had Straus arrested!

Of the 2,000 children who drank Mr. Straus's treated milk, only six died in eight months. If they'd been drinking untreated milk, 890 would have perished in that same period.

When people heard the facts of the test, they began demanding "pasteurized" milk for their families. Governments passed laws and imposed fines, and babies grew up instead of dying.

When you believe in something, stick to it, even if others disagree. The life you save may be your own.

CHOOSE GRACE

Q: Why didn't God destroy Satan?

A: For the same reason He doesn't destroy us. He loves him.
What? God loves Satan?

Yup. But He absolutely *hates* what Satan does.

"But," you say, "if God had destroyed him, all the pain and suffering in the world would never have happened." I take that to mean that if God knows your great-grandson or great-granddaughter is going to murder a neighbor, He should come down and destroy you right this minute so it won't happen.

"Wait a minute," you protest. "I don't want God to kill me off because of something a future relative is going to do."

Exactly. If He'd destroyed Satan back there in Eden, the whole universe would see how unfair that was. Instead, Jesus told His Father, "Let *Me* die. Let *Me* pay the price for Satan's sin, and for everyone's sin. Then death will be only a sleep, and all those who choose to love and obey You will have a bright future waiting beyond the grave."

Satan will ultimately be destroyed along with those who follow him and turn their backs on God's forgiving grace. But it will happen only after *everyone*, including you and me, has had a chance to choose which side they're on, and which future they want—eternal life or eternal death.

"For sin shall not be your master, because you are not under law, but under grace" (Romans 6:14). Choose grace!

TEN THOUSAND VERSUS 41

After suffering defeats at the hands of Joshua Gianavello and his courageous little bands, the marquis of Pianaza decided to send into the Waldensian valleys all the troops under his command—10,000 men!

Although Gianavello and his 40 comrades were able to fight back one group of advancing soldiers as they moved through a narrow mountain pass, two other regiments slipped around the battle and completely destroyed several villages, killing many people. The worst of it for Joshua was the fact that they captured his wife and daughters and carried them away.

The next day a letter from the marquis informed Gianavello of that unsettling fact. Then the writer added, "If you fall alive into my hands, be sure there are no torments so cruel but that you shall undergo them."

Joshua responded with a letter of his own. "There is no torment so cruel that I should not prefer it to giving up my faith; and your threats, instead of deterring me from my faith, fortify me still more firmly in it. As to my wife and children, they well know how dear they are to me; but God alone is the master of their lives, and if you make their bodies perish, He will save their souls."

What wonderful courage! How well do we compare with Joshua Gianavello? Do we willingly give up those things that are important to us in order to serve God? Or do we make compromises, allowing Satan into our hearts when the going gets tough?

Peer pressure, violence on television, smut-filled reading material are trying to slip through the mountain passes of your mind. Protect yourself at all costs!

NEW WORTH

Jesus said,] "The kingdom of heaven is like treasure hidden in a field. When a man found it, he hid it again, and then in his joy went and sold all he had and bought that field.

"Again, the kingdom of heaven is like a merchant looking for fine pearls. When he found one of great value, he went away and sold everything he had and bought it.

"Once again, the kingdom of heaven is like a net that was let down into the lake and caught all kinds of fish. When it was full, the fishermen pulled it up on the shore. Then they sat down and collected the good fish in baskets, but threw the bad away. This is how it will be at the end of the age. The angels will come and separate the wicked from the righteous and throw them into the fiery furnace, where there will be weeping and gnashing of teeth.

"Have you understood all these things?" Jesus asked [His disciples].

"Yes," they replied.

He said to them, "Therefore every teacher of the law who has been instructed about the kingdom of heaven is like the owner of a house who brings out of his storeroom new treasures as well as old."

Matthew 13:44-52

Are you beginning to understand what Jesus was teaching with His parables? "Forget war. Forget overthrowing your enemies," He is saying. *I'll* wage war on the devil. *I'll* exact revenge on your enemies. Your job is to love one another and help friends, family members, and neighbors enjoy My presence in their lives." Sounds like you've got work to do today!

GUILTY!

T hen David said to Nathan, "I have sinned against the Lord." 2 Samuel 12:13.

David had been a very bad boy. *Very* bad. He'd ordered Uriah the Hittite to the front lines against the Ammorites during fierce fighting. Uriah would probably die, which was the whole idea. David wanted Bathsheba, the brave warrior's beautiful wife.

When the prophet Nathan confronted David with his sin, the morally bankrupt king broke down and confessed bitterly.

I live in a small West Virginia town. Our weekly newspaper prints summaries of the criminal cases brought before our magistrate. In almost every case the one who has been charged with a crime pleads, "Not guilty!" Police may have caught them with the goods/money/smoking gun/embezzled funds/missing property hiding in their own pocket/garage/car/closet/storage shed, but still the people scream, "Not guilty!"

Then taxpayers (like me) have to shell out hard-earned money to try these lawbreakers and then send them off to where they belong until they can learn to live like normal human beings.

How much better/faster/cheaper it would be if these guys would admit to their crimes, do the time, and then get on with their lives.

Juniors, if you ever mess up, admit it. Don't point fingers, whine, complain, or obsess over fake innocence. Like David, say, "I have sinned against God." Take your punishment, then get on with life.

The last part of the verse reads: "Nathan replied, 'The Lord has taken away your sin.'"

David paid a terrible price for his mistakes, but he didn't have to pay the ultimate price—eternal separation from God.

JESUS, NEW YORK 8

You've probably heard of *Christian Lifestyle Magazine,* a television program produced by Adventists at Faith for Today in California. Long before CLM existed, Faith for Today was headquartered in New York City, where the husband and wife team of Pastor and Mrs. William Fagal beamed words of hope to viewers.

On one such broadcast they invited young people to write in for their own Junior Bible Course. "You'll love it," Pastor Fagal encouraged. "Just send a postcard to Faith for Today, Box 8, New York 8, New York."

Gary wanted the course and ran for paper and pencil. Grabbing a postcard from his study desk, he began to write. The problem was that he'd forgotten the address. *Wait,* the boy mused. *The man said "New York" a lot of times, so I'll put that down. Hum. He also said something about 8, so I'll include that.* Gary scratched his head and frowned. *What was the name of the television program? Oh yes. He kept talking about Jesus, so I'll jot down that word, too. There, that should do it!*

The most amazing part of this story is that, when the postal clerk picked up the card from his mail sack, he didn't even hesitate. He delivered the card to the correct address, and Gary soon had his Bible course.

How did that clerk know where to send a postcard labeled "Jesus, New York 8"? Simple. He'd seen the Faith for Today programs, too!

If a postcard came to your town addressed to Jesus, would the mail carrier know to bring it to *your* house?

FALLING GRADES

Q: I'm in eighth grade and have been going to an Adventist junior academy. But my grades are falling. My friend, who had the same problem, now attends public school, and she's getting better grades. I enjoy my Adventist school, but I'm afraid if I don't go to public school I won't get a good job because of my grades. What should I do?

A: We are so glad to hear that you enjoy your school. Such things as Bible classes and worship experiences make Adventist schools special!

But we're sorry to hear you're not getting good grades (you're certainly pretty smart for wanting to stay in an Adventist school!). Have you tried talking with your teachers? We feel sure that they will try their best to help you. Also, your public library or local bookstore probably has books on study skills that can help.

It's interesting that your friend's grades went up when she transferred to public school. Maybe the work there is a lot easier. But good grades don't necessarily mean success later on. It's how much you know that makes the difference in the end. Even more important than getting good grades or a good job or knowing a lot is our friendship with Jesus. That counts more toward our success than anything.

Study God's Word and pray for wisdom, and He will bless you!

Art and Pat Humphrey

UNDERSTANDING

Mr. Myers looked down at the furry lumps nestled against the belly of his female cocker spaniel. Five babies. Five squirming, yapping, yawning bundles of energy.

Then he frowned. One of the puppies had a weak, deformed leg and could only limp about, trying to keep up with the others. The man sighed. "No one will want her."

A few days later, after he'd put a "Puppies for Sale" sign in his window, he answered a soft knock at his door. A boy stood looking up at him. "How much for the puppies?" he asked.

"Twenty-five dollars each," Mr. Myers announced.

"Oh," the boy said sadly. "I only have $3. May I at least see them?"

Mr. Myers led the boy to the box. The boy's face lit up as he watched the five little balls of fur. Suddenly he gasped. "Please, mister," he exclaimed, "could I have that one with the bad leg? I'll pay you all I've got and more each week. Please, let me have that one."

"Now, son," Mr. Myers said. "You don't want her. She'll never be able to walk well. Wouldn't you rather have one that can play with you when it grows up?"

That's when the boy lifted his pant leg to reveal shiny metal braces. "I've never been able to walk too good," he said. "I reckon that little puppy will need a bit of understanding. I sure did."

The boy left with the crippled puppy held gently in his arms.

Why did Jesus come to earth? To learn exactly what it's like to be a human being so He could understand us.

VISION TEST

Q: How can we know that when we see a "vision" it's from God and not Satan?

A: First of all, I want to say that the whole idea of "visions" is overrated in our world right now. We've got people having "out-of-body experiences" left and right, others "channeling" with the supposed spirits of departed loved ones, movies depicting lost loves rising from the mists, and dozens of books proclaiming close encounters of the angelic kind.

Even the Bible states that "it shall come to pass in the last days, saith God, I will pour out of my Spirit upon all flesh: and your sons and your daughters shall prophesy, and your young men shall see visions, and your old men shall dream dreams" (Acts 2:17, KJV).

But which are from God? Listen to these Bible words. "Dear friends, do not believe every spirit, but test the spirits to see whether they are from God, because many false prophets have gone out into the world. This is how you can recognize the Spirit of God: Every spirit that acknowledges that Jesus Christ has come in the flesh is from God, but every spirit that does not acknowledge Jesus is not from God" (1 John 4:1-3).

Why does this test work? Because the last thing Satan wants to do is draw you closer to Jesus. The closer you are to Him, the more obvious Satan's counterfeit becomes. If the vision you hear about, read, or experience stays true to Bible teachings and highlights Jesus and not self, you can rest assured that God is delivering the message. If not, ignore it.

BULLETS IN HAY BAGS

Joshua Gianavello defended the Waldenses from persecution with every fiber of his body. Even after enemy soldiers captured his wife and daughters, he fought on. More men joined his army, including Waldenses from another valley.

At last Joshua decided to take the offensive and do some attacking of his own. On the morning of May 28, 1655, Gianavello roused his men before daybreak, and they all prayed for victory. Then they left their mountain fortresses and headed for San Segonzo, a city filled with enemy soldiers.

When the alarm rang, marksmen took their places on the walls and then gasped. Slowly advancing on their positions were hundreds of . . . hay bags! They rolled over the fields, being pushed by unseen men hiding behind them for protection. Bullets whizzed from the walls but only pierced hay, not flesh.

When the bags stopped at the base of the walls, the men above began throwing down anything they could find in order to crush the advancing army, but Joshua and his men set the hay on fire, filling the air with thick, choking smoke. In the confusion that followed, he and his soldiers broke through the gates of the city. Enemy soldiers fell under their flashing swords. An entire regiment of Irishmen who'd hoped to get rich off of dead Waldenses' property perished along with 650 other soldiers.

"Be faithful, even to the point of death," says God in Revelation 2:10, "and I will give you the crown of life." Joshua Gianavello and his people lived and died by those words.

HEAVENLY CLASSIFIEDS,
PART 1

Jesus said,] "The kingdom of heaven is like a landowner who went out early in the morning to hire men to work in his vineyard. He agreed to pay them a denarius for the day and sent them into his vineyard.

"About the third hour he went out and saw others standing in the marketplace doing nothing. He told them, 'You also go and work in my vineyard, and I will pay you whatever is right.' So they went.

"He went out again about the sixth hour and the ninth hour and did the same thing. About the eleventh hour he went out and found still others standing around. He asked them, 'Why have you been standing here all day long doing nothing?'

"'Because no one has hired us,' they answered.

"He said to them, 'You also go and work in my vineyard.'"

Matthew 20:1-7

We'll read the rest of this parable next week, but there's something we can learn from the first part. Jesus (the landowner) needs workers in His fields (the earth) first thing in the morning, and at the third, sixth, ninth, and eleventh hours. Basically all day long.

Did you notice what those hired at the eleventh hour said when the landowner asked them why they were just standing around? They responded, "Because no one has hired us."

Juniors, don't ever think you're "unemployed" when it comes to saving others for the kingdom. Jesus wants you out in the field, demonstrating God's love to everyone. So get up, get out, and get busy. There's work to do!

IF I WERE JUDGE

I f only I were appointed judge in the land! Then everyone who has a complaint or case could come to me and I would see that he gets justice." 2 Samuel 15:4.

These words, spoken by I-want-to-be-king-of-the-world Absalom, echo the hidden desire of a lot of adults and juniors. Here's what I would do if appointed judge in the land.

1. I'd make all divorced parents of junior-age kids get back together. OK, so one of them did something really stupid. Hey, don't we all? Let's show a little forgiveness out there! If physical or sexual abuse was involved, I'd toss 'em in jail so fast that their sunglasses would still be hanging in midair.

2. I'd make all public schools teach "Bible" science along with evolution. Let students decide whether they came from river slime or from God's hand.

3. I'd make Moose Tracks the official ice cream of the world (that's vanilla with mini Reese's Pieces in it—yum!).

4. I'd ban drum kits from church services. If you want to rock and roll, go on a nature hike. God isn't impressed with noise or swaying bodies. He'd much rather listen to the joyful praise generated by a life in tune with His will.

5. I'd make all pastors take one full day and one half day off each week. No phones, no committee meetings, no visits. They've got a life and need to live it.

6. I'd insist that all juniors spend two minutes each day reading something spiritual. Oh yeah, you're reading this book. One down, five to go!

"FALLING" FOR BOYS

S abrina and Lynn like boys. To them, males are the most interesting things on this planet. So when the guys in their school joined the Pathfinder Club, the girls quickly followed.

All went well until crafttime and the boys headed upstairs to the old church attic to work on their weight lifting and tumbling honors while the others stayed below baking bread and painting pottery. None of the other girls had any desire to learn how to bench-press a Buick, and Sabrina and Lynn didn't want to be the only female jocks in the group, so they reluctantly stayed behind.

"I've got it!" Sabrina gasped one evening while she and Lynn were up to their elbows in wheat flour. "Let's sneak out and see what the guys are doing." So when the instructor wasn't looking, the two headed up the steps and soon were settled in an out-of-the-way spot watching the objects of their affection sweat and flex.

Suddenly the tumbling director started heading in their direction. "Quick," Sabrina gasped. "Let's hide behind those boxes."

The attic in the old church wasn't completely finished. Part of the floor, where the boys were, had been covered with strong boards. The other section boasted only a thin layer of plaster and dust between the joists. When the two girls jumped behind the boxes, they sailed right through the floor plaster, slipped between the joists, and landed with a resounding *crash* on the table spread with freshly baked bread in the room below.

No one was hurt. But needless to say, two totally embarrassed Pathfinders decided to start admiring boys from much safer hiding places.

AFTER THE FALL

Q: Why are all adults (and both of you) always saying "Have a lot of casual friends and don't get too serious about one person"? Also, some people make "falling in love" seem out of your own control. Is that true? (I'm a girl.)

A: Time brings change. As young people grow and mature, their interests, likes, and dislikes change. We know a young woman in her mid-20s who said after breaking off a relationship, "I wonder how I could have ever liked him." The person you think may be so cool and awesome today may seem like a nerd a few years from now. And someone who appears a nerd today may one day become the man of your dreams!

Also, a close relationship formed too early may deprive a young person of the opportunity to get to know and enjoy the friendship of other people. Often when people know that a girl or a guy is going steady with one person, nobody else will talk to them. As part of normal, healthy development young people should become acquainted with as many people of the opposite sex as possible in ways that don't force them to make strong attachments to just one person.

As for "falling in love," the expression itself seems to suggest a lack of control, doesn't it? When we fall we lose control, and sometimes we get hurt. The same thing can happen when we "fall in love." *True* love is a relationship based on choice. It's not something that happens instantly. Like caring for a tender plant, it grows, develops, and must be nurtured over a period of time.

Art and Pat Humphrey

LUCKY TO BE ALIVE

Lora Robey wasn't born yet when the story she wrote about took place. But she certainly knows how it ends. Listen:

When my older brother was just a baby, he was diagnosed with a brain tumor. The doctors told my parents in a solemn voice that he'd not live past the age of 16.

My folks were devastated. "Is there anything we can do to save his life?" my mom cried. The doctor told them that there was nothing medically or humanly possible. He said, "Take him home, make him as comfortable as possible, and just love him. Make the most out of every minute."

After a few weeks had passed, Mom and Dad took my brother back to the doctor. He did a MRI scan on him. Thinking that something must be wrong with the equipment, he checked the results repeatedly. In shock he went out to the waiting room "The tumor is gone," he said, shaking his head. Then he added, "But you must keep a close eye on him. It might come back even worse."

Mom and Dad took my brother home and thanked Jesus for the good report. My brother is now 18 years old and in very good health. He has never had any problems since. We thank God every day that he's fine and lucky to be alive.

Lora Robey,
14, California

Sometimes doctors deliver happy news. Other times they don't. But whatever the report, God is there ready to comfort our hearts and strengthen our resolve to live forever with Him in heaven.

SECRET DATE

Q: How come God didn't tell us the day or hour of Jesus' coming?

A: Maybe because of people like me (Pat)! Here's what I mean. As a writer I constantly have deadlines to meet. But sometimes I wait until the last minute to get my assignments done. Even though I get things in on time, and the people I write for seem to like my work, I could probably save myself a lot of headaches and stress by starting on my projects earlier!

Consider this: What if we knew the exact time Jesus would return? Do you think we'd be busy every minute doing the work He has asked us to do (such as helping people and telling others about Jesus), knowing that we have some extra time to get ready? Probably not. Most likely we'd say, "We've got plenty of time. Just before Jesus comes back, we'll get our work done." But think of all the people who might miss out on hearing the good news of the gospel if we take that attitude!

But that's not all. We have no guarantee that we will be alive tomorrow. So let's live and work as though Jesus will come at any moment!

We may not know exactly when Jesus will return, but all we have to do is look around. The signs everywhere are telling us that the time is very near (see Matthew 24). I want to be ready. I hope you do too!

Art and Pat Humphrey

BY THE WATERS

He was a handsome young man, strong and active. But he had some bad habits that left him very sick. Friends took him to doctors and finally to the only place that might help—a pool in Jerusalem at which people said angels stirred the waters. The popular belief was that if you were the first person into the pool when the waters rippled, you'd get better.

So they left the young man by the pool and then forgot him. No one came to see him. Nor did anyone offer to help him get into the water when the ripples appeared. He sat there month after month, year after year, begging for handouts, never able to reach the pool in time.

Thirty-eight years passed. Countless times the waters rippled, countless times the man watched someone else get to the pool before him. And for all those years he longed to be forgiven for the evil ways of his youth.

One Sabbath afternoon a stranger paused at his side. "What do you want most?" the visitor asked.

"Sir," the sick man answered, "I have no one to put me in the pool when the waters move."

Then the stranger spoke words that changed his life forever. "Get up," He told him. "Take your sleeping mat and walk." Something in that voice sounded like forgiveness and hope. Without hesitation, the sick man stumbled to his feet and turned to face the stranger, but He was gone.

He had finally reached the waters. No, not those in the pool. He'd found the water of life in the presence of Jesus Christ and was healed.

HEAVENLY CLASSIFIEDS
PART 2

Last week we read the parable about the landowner who hired workers in the morning and at the third, sixth, ninth, and eleventh hours. Well, the day is done, and it's paytime! Listen as Jesus finishes the story:

"When evening came, the owner of the vineyard said to his foreman, 'Call the workers and pay them their wages, beginning with the last ones hired and going on to the first.'

"The workers who were hired about the eleventh hour came and each received a denarius. So when those came who were hired first, they expected to receive more. But each one of them also received a denarius. When they received it, they began to grumble against the landowner. 'These men who were hired last worked only one hour,' they said, 'and you have made them equal to us who have borne the burden of the work and the heat of the day.'

"But he answered one of them, 'Friend, I am not being unfair to you. Didn't you agree to work for a denarius? Take your pay and go. I want to give the man who was hired last the same as I gave you. Don't I have the right to do what I want with my own money? Or are you envious because I am generous?'

"So the last will be first, and the first will be last."

Matthew 20:8-16

What a fair God we serve! If He were to come right now, you'd receive the same reward as someone who has worked his or her entire life for Him. In God's eyes, sacrifice is sacrifice, whether for a day or a lifetime.

RUN!

He said, "Come what may, I want to run." 2 Samuel 18:23.

Ahimaaz wanted to deliver the good news to King David. He longed to tell him that his enemies had been routed and that his houses and wives and concubines were safe once again. The messenger's feet were just itching to race back to the palace and inform the monarch that all was well in the kingdom. Oh yes, there was one teeny-weeny bit of bad news. Absalom, David's son, had been killed.

Being a missionary is a good news, bad news deal, too. You tell people of a glorious future with the God of the universe and—oh by the way, you've got to change your life completely if you want to be a part of it.

But wait. Is living the Christian life really bad news? You're healthier. That's for sure. Now you have faith in something besides yourself. That's a plus. And you're nicer to others, and that usually makes them nicer to you. Definite benefits there. The future doesn't frighten you because you know that Jesus *is* your future and there's absolutely nothing scary about Him. Ditto.

Then there's the Ten Commandments that, if followed faithfully, can help keep you out of every jail and mental institution in the world. And the "Do unto others" thing you learned as a kid—that alone makes you more friends than enemies.

I guess there really isn't any bad news after all! So slip into your Cross Trainers, do your warm-up stretches, grab your Bible, and *run!*

SABBATHKEEPING HAMMER

Berto Menon, a poor shoemaker, lived in Spain. One day he heard beautiful music coming over his radio. A male quartet was singing, "Lift up the trumpet, and loud let it ring." "Nice music," Menon said to himself. After he heard the speaker present a short talk on God's love, he added, "Hey, nice sermon."

The shoemaker began listening every day to the broadcast. When an Adventist literature evangelist stopped by, he purchased several books and discovered that the messages in the books sounded like those on the radio.

"That's our church's Voice of Prophecy program," the LE explained. "We preach and sing about the beautiful truths found in the Bible."

Menon accepted every doctrine that Adventists teach except one. "You can't convince me that God doesn't want me to work on Saturday," he insisted.

When the shoemaker showed up for work early the next Sabbath morning, he couldn't find his hammer. He looked everywhere, then went home. Without a hammer, he couldn't work. The next day he found it.

A week later he arrived at the shop bright and early on Sabbath morning, picked up his hammer, adjusted his first shoe carefully, slipped a nail between his fingers, took aim, and began tapping. *Crack.* The hammer broke in two.

"All right, *all right!*" Menon moaned. "Someone's trying to tell me something." So instead of working that day, he headed for the local Seventh-day Adventist church. Weeks later he was baptized. To celebrate his joining the family, church members presented the shoemaker with a brand-new hammer—one they knew would never work on Sabbath.

HURTFUL FORMER FRIEND

Q: I'm having trouble with a former friend. Whenever she was in a bad mood she'd talk behind my back, make fun of me, and even throw me on the floor! When I told her we couldn't be friends anymore, she started putting hate notes in my locker and spreading rumors about me. What should I do?

A: It must really hurt to be treated this way by someone you probably still care about.

Your friend may be dealing with some serious personal problems. Often when young people act aggressively and mistreat others, it's because they live in a troubled home.

This girl probably doesn't like herself very well. What she needs more than anything is a close friendship with Jesus, to know that He loves her, and to love Him in return. It will help her form positive relationships with others and feel better about herself.

Ask God to help you forgive her for the wrong she has done. Then ask her if there's some way you can help. Offer to listen. Also, find out if you've done anything to hurt her that would cause her to act mean toward you. Be kind, but at the same time make sure she understands that you won't tolerate mistreatment. You might suggest that she talk to her parents, a teacher, counselor, or pastor who can help her deal with whatever problems she's facing. If she doesn't respond positively to your offer for help, you may want to take the problem to a teacher or counselor who can directly intervene in the situation. (Check out Ephesians 4:32!)

Art and Pat Humphrey

DOG-BONE MYSTERY

Mrs. Hazel Bretman had more to worry about than a stray dog asking for a bone. She had a hundred hungry schoolchildren to feed each day, so when her assistant, Leona, told her that a dog was at the back door of the kitchen begging for a bone, she simply said, "Give it one."

Halfway through the meal, her assistant tapped her on the shoulder. "Sorry to disturb you, ma'am," she said, "but the dog is back begging for another bone."

"Then give it one," her boss responded.

The dog's visits continued for days. Just as the children were filing into the dining room, the dog would appear at the back door and scratch softly. When given a bone, he'd hurry off, only to return 15 minutes later.

The kitchen help were puzzled. "Maybe he's storing them for the winter, like a squirrel," Jocelyn, the woman who ran the dishwasher, suggested. "Maybe he's got babies and has to feed them," chimed in Rodney, the head server.

"Well, I'm going to find out," Mrs. Bretman declared. "Tomorrow, don't give the dog any bones until after the meal, when I can follow him."

The next day the woman trailed the pooch the second time it raced away from the school with his bone. When Mrs. Bretman returned, everyone gathered around to hear her report.

"He keeps only one bone for himself," she said. "The other he gives to another dog that stays chained up all the time. Tomorrow, let's give him an extra-large bone for being so thoughtful."

We can learn a lot from a dog.

SUICIDE

Q: Will a person who commits suicide be in heaven?

A: Keep in mind this simple truth: God is more interested in *why* we act than *how* we act. The Bible states, "The Lord does not look at the things man looks at. Man looks at the outward appearance, but the Lord looks at the heart" (1 Samuel 16:7).

People take their own lives for many reasons. Some kill themselves because life has become more than they can handle. I only wish someone had introduced those people to their friend Jesus, who could help them face their challenges.

Others commit suicide because they're ashamed of something terrible they did. Jesus could help here too by offering forgiveness and teaching them how to live with the results of their mistakes—even if that meant prison.

Still others end their lives because they're afraid of dying of a painful illness they've contracted, such as AIDS or cancer. They'd rather die peacefully than in agony.

We can't judge whether a suicide is sin because we can't read thoughts and understand motives. But God can, and does. Rest assured that our heavenly Father takes into account every aspect of this human tragedy and reserves a place for that person in heaven if at all possible.

If you're tempted to commit suicide, give God a chance to bring you hope and courage. Allow Jesus to place answers in your mind. Be patient and listen for that still small voice that can turn despair into joy, and death into life eternal.

HAPPY BEGGAR

Jesus is coming!" The excited whisper drifts through the gathering like a spark of electricity. "Jesus is coming!"

The breath of a blind man huddled under the protection of a tree catches in his throat. Could it be? Was it true? He'd been waiting for this moment ever since he'd heard about the kind Teacher who traveled throughout his homeland, healing people of all manner of ills. This would be his one opportunity. He might never have another.

"Jesus, Son of David," he calls, voice trembling with excitement, "have mercy on me."

"Be quiet," someone hisses at him. "You're making far too much commotion."

But the man didn't care. His one chance for sight, his one chance for living a normal, productive life, was about to pass by. It was no time to be timid.

"Jesus, Son of David, have mercy on me!"

In the distance he hears a kind, resonant voice say, "Tell the blind man to come to Me."

The beggar leaps to his feet and races for the voice, bumping into people, stumbling over rocks, finally landing at Jesus' feet.

"What do you want Me to do?" he hears the Teacher say. Of course, Jesus knew exactly what the man wanted, but He likes to be asked. He doesn't force Himself on anyone.

"Sight," said the beggar. "I want to see!"

"Your faith has made you well," Jesus responds. And the eyes of the blind man opened wide in wonder.

Today Christ offers unlimited healing power for every spiritual ill. Fall at His feet. Ask. Receive.

KEEPING WATCH

At that time the kingdom of heaven will be like ten virgins who took their lamps and went out to meet the bridegroom. Five of them were foolish and five were wise. The foolish ones took their lamps but did not take any oil with them. The wise, however, took oil in jars along with their lamps. The bridegroom was a long time in coming, and they all became drowsy and fell asleep.

"At midnight the cry rang out: 'Here's the bridegroom! Come out to meet him!'

"Then all the virgins woke up and trimmed their lamps. The foolish ones said to the wise, 'Give us some of your oil; our lamps are going out.'

"'No,' they replied, 'there may not be enough for both us and you. Instead, go to those who sell oil and buy some for yourselves.'

"But while they were on their way to buy the oil, the bridegroom arrived. The virgins who were ready went in with him to the wedding banquet. And the door was shut.

"Later the others also came.'sir! Sir!' they said.'Open the door for us!'

"But he replied,'I tell you the truth, I don't know you.'

"Therefore keep watch, because you do not know the day or the hour."

Matthew 25:1-13

What was Jesus trying to say? That's right—those of us who are watching and waiting for His second coming must be ready at all times. We may sleep the long sleep of death, but if we've filled our hearts with the oil of understanding and service, we'll be ready to welcome Him back with open arms.

THE SERGEANT'S COURAGE

Now go out and encourage your men." 2 Samuel 19:7.

The battlefield at Gettysburg shook with the rumble of cannon and the shouts of men. Southern forces poured over Northern defenses. Lieutenant Frank Haskell knew that if something weren't done immediately, the North would lose.

"Major," Lieutenant Haskell shouted at the brigade leader, "lead your men over the crest."

Major Webb shook his head. "By the rule of battle my place is in the rear of my men."

Haskell nodded angrily. "I see *your* place is in the rear of men." Then he noticed a low-ranking officer standing nearby. "Sergeant," he ordered. "Forward with your color."

The lower-ranked officer seized the flag and ran for the enemy's line. One by one, then as a group, the soldiers followed the brave sergeant into battle, fought the enemy, and won.

Faced any foes lately? Got bad habits attacking you day after day? The same thing is happening to every junior. The battle rages. More and more "high-ranking" teens and preteens are refusing to mount a counterattack. "You," God shouts, "lead your friends, your family, your classmates. They will follow." How do you answer?

Are you like Major Webb, who chose to cower behind brave men? Or are you like the sergeant who seized the flag and ran straight at the enemy?

Don't worry if your parents aren't rich or powerful. And don't be concerned if you don't live in the grandest house or ride in the coolest car. In the battle against evil, the only thing that matters is your courage. Grab the flag. Gather your army. *Charge!*

GEM OF GREAT PRICE

The gun felt heavy in Philip's hand as he sighted down the barrel. Nearby, unaware of the danger, stood Martino, a man Philip knew was the thief who'd stolen a precious gem from his house. The police were doing nothing, so the victim of the crime had decided to take matters into his own hands.

Just a little pressure on his trigger finger would end the hunt forever. Martino would pay for his crime.

But Philip hesitated, and in that brief moment Martino moved back into the crowd. It wouldn't be safe to fire now. Disgusted, the would-be shooter walked away and soon vanished into the crowded Rio de Janeiro marketplace.

Days passed. Once again Philip stood with gun leveled at his enemy. But again he couldn't pull the trigger. What was wrong? Martino had done a terrible thing, robbing Philip of his future. He'd spent everything to buy the gem. Now it was gone, and Martino had taken it.

Three months later Philip passed a church. "Maybe I ought to go to services before I kill Martino. The preacher may have something worthwhile to say."

The preacher did, as all good Seventh-day Adventist pastors do. He spoke about forgiveness, about loving our enemies and doing good to those who hurt us. The Holy Spirit must have shouted in Philip's ear that night because when he returned home he put his gun away for good. "Instead of taking a man's life," he told the preacher, "I'm accepting a new life in Christ."

Did he ever get his gem back? No. But he found something much more valuable. He found Jesus.

HELPING THE WAYWARD FRIEND

Q: I'm a 13-year-old girl. I have a friend who hangs around with a person who does drugs, smokes, drinks, and other bad things. My friend is nice and says she wants to help this person. But I'm worried that my friend will get pressured to start using drugs.

A: You're a wise friend! Statistics show that many kids who come from good homes end up getting involved in drugs simply because of the influence of a peer. (The Bible warns us to be careful about the company we keep.)

We think you should encourage *your* friend to encourage *her* friend to get some help. If the friend is really heavy into drugs, then just trying to convince the person that it's wrong isn't enough. This friend needs the help of an expert, someone who knows how to help people in these situations. Drugs, alcohol, and tobacco are powerful and addicting, and a person needs more than simple willpower to get unhooked. All this depends on whether or not the person *wants* to be helped in the first place.

Aside from suggesting professional help, suggest that *your* friend pray for and with this person. Also, how about the two of you joining together in praying for him or her, asking God to show you how you can help? If your friend is a church member, maybe she could invite her friend to church too. There's lots of good reading material available that she could share with the other person, such as *Listen* and *Winner* magazines.

Art and Pat Humphrey

MOLDY MELON

Kenneth pawed through the melon display, trying to find the one fruit that would fit his needs. "Nope," he said, holding one near his nose, "not old enough." Then he saw a melon sitting off to one side. It looked like it had been there for days. "Perfect!" Ken said with a smile.

At the checkout counter, the storekeeper didn't want to sell him the fruit. "It's totally rotten," he gasped.

"I know," Ken grinned.

"That's what you'd expect when you send a *man* to do your shopping," two women standing nearby whispered to each other.

Ken hurried from the store to his office in the U.S. Department of Agriculture and handed the moldy melon over to technicians who quickly ran to their laboratory. The year was 1939. Not long before, researchers had found that penicillin helped people fight infection. But only bread mold seemed to work. Not much penicillin was available, and the department was trying to find new sources from which they could create the much-needed and terribly expensive substance.

A few days later the results were in. Melon mold worked great. Penicillin could now be produced in greater volume and inexpensively. Many lives would be saved in the war about to sweep across the world.

A moldy melon. The grocer saw in it only junk. But Kenneth saw in it a million miracles.

How about you? Do you sometimes feel worthless? Remember the melon. If such a discarded fruit can create a million miracles, what can *you* do with God's help?

FASHION STATEMENT

Q: Where in the Bible does it say you should not wear jewelry and not adorn yourself?

A: You're probably thinking of 1 Timothy 2:9, in which Paul states, "I also want women to dress modestly, with decency and propriety, not with braided hair or gold or pearls or expensive clothes, but with good deeds, appropriate for women who profess to worship God."

Like everywhere else in the Bible, a deeper meaning hides behind this verse.

When I was a junior, a rock group from England took America by storm. They were called the Beatles, and I, like millions of teenagers, thought they were the next best thing to sliced bread (which only *sounds* like the name of a rock group). The stores soon started to carry tons of Beatles merchandise—Beatles wigs, Beatles coats, and most attractive to me, Beatles shoes. I wanted a pair of Beatles shoes so I could look like John Lennon.

You see, I wanted to adorn myself with something that had no *real* value. Beatles shoes didn't help me climb mountains, or play football, or even walk to school. They were only good for looking like a Beatle.

Any article of clothing, any piece of jewelry that we as Christians wear should be more than something that just draws attention our way. When fashion ignores modesty, good taste, and usefulness, it's time for us to ignore fashion. "A wicked man puts up a bold front, but an upright man gives thought to his ways" (Proverbs 21:29). That includes how we adorn ourselves.

COUPLING PIN MYSTERY

James and Ellen White boarded the train bound for Michigan with some misgivings. Pastor White had felt uneasy that afternoon, wondering if they should make the journey at all. "I feel strange about starting this trip," he told his wife.

"But we've promised the believers we'd come," Ellen responded.

To relieve their uncertainty, the young couple did what they usually did under such circumstances. They knelt and prayed, thanking God that He'd be traveling with them.

At the station James placed his trunk filled with printed religious materials in the baggage car and then the couple settled themselves in a coach. Ellen hadn't been there more than a minute when she told her husband, "I can't stay here. I must find a new seat."

They moved to the last passenger car in the train. Even that didn't make Ellen completely comfortable. "I don't feel at home," she admitted.

They'd traveled only three miles when *BANG, BOOM, CRASH!* a terrific jolt threw them forward in their seats. The car filled with choking dust, and then all was silent. James hurried out to see what had happened. The locomotive had hit an ox lying on the tracks, derailed, flipped over, and then come to rest—upside down. The cars immediately behind it had been crushed. But the last passenger car remained safely on the rails because the coupling pin, the device that linked train cars together in those days, had somehow slipped out. The brakeman said he hadn't removed it. Perhaps a quick-thinking passenger had saved their lives. No one knows for sure.

Was it luck? You decide.

LAST-PLACE WINNERS

T hen the mother of Zebedee's sons came to Jesus with her sons and, kneeling down, asked a favor of him.

"What is it you want?" he asked.

She said, "Grant that one of these two sons of mine may sit at your right and the other at your left in your kingdom."

"You don't know what you are asking," Jesus said to them. "Can you drink the cup I am going to drink?"

"We can," they answered.

Jesus said to them, "You will indeed drink from my cup, but to sit at my right or left is not for me to grant. These places belong to those for whom they have been prepared by my Father."

When the ten heard about this, they were indignant [mad] with the two brothers. Jesus called them together and said, "You know that the rulers of the Gentiles lord it over them, and their high officials exercise authority over them. Not so with you. Instead, whoever wants to become great among you must be your servant, and whoever wants to be first must be your slave— just as the Son of Man did not come to be served, but to serve, and to give his life as a ransom for many."

Matthew 20:20-28

"Drinking the cup" brings the possibility of suffering. You may be scorned by friends, fired from your job, or even persecuted. But don't give up. God's people know that being good, faithful servants will transform their last-place finish into eternal victory!

BLESSING OTHERS

T hen [Jesus] went down to Nazareth with [His parents] and was obedient to them. Luke 2:51.

Benjamin Franklin is one of American history's most beloved individuals.

While he was a schoolboy his teacher ordered the students in his class to learn some popular stories in preparation for Visitation Day, a special event attended by dignitaries in the community. The schoolmaster insisted that they memorize the stories and recite them in Latin.

"I can't do this," Benjamin's friend Nathan moaned, pointing at the printed version of his story, "The Wolf and the Kid." "I've already been whipped for not keeping up with the others."

"Don't worry," Benjamin encouraged. "I've learned my story, 'The Dog and His Shadow.' I'll help you memorize yours."

The two worked hard until Nathan could get through his presentation fairly well. When the big day arrived, the important men of Boston showed up in their fancy velvets and silks. Even the governor came.

At the appointed time the schoolmaster rose shakily to his feet. He was very nervous with the dignitaries staring up at him. "And now," he announced, "Benjamin will take his place onstage and recite 'The Wolf and the Kid.'"

Benjamin stood and then froze. *Wait*, he thought. *That's Nathan's story! Even though I can recite it, that will leave Nathan with nothing to present. And if I point out the teacher's mistake, he'll be embarrassed in front of these important men.* So Franklin just stood silent. "You're a wicked, stubborn boy," the governor snarled. "Take this child and whip him."

Sometimes, living to bless others exacts a price.

THE MAN IN THE BARN

Vaino Kilpinen didn't like horses. When he was 20 years old his country drafted him into the Army and told him he must ride one. The year was 1921, and horse riding was a common mode of transportation for soldiers.

Try as he might, he couldn't learn to ride. The horses kept bucking him off, leaving him bruised and sore. "I quit," he grumbled to himself and ran away from the army camp.

"You can't desert the Army!" his parents told him. "They'll shoot you."

"I'm not going back," the young man stated firmly.

When Mom and Dad couldn't convince him otherwise, they reluctantly agreed to hide him in their barn. Day after day Vaino's parents brought him food. Sometimes he'd venture out at night, but not very far. His teeth began to ache, but he dared not visit a dentist, so they eventually fell out. His father died and, six years later, his mother. He watched their funerals through a crack in the barn wall. After that, his brother and sister delivered the food.

For 40 years Vaino stayed cooped up in that smelly, drafty barn, afraid to leave.

One day a police officer stopped by to inquire about the family's long-lost son. Thinking their secret had been discovered, the deserter surrendered. "Will I be shot?" he asked.

The police officer laughed. "If a deserter is not found after a certain number of years," he said, "he's pardoned. You've been free to leave this barn for a long time!"

Ever wonder what it's like to live in constant fear with a guilty conscience? Ask a sinner who hasn't found forgiveness and freedom in Jesus.

PEER PRESSURE

Q: I'm under a lot of pressure from my friends at public school to dress the same way they do and do stuff with them that I know isn't right. How can I be a Christian and still have friends at school?

A: I remember experiencing that kind of pressure when I was in the Army. Whenever I would go through the food line in the mess hall, a group of guys who were serving always noticed that I would avoid the meat. As soon as they saw me coming, they would snicker, point at me, and yell, "Hey, here comes that guy who don't eat no meat!" Then they would fall over laughing. Boy, was that embarrassing!

But after about six months of teasing, the guys realized I wasn't going to bend. So instead of harassing me, they began to go out of their way to find something I *could* eat. Then they would say, "Hey, get this guy some cheese!"

Get the point? Stand up for what you believe, don't bend to peer pressure, and you'll earn your peers' respect. Remember, a true friend will never encourage you to dishonor God or your conscience.

Art and Pat Humphrey

DESERT TUNAS

What kind of berry is the size of a large egg, is covered with spines, is bright-red inside, and tastes like a honeydew? Give up? It's a tuna. No, not the fish. Tuna is the name of the fruit of the prickly pear cactus.

Most people think of cacti as desert plants. But some of their almost 2,000 species grow as far north as Ontario and northern Europe. They live in such states as Massachusetts and Minnesota—surviving bitter winters. Others thrive in the subtropical climate of Florida. Cactus plants are more versatile than most people know, and have unique features that help them survive.

It didn't take explorers of America long to discover that cattle ate prickly pear cactus pads, called nopals. As long as the spines were burned off, the cattle liked them.

One day someone cut off some nopals, shipped them to Australia, and transplanted them into arid Australian soil in which other food wouldn't grow. Then they discovered that too many nopals made the cattle unhealthy.

But by the time ranchers realized this, it was too late. The fast-growing prickly pear cactus had taken over the countryside. Efforts to control the rampant growth failed until they discovered an insect to do the job. The little creatures burrowed holes all over the cactus stems until enough plants died to keep them under control.

God's nature thrives on balance. So when human beings move plants and animals from their native habitats to different parts of the world, trouble usually follows. That's why you and I have such a hard time with sickness and stress. We were created to live in heaven!

Jane Chase

HOW OLD IS HISTORY?

Q: How long ago did God create Adam and Eve?

A: Seventh-day Adventists believe that God created life on the earth about 6,000 years ago. We know, according to the biblical record, that Christ was born about 2,000 years ago, and that Abraham was born about 2,000 years before the birth of Christ. Going back to Adam another 2,000 years before Abraham makes it about 6,000 years ago that God brought Adam and Eve into being.

People have different beliefs about the actual time period in which the creation of the world took place. Some people believe that it happened over a period of thousands or millions of years. But the Bible seems clear that God made the world in six literal days. (The Sabbath would certainly seem less meaningful if Creation took place over a long period of time.)

When we get to heaven we'll have the opportunity to ask God all our unanswered questions about the wonders of creation. For example, Ellen White has written that in heaven the student of science will be able to "read the records of creation" (*Education*, p. 303). How exciting!

Art and Pat Humphrey

RESTLESS FISHER

The sea lay placid the day the cousins arrived to play on its northern shore. Two pairs of brothers, Andy and Pete and John and Jim, settled under the shade of a tall tree guarding the gentle curve of their favorite beach. They came here often to make castles, roads, and entire villages with the rocks and pebbles at the water's edge and to listen to the lullaby of the water.

"We'll end up being fishers like our fathers and grandfathers and great-grandfathers," one of them said.

"That's not so bad," another responded, placing a leaf roof on his sheep barn. "They make pretty good money."

A louder voice rose in protest. "No! I don't want to be a fisher. It's boring. I want excitement and fun. I want to travel and see new things."

The other three looked at each other and chuckled. Pete was always spouting off about how he was going to leave the fishing life and seek adventure beyond some distant horizon.

"Come along, boys," someone called from the road beyond the trees. "We've got to get the boats ready for tonight's work." Pete's father waved at the youngsters. Playtime was over. They had nets to arrange and oars to mend.

Years passed. The four cousins became successful fishers, providing a comfortable living for themselves. But Pete never seemed to settle down, especially after he heard about a man who roamed the highlands to the south, a preacher who spoke words of hope to people in need. The man lived outdoors and traveled throughout the region. To the young fishers, that seemed like the perfect life. Yes, that's what he longed for. Freedom!

We'll discover what happened in the coming weeks.

HOSANNA!

As they approached Jerusalem and came to Bethphage on the Mount of Olives, Jesus sent two disciples, saying to them, "Go to the village ahead of you, and at once you will find a donkey tied there, with her colt by her. Untie them and bring them to me. If anyone says anything to you, tell him that the Lord needs them, and he will send them right away."

This took place to fulfill what was spoken through the prophet: "Say to the Daughter of Zion, 'See, your king comes to you, gentle and riding on a donkey, on a colt, the foal of a donkey.'"

The disciples went and did as Jesus had instructed them. They brought the donkey and the colt, placed their cloaks on them, and Jesus sat on them. A very large crowd spread their cloaks on the road, while others cut branches from the trees and spread them on the road. The crowds that went ahead of him and those that followed shouted, "Hosanna to the Son of David! Blessed is he who comes in the name of the Lord! Hosanna in the highest!"

When Jesus entered Jerusalem, the whole city was stirred and asked, "Who is this?"

The crowds answered, "This is Jesus, the prophet from Nazareth in Galilee."

Matthew 21:1-11

The whole city is in an uproar. They're welcoming Jesus. But did you notice something sad? Through their gates rides the Saviour of humanity, the Messiah, the Promised One. And who did they say He is? A prophet.

As you share Jesus with others, be sure to explain that He's much more than a prophet. He's God on earth!

BENJAMIN AND THE WHIP

When [Jesus] arrived in Galilee, the Galileans welcomed him. They had seen all that he had done in Jerusalem. John 4:45.

Benjamin stood facing the room of dignitaries. The nervous schoolmaster had asked him to recite the wrong story, one assigned to Nathan, a fellow classmate who'd barely been able to learn it in time. If he gave it, his friend would be in trouble. But if he pointed out the schoolmaster's mistake, he'd embarrass the man terribly. The governor, thinking Benjamin was being stubborn by not speaking, had ordered that the teacher whip him.

Just then they heard a disturbance in the back of the hall. Nathan had become sick and his dad was leading him out. Benjamin took this opportunity to lean close to his teacher's ear. "Excuse me, sir," he whispered politely. "I think you asked me to recite the wrong story."

"Did I? Oh, I'm sorry!" stammered the schoolmaster. "I'm very nervous with so many important men here. Thank you."

"And sir?" Benjamin cleared his throat. "Please don't whip me."

Of course the teacher didn't whip him. Such unselfish loyalty through the years helped Benjamin Franklin win the respect and friendship of many people.

Being a friend, even to adults, can cost you. You may have to receive ridicule that should go elsewhere. Or you may get punished because someone made an error. But isn't that exactly what Jesus did? He died for *our* sins, suffered for *our* mistakes. Jesus was treated as we deserve so we could be treated as He deserves.

Go ahead. Do a brave thing today. Be someone's friend.

GUIDE IN THE FOG

Mr. William D. Boyce, a wealthy Chicago-based publisher, was lost in a London fog. He didn't know his way around, and the lack of visibility only made matters worse.

"May I be of service, sir?" a young male voice called from nearby. Boyce turned to see a street urchin—the kind of child most wealthy men try to avoid—standing at attention.

"Well, yes," the publisher responded. "I'm late for a meeting, but I don't know where the building is. If you could help, it would be a real service."

"I'll gladly lead you there," came the quick reply.

Before long, man and boy stood outside the building where Boyce was scheduled to transact some business. "Here," the man said, handing the child a coin. "Thanks for your help."

"No, sir," said the boy. "I'm a Scout. Scouts don't accept tips for courtesies." The young speaker leaned forward slightly. "You do know what a Scout is, don't you?"

"Well, no."

"Then I'll take you to someone who can explain everything after you've finished your meeting. I'll wait right here for you."

Boyce agreed, completed his business, and allowed the boy to take him to Lord Baden-Powell, the man who started the Boy Scout movement. So impressed was the publisher with what he heard and saw that the director gave him many books and pamphlets about Scouting. The publisher returned to Chicago and launched the Scouting movement in the United States.

For almost 100 years boys have enjoyed the benefits of Scouting. What a tremendous amount of good resulted from one act of "no-charge" courtesy on a far-off foggy street.

I LOVE THEM THE SAME

Q: My parents are divorced, and I live with my mom. When I go to spend time with my dad, I get the feeling Mom thinks I don't love her anymore. How can I help my parents understand that I love them both the same? I'm a 13-year-old girl.

A: Here's something to think about. Imagine you own the cutest, funniest, and most lovable pet dog in the world. But unfortunately, you have to share it with another kid way across town. So the dog lives mostly with you, but sometimes goes away to visit the other kid. When the dog is with you, you feel loved and happy. But when it's gone, you really miss it. Such a situation isn't exactly the same as yours, but in a way it shows how your mom probably feels when you're visiting your dad.

You can help by reassuring your mom that you really do love her. Try doing something to let her know she's special. For example, set aside a day every week when the two of you go to a favorite spot or do something together you both enjoy. Or you could make her "queen for a day" by treating her to a day off from housework and cooking. You can probably come up with more—even better—ideas. But whatever you do, remember often to say these three little words (to *both* of your parents): "I love you."

Art and Pat Humphrey

DOG IN THE DESERT

We're lost!" little Colleen whispered as she gripped her older brother's hand. "I don't see our car or the road. I'm scared!"

Danny Greenwood looked down at his sister. "Don't cry. We'll be OK." But he didn't feel as confident as he sounded.

The children and their parents had been traveling through a lonely stretch of Nevada. As night approached, they'd stopped to camp. While Dad and Mom set up the tent, Colleen and Danny had wandered off in search of adventure. Somehow, they'd become disoriented and gotten lost in a featureless land filled with rattlesnakes and scorpions.

"I think we'd better pray," Danny encouraged. "God knows where we are, even though we don't."

The two children knelt on the sand. "Dear God," he said, "we're lost and don't know our way back. Please help us." Colleen tried to pray, but she was too scared. So she just said, "Amen."

When they stood up, everything looked the same except it was getting even darker. Suddenly Danny lifted a finger. "Listen!" he whispered. "I hear a dog."

"We don't have a dog," Colleen reminded him. Then she heard a distant barking.

The children began following the sound, moving cautiously around bushes and rocks, scampering up hills and running through shallow depressions. Finally they arrived back at the campsite, where a dog stood off to one side barking at their parents. There were no houses around. No one seemed to own the mutt. But there it stood, barking.

Prayer opens our eyes and ears to what can save us, even if it's the persistent barking of a mysterious dog in a darkening desert.

DOING RIGHT

Q: How do you know you're doing the right thing?

A: A text in the Bible used to make me nervous. "There is a way which seemeth right unto a man, but the end thereof are the ways of death" (Prov. 14:12, KJV).

Excuse me? You mean I can go through life thinking I'm doing the right thing when I'm really not?

Solomon, who wrote Proverbs, wasn't exactly Mr. Sinless. He lived his life the way he saw fit, disregarding God most of the time. The king firmly believed he was doing the right thing, but it was *his* thing, not God's.

Later in life, he wrote, "I denied myself nothing my eyes desired; I refused my heart no pleasure. My heart took delight in all my work. . . . Yet when I surveyed all that my hands had done and what I had toiled to achieve, everything was meaningless, a chasing after the wind; nothing was gained under the sun" (Ecclesiastes 2:10, 11).

Poor King Solomon. He hadn't learned the lesson you can right now. Doing the right thing begins by discovering what God considers to be the right thing. That's why He handed down the Ten Commandments and His many ideals and formulas for living a satisfying life. Solomon thought he knew better than God. But he didn't.

You're doing the right thing when you're living by God's laws as clearly outlined in the Bible. Everything else is meaningless.

AMBITIOUS FISHER

I don't know why I let you talk us into this," Andy whispered to Pete as he and their cousins, Jim and John, hurried toward a spot by the river where a man stood preaching. The speaker was powerfully built with sun-tanned face and resounding voice. His clothes were handmade and hardly fashionable.

"Do violence to no man," the preacher was saying to the assembled crowd. "Beware of our religious leaders. They're a generation of vipers."

Pete gasped. Talk about guts. This guy had just called the spiritual bigwigs of their nation "sons of snakes"! This was his kind of preacher.

The cousins talked it over and decided that the fishing life paled in comparison to life on the road with the man many were calling the "Baptist." He dunked repentant sinners in the river and ate wild berries.

But the Baptist kept talking about Someone else, Someone of whom he said, "I'm not worthy to untie His sandals." Then he said the magic word: "Messiah." Everyone was looking for the Messiah, the person who'd come and end Roman rule in the land, setting the Jewish nation back on its feet.

One day the Baptist pointed at a Man in the crowd and announced, "There He is!" Pete and the others turned to look and almost burst out laughing. *That's* the Messiah? they giggled. "He's just a common, ordinary man, like us!"

But when the Stranger asked to be baptized and the Baptist dipped Him under the water, something amazing happened. A white dove appeared and hovered over the Man's head while a voice unlike any they'd ever heard rumbled, "This is My Son. I'm pleased with Him."

What would happen next? We'll find out next week.

ANOINTED ONE

While Jesus was in Bethany in the home of a man known as Simon the Leper, a woman came to him with an alabaster jar of very expensive perfume, which she poured on his head as he was reclining at the table.

When the disciples saw this, they were indignant. "Why this waste?" they asked. "This perfume could have been sold at a high price and the money given to the poor."

Aware of this, Jesus said to them, "Why are you bothering this woman? She has done a beautiful thing to me. The poor you will always have with you, but you will not always have me. When she poured this perfume on my body, she did it to prepare me for burial. I tell you the truth, wherever this gospel is preached throughout the world, what she has done will also be told, in memory of her."

Then one of the Twelve—the one called Judas Iscariot—went to the chief priests and asked, "What are you willing to give me if I hand him over to you?" So they counted out for him thirty silver coins. From then on Judas watched for an opportunity to hand him over.

Matthew 26:6-16

A woman spends a large sum of money to buy sweet-smelling perfume that she pours on Jesus' feet. The disciples refer to it as a "waste." Jesus calls it a "lasting memory."

Juniors, don't be afraid to give your life to Jesus. While others may point and giggle, He'll smile proudly at your sacrifice.

The woman also took part in the first act of a terrible tragedy. It begins next week.

MIDNIGHT RIDER

T his man deserves to have you [heal his servant], because he loves our nation." Luke 7:4, 5.

A man stood beside his horse on a dark hillside and stared across a stretch of water to a church rising above the trees. The lives of hundreds of people and possibly the future of his beloved country lay on his shoulders.

"One if by land. Two if by sea." He repeated those words over and over, not wanting to forget their grave meaning.

War between America and England was inevitable. American farmers felt that everything they'd worked for was in jeopardy. All had armed themselves and were ready to fight if British soldiers appeared. That's why Paul Revere stood on that hillside waiting for the signal. Spies at the British fort were watching troop movements. If the soldiers marched by land, one lantern would shine from the church steeple. But if the men took boats and crossed the water, two lanterns would glow.

Suddenly one . . . and then two lights sparkled across the water. The British were on the move, and they were coming by boat.

Paul Revere rode as he'd never ridden before, his voice calling the sleeping farmers to battle. "The British are coming. The British are coming! Prepare to fight!" His warning saved lives and launched a nation.

Today millions fear the future. They know something evil is trying to invade their lives. But we've seen the signal—the falling stars and blood-red moon. "Jesus is coming. Jesus is coming soon!" we shout. With these words, the battle against Satan begins.

HERO AT THE HELM

John Maynard didn't look like a hero. He was a very ordinary man doing a very ordinary job. As pilot of the *Ocean Queen*, a small passenger boat carrying people across Lake Erie from Detroit to Buffalo, John's only task was to steer the vessel on a safe course.

One day the crew saw smoke rising from the lower decks. "The ship's on fire!" the mate reported to the captain. "And we have no lifeboats."

"How far to land?" a crewman asked.

"Seven miles and 45 minutes," the captain replied. "We'll be burned up in that time unless we move everyone to the front of the ship." But there was a problem. The wheel that steered the boat—the one in John Maynard's hands—was at the back.

After everyone had been rushed forward, the captain shouted through his voice trumpet, "John Maynard? Are you at the helm?"

"Aye, aye, sir," came the reply from the billowing smoke.

"And what direction are we going?"

"East southeast, sir."

"Head her southeast and run her ashore."

John Maynard turned the wheel and headed in that direction as flames crept closer and closer. Again and again the captain called, and each time John responded in a voice growing weaker. His hair shriveled in the terrible heat, his hands and arms blistered. Finally the bow crunched over the gravel boundary separating lake from land, and everyone scurried to safety—everyone except John Maynard. Overcome with pain and smoke, he died at his post. Think of this story the next time you sing the song "Jesus, Savior, pilot me, over life's tempestuous sea."

SMOKE SIGNALS

Q: My dad smokes cigarettes, and now my brother is starting the habit. He says, "Well, Dad hasn't died yet from smoking." What can I do to help both my brother and my dad?

A: You're right to be concerned about your dad and your brother. They're both literally "playing with fire." Each of them probably smokes for different reasons, but the sad fact is that the end result—early death—could be the same unless they quit the habit.

It sounds as though your brother is misinformed about what smoking really does to the body. An article for kids on the dangers of smoking, such as the ones in *Winner* magazine, just might help to open his eyes. Many kids think it's cool to smoke, but the truth is, smoking gives you bad breath, makes you look old, turns your teeth yellow, and leaves you stinky. Now, *that's* not cool!

With your dad you might try another approach. Let him know how much you love him and want him around for a long, long time. Ask if he would consider attending a Breathe Free program at your local church, or a similar program in your community. Remind him of what secondhand smoke does to others, and make sure he knows about the new habit your brother has started.

Most of all, be patient and loving. And remember to pray for your dad and brother. Only God's power can help them quit smoking.

Art and Pat Humphrey

TWO STORIES TALL

When Jim Lillie enters the giraffe enclosure at the National Zoo, he never wears a hat with a visor. The giraffes he cares for aren't mean, but some of them *will* feel especially frisky or be in a bad mood. Then the giraffe may kick or swing its neck down and smack Jim with its head! So when Jim cleans the floor or tosses alfalfa into the high feeding racks, he doesn't wear a hat. It might block his view of what's happening 10 feet above him.

When God made giraffes grow 17 feet tall—the world's tallest living animal—He knew they would need special characteristics in order to survive. If a giraffe's heart and arteries were like other animals', the slender giant would faint every time it lowered its head to drink. But God gave giraffes a unique circulatory system. He put extra valves in the neck to keep the blood from rushing into the animal's head when it bends over.

He also gave giraffes a unique heart. It is two feet long, weighs 24 pounds, and beats 150 times per minute. Every minute it pumps 20 gallons of blood 10 feet up the neck into the brain. The blood pressure necessary to accomplish this would kill other animals, but not the giraffe. Its extra-tough arteries easily handle the pressure.

The giraffe is unlike any other creature in the world. Yet it is graceful, harmless, friendly, and as intelligent as a horse. Who else but God could think of inventing a speckled creature with golf-ball-sized eyes . . . that's two stories tall?

Jane Chase

WHEN WE DIE

Q: What happens to us when we die?

A: Years ago I worked at Faith for Today, our church's longest-running television ministry. We were filming a documentary on the subject of suicide and paid a visit to a most unsettling place—the Los Angeles County coroner's office.

Several portions of the show were shot in the morgue (the facility where dead people are brought for examination before being handed over to funeral homes or other agencies for burial). I probably saw more than 100 corpses that day, some waiting to be identified by relatives, some undergoing autopsies to find out the cause of death, and others lined up on gurneys along the hallways waiting to be studied.

After seeing all those bodies lying around like abandoned shells on a seashore, I began to see how useless we are without God's breath of life in us. We're just a collection of tissue and bone. Nothing more.

But when God breathes life into us, as He did for Adam and Eve, something wonderful happens. Our arms move, legs kick, the heart beats, lips smile, the voice speaks, lungs expand, eyes blink, toes wiggle—everything that makes us who we are comes with that glorious infusion of life-stirring power.

The moment we die, that breath (or ability to live) returns to God for safekeeping until the resurrection. Our bodies eventually crumble into useless piles of dust. But don't worry. On that wonderful day God will breathe again. And so will we.

UNCERTAIN FISHER

Pete watched the waves slap against the bow of the boat and sighed deeply. Life with the Messiah had started off with a bang. First this Man called "Jesus" had turned water to wine at a wedding. Then He'd driven a bunch of money-grubbing con men out of the Temple in Jerusalem. What a Guy! However, things had calmed down to a dull routine after that. Listening to Him preach and teach had become a little boring, so Pete and the others had headed back to their fishing business.

The cousins had just spent a particularly frustrating night on the sea. No fish. Not even a guppy had appeared in their nets. In the morning they saw Jesus walking along the beach followed by a large crowd. "Pete," the Man called, "may I use your boat? I need it to preach from."

"Be my guest," the burly fisher chuckled. "It's no good for fishing."

"So," Jesus said as He stepped into the vessel, "are you going to spend your life catching fish, or would you like to capture something much more interesting?"

"Like what?"

Jesus motioned toward the crowd. "People. I can teach you to be a fisher of men."

Those words rang like a bell in Pete's ears. Anyone can catch fish. But to bring hope and joy to another human being—now that's excitement. Even if this Jesus didn't turn out to be the hoped-for deliverer of the Jewish nation, He offered something the fishing life could never deliver.

From that day forward, Pete and the others were constant companions of the Messiah, beginning ministries of their own. But leaving their nets would cost them dearly.

SERVANT GOD

I t's Passover time in Jerusalem. Jesus and His disciples gather in a rented room to enjoy the Passover meal. But this supper will be unlike any they'd ever had. Let's watch!

The evening meal was being served . . . [when Jesus] took off his outer clothing, and wrapped a towel around his waist. After that, he poured water into a basin and began to wash his disciples' feet, drying them with the towel that was wrapped around him.

He came to Simon Peter, who said to him, "Lord, are you going to wash my feet?"

Jesus replied, "You do not realize now what I am doing, but later you will understand."

"No," said Peter, "you shall never wash my feet."

Jesus answered, "Unless I wash you, you have no part with me."

"Then, Lord," Simon Peter replied, "not just my feet but my hands and my head as well!". . .

When he had finished washing their feet, he put on his clothes and returned to his place. "Do you understand what I have done for you?" he asked them. "You call me 'Teacher' and 'Lord,' and rightly so, for that is what I am. Now that I, your Lord and Teacher, have washed your feet, you also should wash one another's feet. I have set you an example that you should do as I have done for you. I tell you the truth, no servant is greater than his master, nor is a messenger greater than the one who sent him. Now that you know these things, you will be blessed if you do them."

John 13:2-17

DOGS AND CRUMBS

Y es, Lord," she replied, "but even the dogs under the table eat the children's crumbs." Mark 7:28.

Jesus loved to talk in double meanings. He also liked to use words that society bantered about. In the above conversation, *dogs* meant "Gentile" or "non-Jew" and *crumbs* hinted at "salvation." The woman was saying to Jesus, "Even Gentiles need salvation."

Jesus had a thing about non-Jews. He ate with them, visited with them, told stories about them, and eventually died to save them. It miffed His followers who thought that Jews were God's people and everyone else wasn't. Arrogant, huh?

The other day I read an article about a guy who hated Jews and Blacks so much he went on a shooting rampage, killed several people, then turned the gun on himself. In his twisted mind, "dogs" weren't worthy of life. He apparently didn't think much of himself, either.

But we Christians have a whole different slant on the world. We take the "Jesus" view that all people are worthy, that all life is sacred, and that we exist to bless others.

Here's an old poem I love to recite:

You are writing a gospel, a chapter each day,
By deeds that you do, by words that you say.
Men read what you write, whether faithless or true.
Say! What is the gospel according to YOU?
—Paul Gilbert

Why not spread a few crumbs today?

SHADOWY SCARE!

Alice and Jeanie lived in the country where they enjoyed roaming the fields and taking care of their pet horse.

One day Mother became ill and had to go to the hospital. Daddy wasn't home at the time, so the two sisters decided to stay at a neighbor's farm at night. "Remember to hurry home after school to feed and comb the horse," their mother instructed. "Then you'll have plenty of time to get to the neighbors' before dark."

The two girls kept to the schedule for a few days, then got so involved in a ball game one afternoon that the sun was setting by the time they reached home. When they finally headed out for the neighbor's house a half mile away, it was dark.

Grabbing the little lantern hanging by the back door, they left, but the going was slow. The lantern didn't give off much light. The girls were nervous. Someone had sighted a mountain lion in the area, and a mental institution nearby was always reporting that someone had escaped.

Suddenly Alice screamed. There in the shadows, over against the fence, was a low, dark form swaying back and forth. It grew as they came nearer and moved as they moved. "Is it a monster?" the girl gasped.

Then a puff of wind blew Jeanie's skirt, and the lantern's light chased the "monster" away. They'd been frightened by the shadow of her skirt on an old wooden gate.

King David called the Bible a light shining on his path. Sometimes that light reveals the shadows of our sins. But remember, the same light that casts a shadow can chase it away.

KILLER KINDNESS

Q: I'm a 10-year-old boy. At school some of the other kids in my class pick on me and take my things without asking. I don't want to get in a fight, so I usually don't do anything back. But that only seems to make things worse for me. What can I do?

A: You've made a wise decision not to fight back. Proverbs 20:22 says: "Do not say, 'I'll pay you back for this wrong!' Wait for the Lord, and he will deliver you." So if you can't fight back, what should you do? *Kill them with kindness!*

We heard a story recently about a family who moved onto a farm next to a mean old man. For years he had scared away every family who had lived in the farmhouse before them. Now the old guy was doing every evil thing he could think of to run the new family off. He cut their water lines, killed their dog, and broke the fence so their cows would get out.

How do you think the family responded? Well, every time the man did something mean they simply repaid him with kindness. They baked bread and left it on his doorstep, painted his house and weeded his garden while he was away, and helped him out of the mud when he got stuck. Finally the man couldn't stand it any longer. "You're killing me!" he said. "Every time I do something mean, you treat me nicely. I can't take it!" From that point on they became the best of friends. Get the idea? See if it works for you.

Art and Pat Humphrey

BLOWING IN THE WIND

Here's a happy story about being at the right place at the right time.

A family of four was fairly wealthy and lived in a nice home. Even though they were rich, they still believed in God.

One day the mother, Diana, decided to quit her job and stay home. Things went pretty well for about six or seven months. Then the family's money began to run out. When one of the daughters had a birthday, they used up quite a bit of money. The father, Gary, noticed the problem but didn't want to worry the family.

Before long, they were bankrupt! They'd used up all their savings and were too proud to accept money from church members or neighbors.

One morning, right before Gary left for work, the electricity went off and Diana began to cry. Gary comforted her, saying everything would be OK. Before he got in his car, he prayed to God for help. As he said amen he looked up and saw a $20 bill blowing down the street. He picked it up and saw another one drifting through the air. When he was sure there were no more, he immediately got in his car and drove to the supermarket where he bought enough food to last until his next paycheck. The money left over filled his gas tank. Then he arrived at work with a thankful prayer on his lips.

Evelyn Moore,
11, California

Not everyone in need finds money blowing in the wind, but they'll always find God's loving presence in their hearts.

GOING FOR THE GOLD

Q: I don't feel like I'm ready for heaven. This bothers me a lot. What can I do?

A: We're glad to hear that you're thinking about heaven, because guess what? The first step to getting there is wanting to go! But it sounds as though you're worried whether you will make it or not, and that's not so good.

First, it's important to realize that it is Jesus' death on Calvary that gains you entrance into heaven, not your own good deeds. When you accept His gift, this promise becomes your own: "I have written this to you who believe in the Son of God *so that you may know you have eternal life*" (1 John 5:13, TLB).

Here's something to think about that may help as your friendship with Jesus grows each day. Imagine you pick up the daily newspaper and find this announcement: "Hidden in the Midwestern city of Wannaget is a gold treasure worth $1 million. Anyone locating it can keep it—tax-free!"

Wouldn't you start to think about "going for the gold"? We sure would! But what would we need to find it? A map, of course! In a way, going to heaven is like going for that treasure. The Bible is our map (free, again!) and comes with a built-in Guide—Jesus working through His Holy Spirit.

When we follow the instructions on our "map" and go only where our loving Guide leads us, He automatically helps us be ready for heaven—every step of the way.

Art and Pat Humphrey

REPENTANT FISHER

Pete loved his new life. The Messiah taught him how to cast out devils—something that's always exciting. One night he even walked on water. Now, how many fishers did that?

Then things got very scary. First, Jesus was arrested. When people accused Pete of being a follower of the Messiah, he denied it. He swore he didn't even know Jesus! At that moment he glanced up to see his Master looking at him, and he realized that he'd lied. In fact, he'd betrayed his friendship with the one Man who had given him hope for the future.

Soon after that, they crucified Jesus.

Gloom, misery, and shame followed the big fisher back to Galilee, where he and the others returned to their fishing business. The Baptist was gone. The Messiah was gone. And hope itself was gone.

"Did you catch anything?" a voice called from the beach early one morning as Pete and the others were guiding their boat back to port.

"No," he responded with frustration. "Fished all night. Nothing."

"Put your nets down on the *right* side of your boat."

Nothing else had worked, so they tried it. In an instant their nets were full! Pete blinked and strained to recognize the stranger who'd led them to the early-morning school of fish. "It's the Messiah!" he breathed.

With a happy shout, Pete plunged into the water and swam for shore. Jesus had returned! The burly fisher fell at the Messiah's feet and wept. Could He forgive the denial, the lies, and the betrayal? Was there still hope?

BREAD AND WINE

When evening came, Jesus was reclining at the table with the Twelve. And while they were eating, he said, "I tell you the truth, one of you will betray me."

They were very sad and began to say to him one after the other, "Surely not I, Lord?"

Jesus replied, "The one who has dipped his hand into the bowl with me will betray me. The Son of Man will go just as it is written about him. But woe to that man who betrays the Son of Man! It would be better for him if he had not been born."

Then Judas, the one who would betray him, said, "Surely not I, Rabbi?"

Jesus answered, "Yes, it is you."

While they were eating, Jesus took bread, gave thanks and broke it, and gave it to his disciples, saying, "Take and eat; this is my body."

Then he took the cup, gave thanks and offered it to them, saying, "Drink from it, all of you. This is my blood of the covenant, which is poured out for many for the forgiveness of sins. I tell you, I will not drink of this fruit of the vine from now on until that day when I drink it anew with you in my Father's kingdom."

When they had sung a hymn, they went out to the Mount of Olives.

Matthew 26:20-30

Jesus knew what was about to happen. His disciples, as usual, were clueless. When He called the bread and wine His "body" and "blood," they shrugged it off as some parable He'd probably explain later.

Soon they would all understand the horrible meaning.

THE LORD'S WIND

In the beginning was the Word, and the Word was with God, and the Word was God. John 1:1.

God's love is like the wind.
    It whirls and twirls and runs actively to people like a toy;
    Something that is admired by young Christian boys.
They too spin in the love that God has shared.
    They leap and bound, without knowing how.
The loving wind gave a large howl and prowled to the east.
    It flowed past the leaves that seemed to wave at its passing.
The wind made a turn to the north, but people rose in scorn,
    For those were not the Christian type.
But when they felt the power of God's love,
    Most of the people turned from their wicked ways.
But those who refused God's love
    Were swept away in a flash by a terrible spin.
The people knew what it was.
    It was the storm of sin.
This funnel was dark and terribly frightening,
    But still the people would not repent and back away
        from their sins.
His love could do nothing,
    For He had given them a choice.
They're gone now,
    Gone from the light, swallowed in a sea of darkness.
But those who respected and trusted God's loving wind will
    walk on glory. God's glory.

Tucker Burnett,
10, Arizona

LOST ABOVE THE SWAMP

Carter glanced at the fuel gauge and gasped. It showed almost empty! In a car, that's a nuisance. But he wasn't in a car—he was flying above an endless swamp in a small airplane.

He'd only wanted to practice some of the maneuvers his instructor had taught him earlier in the week. But so intent was he on getting the airspeed and bank angles just right that he'd lost track of the one thing pilots always need to know—their location.

"Which way back to the airport?" he asked himself. "The last time I saw it, it was right below me. Now it's gone, and I'm lost with nothing but sky above and swamp below." He bowed his head. "Lord, please help me. Please."

When he opened his eyes, he suddenly remembered something his instructor had told him. "In any emergency, first fly the airplane. Second, try to remember what you were doing when the problem began. Third, stop doing it."

"Well," Carter said to himself, "I've got the plane under control. I was flying maneuvers with the sun behind me and . . . That's it! I've got to turn around and fly with the sun in my face. That should take me in the direction of the airport."

Sure enough, in about 10 minutes the landscape began to look familiar, and before long, the runway appeared under his wings.

Great advice, wouldn't you say? If you find your life getting a bit confusing, first stay in control; second, review what you'd been doing when things got crazy; and third, stop doing those things. Works for pilots. And it works for juniors.

SHUNNED BY SISTER

Q: I'm a 13-year-old girl. Last year my sister, who is 16, went away to boarding academy. Before she went away, we were extremely close. But now when she comes home during breaks it seems as if she doesn't want to do anything with me. Do you have any suggestions?

A: It's great that you and your sister had such a special relationship. The not-so-great part is having to deal with the natural changes that come as a result of her going away to school. Here are a few ideas for keeping your friendship strong:

1. Visit her school. Some boarding schools hold special events to which students can invite their younger brothers and sisters. Even if her school doesn't host such events, ask if it's OK for you to spend a weekend with her (make sure she first gets permission from the dean).

2. Write often. Include in your letters pictures of things that are happening back home.

3. Focus on the things you share in common. For example, if both of you are into music, send her copies of tapes that you know she'll enjoy.

4. Share news. When something great (or not so great) happens in your life, let your sister be the first to know.

Be open to new relationships. As you both grow and move on to new experiences in life, you'll meet new and different people. Nobody will ever take the place of your sister, but it would make her happy to know that you're meeting and making other good friends.

Art and Pat Humphrey

SEEDS OF WITNESS

When American settlers in the early 1800s saw a man wearing an odd-looking hat and carrying tree seedlings slung over his back, they knew they were in for a visit from Johnny Appleseed. Johnny's real name was John Chapman, and his goal in life was to provide apple trees for every farm in the Midwest.

He got free apple seeds from the cider presses in Pennsylvania. Then he would take his bags of seeds and travel by foot or canoe, planting seeds in any good soil. Farmers let him plant on their land, and sometimes he purchased land, paying for it with young apple trees.

Johnny Appleseed was more than just an odd-looking man on a mission. He was also a God-fearing man. When he stopped at farms and homesteads, people would give him dinner and a place to stay. Then he would tell the children stories about nature and God's love, sharing how to care for God's creation.

For nearly 50 years Johnny spread apple trees and the word of God until his death in 1845.

Apple trees are unique because they don't "breed true." That means if you take 10 seeds from the same apple, plant them, and grow 10 trees, each tree will produce a different kind of apple. It's God's way of adding variety to creation.

Apple growers and scientists are constantly working to reproduce uniform apples that have consistent taste and texture. But when God grows apples, He gives us variety and unexpected wonders, since He creates no two apple trees alike.

He does the same thing with people, doesn't He?

Jane Chase

A MILLION MIRACLES

Q: How come God doesn't send miracles other than saving lives?

A: I've got good news. God does send miracles! Most people simply don't recognize them.

Listen to this rather frightening Bible verse: "Your enemy the devil prowls around like a roaring lion looking for someone to devour" (1 Peter 5:8). Romans 6:23 warns that "the wages of sin is death."

Devour? Death? Not a pleasant thought. Haven't you ever sinned? I know I have. The Bible says that "all have sinned, and come short of the glory of God" (Romans 3:23, KJV). But you're not dead. I'm not dead. Why? Because of a miracle.

You see, the devil would have us in constant pain, constant turmoil, and constantly dead. Thus *anything* other than being dead is a miracle from God.

The fact that you can learn interesting stuff at school is also a miracle. When your mom or dad does something that makes you laugh and laugh, that's a miracle. Or when you feel love for an animal or person, when you enjoy your favorite food, or when you feel the cool breezes of summer or soak in the warmth of a crackling winter fire—those are miracles too.

Paul says, "I pray that you may be active in sharing your faith, so that you will have a full understanding of every good thing we have in Christ" (Philemon 6).

The next time you take in a breath or experience joy, remember, you've received yet another miracle from God.

TRIUMPHANT FISHER

Jesus looked long into the tear-stained eyes of His friend Pete. "Do you love Me?" He asked.

The fisher nodded, guilt weighing heavily on his shoulders. "Yes."

The Messiah asked the question again and again. Each time Pete responded with a humble, heartbreaking "Yes."

Then Jesus said something that Pete understood immediately. In words filled with forgiveness and comfort, the Messiah invited, "Pete, feed My sheep."

The fisher grabbed his friend in a big bear hug. He was forgiven, he knew it! Jesus had just asked him to get back to work, to continue the ministry he'd started three years ago when he'd first joined the Messiah's band of disciples. Oh, how happy he was! How good it felt to know that his Master didn't hold grudges, didn't condemn his human mistakes, didn't punish those who deserved to be punished. Pete's newfound hope came from the realization that in spite of his error in judgment and his rough, sometimes sinful, ways, Jesus had forgiven him.

Right then and there Pete, the catcher of fish, determined to change his life fully so he could become Pete, the fisher of men.

Did he succeed? The Bible says that one day Pete preached a sermon that converted 3,000 people. People carried sick men and women, boys and girls, many miles to his house, and he healed them all! Once when he was in jail, an angel got him out. And when Dorcas, a kind woman, died, Pete used the power of God to bring her back to life.

Pete lived a full, useful, and successful life. Why? Because he left his nets and followed Jesus.

KISS OF DEATH

On the Mount of Olives] a crowd came up, and the man who was called Judas, one of the Twelve, was leading them. He approached Jesus to kiss him, but Jesus asked him, "Judas, are you betraying the Son of Man with a kiss?"

When Jesus' followers saw what was going to happen, they said, "Lord, should we strike with our swords?" And one of them struck the servant of the high priest, cutting off his right ear.

But Jesus answered, "No more of this!" And he touched the man's ear and healed him. . . .

Then seizing [Jesus, the mob] led him away and took him into the house of the high priest. Peter followed at a distance. But when they had kindled a fire in the middle of the courtyard and had sat down together, Peter sat down with them. A servant girl saw him seated there in the firelight. She looked closely at him and said, "This man was with him."

But he denied it. "Woman, I don't know him," he said.

A little later someone else saw him and said, "You also are one of them."

"Man, I am not!" Peter replied.

About an hour later another asserted, "Certainly this fellow was with him, for he is a Galilean."

Peter replied, "Man, I don't know what you're talking about!" Just as he was speaking, the rooster crowed. The Lord turned and looked straight at Peter. Then Peter remembered the word the Lord had spoken to him: "Before the rooster crows today, you will disown me three times." And he went outside and wept bitterly.

Luke 22:47-62

BEING CHRISTIAN

A nd they will call him Immanuel"—which means, "God with us." Matthew 1:23.

Is God "with" you?

Being married is a kick. I love it. I've got an instant date for anywhere I want to go, I don't have to dress up for supper, and when I get to feeling romantic I can just go find my wife and snuggle for a few minutes.

Since I run my own business, I sometimes have to travel away from home to take pictures or make a video or hold a seminar. Since my lovely wife doesn't feel much like sitting in hotel rooms all day waiting for me to get back, she stays in West Virginia with her garden and ducks. I call her every night, and we tell each other that we're lonely.

Now, let me ask you a question. When I'm away, am I still married? "Of course," you say. "But I'm not with my wife," I counter. "Yes, you are," you insist. "You're with her in your mind and heart."

Exactly! Being married means I am a *married man,* no matter where I am. I don't have to wear a wedding ring to let available females of the world know what's going on. Instead I act married. I speak married. My whole life is a wedding ring.

Let me ask you another question. Can you be a Christian without Jesus living next door to you? Of course. God is in your mind and heart. You act Christian, you speak Christian, you *are* Christian.

Remember that, no matter how far from home you wander.

LIGHT OF THE WORLD

Jesus said, "You are the light of the world. . . . Let your light shine before men, that they may see your good deeds and praise your Father in heaven." Matthew 5:14-16.

On the farthermost southwest corner of England stands a lighthouse with a rather strange name. The Lizard Light can send a beam 20 miles out to sea and keeps passing ships from running aground on the deadly rocks at its base.

One night a frightening message sounded throughout the lighthouse. "Fire! Fire!" Sure enough, the building housing the fuel supply that ran the generators that kept the light glowing was on fire. Those manning the facility knew that any second the whole thing could blow up in their faces. The fire department was five miles away and would never reach them in time.

"We can run or we can stay and fight the fire," Mr. Stephens, the lighthouse keeper, stated to his staff. If they left, the fire would blow up everything, including the lighthouse that was, even then, sending its beam across the waves. But if they stayed, each and every person risked losing their own life.

Everyone stayed and fought the fire. Fortunately, they got it out in time.

As you try to warn others about sin, Satan loves to start fires around you. He's got temptations and confusing situations galore just waiting to wreck your day. Do you run, leaving your light to fade? Or do you fight the fires in order to keep your saving beam of love shining bright? It's your light. And it's your choice.

BOSSY BUDDY

Q: My buddy bosses me around. It's as if he has to be the one in charge all the time. I like my friend, but his "big shot" attitude bugs me. What can I do? I'm a 12-year-old boy.

A: Sounds as though you and your buddy need to have a talk. It could be that he doesn't even realize what he's doing.

The next time he starts bossing you around, find a place where nobody else can hear, and tell him calmly but honestly how you feel. Let him know in a nice way that you really appreciate his friendship, but that you can't stand being bossed around. Be careful not just to make a blanket statement, such as "You really are bossy!" Instead, try to give a specific example of what he's doing. For instance, you might say, "I really felt embarrassed when you told me—in front of the other kids—to get lost." Ask him if he's willing to change his style of communication, and get his permission to remind him when he's getting out of line. Above all, let him know that despite everything, you still accept him as he is—faults and all.

Art and Pat Humphrey

"EGGING" A FRIEND

Perhaps you may have heard the old expression that when someone wants you to do something and tries to convince you, they are "egging you on." Check out this story.

Rover (a dog, of course) lived on a working farm in North Dakota. He performed many chores such as helping to round up cattle, chasing off coyotes, and guarding the henhouse. But he did have a problem. The dog loved eggs, and every once in a while he'd steal one from the very place he was supposed to guard. When he got caught, the farm family punished him, but he still loved eggs.

When Rover got old, the farmer brought home a puppy named Rags. The newcomer was to learn the ways of the farm from old Rover, which he did. According to the people who witnessed it, Rags learned a little too much from his aging master.

One day the farmer saw Rover and Rags in what looked like deep conversation. Suddenly Rags ran to the henhouse and soon returned with a big egg held gently in his teeth. He carefully placed the meal at Rover's paws. The older dog gratefully gobbled it up.

Whether you believe such a thing actually happened isn't important. (The farmer firmly sticks by his story.) It does illustrate an important point. Not everything someone tells you to do is something you should do. Sin is still sin whether we choose to commit it on our own or whether a best friend, a parent, or even a schoolteacher "eggs us on." We're to obey God first in all things!

HEAVEN-BOUND!

Q: Will I be in heaven?

A: I once had a dream. In it I stood on a mountaintop watching the Second Coming. There was Jesus, and the angels, lots of clouds, and even someone blowing a trumpet.

Everyone around me started rising up into the air, happy smiles on their faces. I waited . . . and waited . . . and nothing happened. For a second I made a little jump—you know, to get my journey to heaven started—but it didn't work. Suddenly I realized that I wasn't going to go.

With terrible sadness I sat down on a rock and began to cry. I woke up and found warm tears on my cheeks. Boy, was I glad that was just a dream!

Since then I've discovered something wonderful about God, and something terrible about Satan. God wants us to look forward to our new home with eager anticipation. Satan tries to get us to keep asking the question "Will I be in heaven?" *He's* the one that makes us doubt. And *he's* the one who planted that horrible thought in my mind that turned into a frightening dream.

We must fight such fearful ideas. We must say to ourselves, "I've given my life to Jesus, and He's building a mansion for me. The decision has *already been made.* I'll be in heaven because Jesus paid for my ticket with His own blood. As long as I give my will to God, as long as I allow Him to teach me new things from my mistakes, as long as I recognize that Jesus' perfect life makes up for my imperfect one, heaven is my future home." Forget doubts. Forget dreams. And remember Jesus.

CLOUD OVER THE MOON

William Smith sat by a small pond, reading by candle-light. He didn't dare return to his home, because the king's henchmen were out looking for people who worshiped God in a way contrary to the Scottish monarch's beliefs. "Kill them all," he told his soldiers.

So engrossed was William in his book that he didn't hear foot-steps behind him. "We are arresting you for reading the Bible," the captain of the guard announced, startling William.

"I'm not reading the Bible," Smith protested, holding up his book.

"We are arresting you anyway," the captain snapped. "We know who you are. We also know that there will be a religious meeting tonight in a nearby town. We're not sure in which building, so *you're* going to take us there." He poked the barrel of his rifle into William's chest. "Understand?"

The group made their way along the road leading to town. A full moon illuminated their way, bathing the countryside in silvery light. However, unknown to the dangerous band, something was happening behind them. Something silent.

Just as they reached the hillside overlooking a quiet Scottish town, thick clouds slipped between them and the moon, throwing the world into utter darkness. "OK, Smith," the captain called out. "Which building is it?" But they received no answer. Their prisoner had used the sudden darkness as an opportunity to escape.

"*Find him!*" the officer ordered. When the search proved un-successful, he commanded his men to fire into the bushes. Every bullet missed the hiding man, and the sound of gunfire warned the gathered Christians in town, so they quickly disbanded.

William Smith escaped. The Christians fled. The king wasn't pleased.

PLACE OF THE SKULL

They came to a place called Golgotha (which means The Place of the Skull). . . . When they had crucified him, they divided up his clothes by casting lots. And sitting down, they kept watch over him there. Above his head they placed the written charge against him: This is Jesus, the king of the Jews. Two robbers were crucified with him, one on his right and one on his left. Those who passed by hurled insults at him, shaking their heads and saying, "You who are going to destroy the temple and build it in three days, save yourself! Come down from the cross, if you are the Son of God!"

In the same way the chief priests, the teachers of the law and the elders mocked him. "He saved others," they said, "but he can't save himself! He's the King of Israel! Let him come down now from the cross, and we will believe in him. He trusts in God. Let God rescue him now if he wants him, for he said, 'I am the Son of God.'" In the same way the robbers who were crucified with him also heaped insults on him.

From the sixth hour until the ninth hour darkness came over all the land. About the ninth hour Jesus cried out in a loud voice, . . . "My God, my God, why have you forsaken me?" . . .

And when Jesus had cried out again in a loud voice, he gave up his spirit.

Matthew 27:33-50

Juniors, He did this so that you could have eternal life with Him in heaven. He went to the Place of the Skull for you!

ETERNITY

G lory to God in the highest, and on earth peace to men on whom his favor rests." Luke 2:14.

Satan must have been really confused when Jesus was born. Suddenly, here was a person walking around on earth that he couldn't tempt into sinning.

Oh, he tried . . . and tried . . . and tried. But each time Jesus would throw Bible texts at him like a warrior hurls a lance. Like it or not, Jesus became a living, breathing reminder to Satan that his days were numbered, that his destructive reign would some-day end. And that end wouldn't be pretty.

Listen to this beautiful invitation to become a member of God's family written by a junior who is very glad Jesus came to earth to show us the way to heaven:

> Just like a newborn baby cradled in its mother's arms,
>> God wants to make you new again, and keep you safe from harm.
> "You must be born again," He said. And if that's what you choose,
>> You must want it with all your heart. If so, you cannot lose!
> You're wanting to be baptized? What does that really mean?
>> You're going under water; saying yes to things unseen.
> Peace and love come over you; a love for all mankind.
>> A peace that only God can bring. Eternity is mine!

Jaime Myers,
13, Tennessee

THREE BOTTLES OF RUM

Nothing like a little riot to make life interesting," Carlos Monroy shouted as he picked up a brick and heaved it though the window of a liquor store.

Carlos wasn't sure what the riot was about. People carried banners and shouted, "Down with the government," or "Kill the governor." The only thing Carlos was interested in was getting his hands on those three bottles of rum in the window.

Grabbing the first, he smashed off the top and gulped down the burning liquid. "Yeah. This is great. Kill the government!" He followed the surging throng as it swept along the streets of Bogotá, Colombia. "Hang the leaders. Burn the capital!"

Then he downed the second bottle. "Hurrah for the revolution! Down with everything!" He was feeling pretty good about life as he polished off the third bottle.

Suddenly someone shouted, "The army's coming. Soldiers! They're shooting!"

The crackle of gunfire and screams of injured and dying people filled his alcohol-soaked brain. "Hang the revolution and kill the . . ."

Carlos slumped to the ground amid the victims of gunfire.

When he woke up, all was silent. He seemed to be in a room somewhere. "Hey, buddy, where are we?" he asked the man lying beside him. No answer. "Hey, you, what's going on?" he queried another prone figure.

Suddenly he realized why he was the only one in the room talking. He was in the city morgue. Everyone else was dead!

"HEEEEEELP!" Carlos screamed. "I'm not dead. Get me out of here. I'll never drink again. I promise." And he didn't.

STICKY-FINGERED FRIEND

Q: My friend and I went into a store, and when he came out he showed me a couple packs of gum he'd stolen. I told him it wasn't right, but he said nobody would miss them. What should I do?

A: Let's look at the choices you're facing. As we see it, you have three options. First, you could ignore the fact that your friend took the gum and say nothing to anyone. On the other hand, you could tell somebody else what happened. Or you could reason with your friend and encourage him to confess and make things right.

What do you think the consequences would be in each situation? In the first instance, if you say nothing, your friend might develop a false confidence, thinking that it's easy to steal and get away with it. It might even encourage him to continue being dishonest!

What if you tell on your friend? You'll clear yourself, but your friendship may be at stake.

Finally, if you try to reason with your friend, he might not appreciate it or take your advice—but then again, he might. That's up to him.

Now, what should you do? Pray about your decision and then do what you feel God wants you to.

Art and Pat Humphrey

MYSTERY UNDERGROUND

Jim White was riding the range near sunset when he saw what appeared to be a cloud of smoke rising from the ground. Puzzled, he watched the "smoke" disappear into the hot June night. The next evening he saw the cloud again and decided to investigate. The third evening he went to where he thought the smoke had come from and found nothing but a hole in the ground. So he sat and waited for nightfall.

Sure enough, from the hole poured the smokelike cloud—a cloud composed of millions of bats that emerged at dusk to hunt. How could they have all come from that hole in the ground? Jim White didn't tell the other cowboys what he had seen because he knew they wouldn't believe him. Instead, he built a ladder out of mesquite sticks, wire, and rope to use to lower himself into the pit.

The pit led to a large cavern whose floor was covered with mounds of bat dropping. Until his lantern ran out of kerosene, Jim explored passages and discovered fantastic stone formations. He went back to the cave many times and finally convinced his skeptical friends of his amazing discovery. Twenty-two years later, in 1923, the government declared Jim's cave—Carlsbad Caverns—a national monument.

Caves all over the world are filled with beautiful, mysterious formations. But God didn't create caves just for people to admire. They provide a unique environment for many plants, animals, and organisms that can survive only there. Caves also provide vital channels for conducting groundwater.

God formed every creation to serve a purpose—including you and me.

Jane Chase

MEETING SATAN

Q: Will I meet Satan before I go to heaven?

A: I'm assuming you mean face-to-face, for we meet Satan every day through the sinful acts we witness and sometimes take part in.

Our friend Ellen White mentions a terrible temptation that will come to God's people prior to Christ's second coming. Listen: "In the last days he [Satan] will appear in such a manner as to make men believe him to be Christ come the second time into the world. He will indeed transform himself into an angel of light" (*Last Day Events*, p. 163).

We're longing for Christ's return. Then suddenly someone shouts, "He's here! He's finally come back! Glory, glory!"

The Bible warns: "If any man shall say to you, Lo, here is Christ, or, lo, he is there, believe him not. For false Christs and false prophets shall rise, and shall show signs and wonders, to seduce, if it were possible, even the elect" (Mark 13:21, 22).

Will we fall for such a terrible trick? Will we drop to our knees before the very being who has caused so much suffering and death in this world? "But while he will bear the appearance of Christ in every particular, so far as mere appearance goes," says Mrs. White, "it will deceive none but those who . . . are seeking to resist the truth" *(ibid.)*.

Satan will not take us in, because we've gotten to know the real Jesus, the real Saviour, the real coming King.

TWO MEN AND A VISION

Mr. Sargent and Mr. Robbins weren't what you'd call Ellen Harmon fans. (Ellen Harmon was Ellen White's name before she got married.) They insisted she had a devil possessing her and that no one could trust her visions. When they heard that she'd be speaking at a church in Boston, they made arrangements to be somewhere else.

As they were settling in for a meeting at a friend's home in Randolph, a town 13 miles away, who should walk in but Ellen Harmon! God had given His young prophet a vision explaining that she should attend this gathering instead.

Robbins and Sargent made sure the visiting girl didn't get a chance to say anything. They hogged the whole meeting, telling personal stories and keeping attention away from Ellen. Suddenly Miss Harmon cried out, "Glory, glory, glory"—words she often spoke when the Lord was showing her something.

"She's in vision!" the people gasped.

"No, she's not," the two men insisted. They tried to drown out her words, but everyone was interested in what the young woman was saying and told them to hush up. Someone brought a large Bible and handed it to Ellen, thinking that if her vision was from the devil, the Bible would end it. But the girl took the Book, held it above her head, and began reciting passages and turning the pages.

The vision lasted nearly four hours. Robbins and Sargent didn't have an opportunity to speak. But no one wanted to listen to them anyway. Many were convinced that Miss Harmon's visions were from God.

Our heavenly Father always finds ways to reach us, no matter what others say and do.

GUARDED TOMB

At that moment [of Christ's death] the curtain of the temple was torn in two from top to bottom. The earth shook and the rocks split. . . .

When the centurion and those with him who were guarding Jesus saw the earthquake and all that had happened, they were terrified, and exclaimed, "Surely he was the Son of God!"

Many women were there, watching from a distance. They had followed Jesus from Galilee to care for his needs. Among them were Mary Magdalene, Mary the mother of James and Joses, and the mother of Zebedee's sons.

As evening approached, there came a rich man from Arimathea, named Joseph, who had himself become a disciple of Jesus. Going to Pilate, he asked for Jesus' body, and Pilate ordered that it be given to him. Joseph took the body, wrapped it in a clean linen cloth, and placed it in his own new tomb that he had cut out of the rock. He rolled a big stone in front of the entrance to the tomb and went away. . . .

"Take a guard," Pilate [ordered]. "Go, make the tomb as secure as you know how." So they went and made the tomb secure by putting a seal on the stone and posting the guard.

Matthew 27:51-66

The Sabbath had come. In keeping with the law He created long before that terrible day, Jesus rested.

Can you imagine the grief of His devoted followers? They had thought He was a king, that he was the Son of God. Now He was dead and buried along with their dreams. But a new week was about to begin. The sun would soon rise.

HEAVEN

Behold, I am coming soon! My reward is with me, and I will give to everyone according to what he has done. . . . Blessed are those who wash their robes, that they may have the right to the tree of life and may go through the gates into the city." Revelation 22:12-14.

What's heaven going to be like? Of course, we can only dream for now. The Bible says it will be even better and prettier and more fun than we can imagine. However, imagining heaven is still a great way of looking forward to being there. Just listen to this junior:

We can fly over a hill with the birds.
    What a thrill!
When we pick a flower
    It won't die,
In heaven we'll never cry!

We will live in a mansion beside Jesus,
    And make new friends.
We can play with some deer.
    They'll have no fear!
Even with a bear or a big cat
    We won't have to worry about that.

We can climb and swing from tree to tree.
    Jesus will tell how He died for you and me.
Someday, heaven will be here on earth.
    Life is much more than we think it's worth!
I just can't wait to go to heaven!

Megan Elyse Myers,
9, Tennessee

AUNTIE'S WILL

S top preaching to me," Colby snapped. "You're my aunt and I love you, but enough with this God stuff!"

Trouble had been brewing between him and his aging aunt for several years. Colby had stayed away as much as possible, because whenever they'd been together, she'd talk to him about his life and the lack of God in it.

Then came the news that Auntie had died. Everyone was sad, including Colby. After the funeral the family lawyer called a meeting for the reading of the will. The young man was happy to see that everyone was getting large sums of money. Then the lawyer looked straight at him. "To Colby, my wayward nephew," he said, reading from the document, "I bequeath my Bible and all that it contains."

"Her Bible!" Angrily Colby stomped to the desk and snatched the book from the lawyer's hand. "She just never quits, even in death," he fumed.

Hard times followed. Years passed. The Bible stayed in the old trunk where he had thrown it unopened the day he received it.

Finally, broken and ill, Colby returned to his childhood home and one day opened the trunk. There lay Auntie's Bible. "Maybe I should have listened to you," he breathed as he picked up the Book. Opening it, he found some money. As he thumbed through the pages, hundreds and then thousands of dollars slipped out. Tears burned Colby's eyes. "To think that all this treasure was hidden inside and all I had to do was open it. What a fool I've been!"

Do you have a Bible? Have you discovered its treasures for your life?

LITTLE SISTER IN MY STUFF

Q: I'm 14, and my 9-year-old sister is always getting into my stuff without asking. I really want to get along with her, but she gets us both into trouble. What can I do?

A: That sounds a lot like my sister and me. Except in my case I was the little sister! There's just something awesome about big sisters. In my case it seemed as though everything my big sister had—from perfume to clothes—was way more cool than my old stuff. Everywhere she went I wanted to go, and everything she did I wanted to do. I'm sure I really bugged her sometimes.

Here's an idea: try to determine at least one *affordable* item of yours that your sister seems to get into the most. Then go to the store and buy her an identical one, along with some pretty wrapping paper. When you get home, wrap up the gift and hide the box in a place where she usually gets into your stuff. Put her name on it and attach a note that reads: "Dear Sis, since you like my _____ so much, I decided to buy you one for your very own. I don't mind you borrowing my stuff, but please do me a favor. Please ask first, and be sure to put my things back when you're done, OK? Love, [your name]."

Art and Pat Humphrey

DARE TO DREAM

A boy stood on a beach gazing out across the ocean. In his imagination he saw himself guiding the first ship ever to China, where spices, ointments, gold, and silver waited. On his return everyone bowed to him and congratulated him for his great courage.

The boy grew and one day led three ships called the *Niña, Pinta,* and *Santa Mariá* to a new world. Christopher Columbus dared to dream.

Do you dream? You should! In the quiet moments of your day or just before you drift to sleep at night, think long, long thoughts about what you'll be in the years to come.

Dream of being a teacher or minister. In your imagination, see people seated before you waiting to hear words of wisdom, wanting to learn how to live better, healthier, happier.

Dream of being a doctor or nurse, bringing healing to hurting bodies in your town or on the far side of the world.

Dream of being a computer programmer, creating software that makes life better for your community.

Dream of being a builder or mechanic, firefighter or veterinarian, scientist or writer. Every dream can come true if you work hard toward your goals.

In all your planning, aim high. Don't be satisfied with second best. And here's the most important part. Don't ever dream without God. "Higher than the highest human thought can reach is God's ideal for His children" (*Education,* p. 18).

People without Jesus in their lives can only reach so far. But when you put God on your dream team, you can reach the stars—and beyond!

HIDDEN TEXTS

Q: Could you find some new texts in the Bible? All people do is preach the same stuff again and again.

A: The Bible isn't a work in progress. It was completed a couple thousand years ago.

However, I'll bet there are tons of texts you didn't even know were in there, passages that could teach you important stuff. Let's see if I can dig up a couple in just one book.

Did you know that loving God helps fight sickness? "Fear the Lord and shun evil. This will bring health to your body and nourishment to your bones" (Proverbs 3:7, 8).

I'll bet you weren't aware that the Bible contains a sure formula for getting rich. Here it is. "Lazy hands make a man poor, but diligent hands bring wealth" (Proverbs 10:4).

Want to know how to keep other people's words from hurting you? "With his mouth the godless destroys his neighbor, but through knowledge the righteous escape" (Proverbs 11:9).

Worrying about someone cheating you? "He who puts up security for another will surely suffer, but whoever refuses to strike [shake] hands in a pledge is safe" (Proverbs 11:15).

Tempted by get-rich-quick opportunities? "He who works his land will have abundant food, but he who chases fantasies lacks judgment" (Proverbs 12:11).

Want to accomplish something great? "Plans fail for lack of counsel, but with many advisers they succeed" (Proverbs 15:22).

Why not discover some treasures of your own?

POLE-SITTING SINNER

Fifteen-year-old Simeon had a problem. He felt guilty all the time. Even while watching his father's sheep, he felt that God couldn't possibly love him. So he asked a preacher what he should do.

"God *is* angry at you," the parson pontificated. "The only way you can be saved is to live in a monastery and spend all your time doing religious things." That was common advice 1,500 years ago.

Simeon said goodbye to his family and friends. At the monastery, he obeyed all the rules, read piles of holy books, sang boring hymns, and starved himself often.

Still, he felt that his sins weren't forgiven, so he found a high desert rock and lived on top of it for a few years. People came from miles around to look up at the holy man and ask him questions.

When he got so busy advising others that he didn't have time for his prayers, he built a pillar to lift him "closer to God." The crowds still came.

So he erected a tall pole with a platform on top and stayed up there in all kinds of weather, fasting and praying, begging God for forgiveness, for 36 years. Yes, *years!* Then, like everyone else, he died.

"What a faithful, wonderful man was Simeon," the people cried.

Faithful? Wonderful? Or foolish? God doesn't require anyone to sit on a pole before He'll forgive him or her. "If we confess our sins, he is faithful and just to forgive us our sins, and to cleanse us from all unrighteousness" (1 John 1:9, KJV).

The world needs more confessors and fewer pole-sitters.

HE HAS RISEN!

After the Sabbath, at dawn on the first day of the week, Mary Magdalene and the other Mary went to look at the tomb.

There was a violent earthquake, for an angel of the Lord came down from heaven and, going to the tomb, rolled back the stone and sat on it. His appearance was like lightning, and his clothes were white as snow. The guards were so afraid of him that they shook and became like dead men.

The angel said to the women, "Do not be afraid, for I know that you are looking for Jesus, who was crucified. He is not here; he has risen, just as he said." . . .

So the women hurried away from the tomb, afraid yet filled with joy, and ran to tell his disciples. Suddenly Jesus met them. "Greetings," he said. They came to him, clasped his feet and worshiped him. Then Jesus said to them, "Do not be afraid. Go and tell my brothers to go to Galilee; there they will see me." . . .

Then the eleven disciples went to Galilee, to the mountain where Jesus had told them to go. When they saw him, they worshiped him; but some doubted. Then Jesus came to them and said, "All authority in heaven and on earth has been given to me. Therefore go and make disciples of all nations, baptizing them in the name of the Father and of the Son and of the Holy Spirit, and teaching them to obey everything I have commanded you. And surely I am with you always, to the very end of the age."

Matthew 28:1-20

BE PREPARED

Here's an insightful verse written by a junior in faraway Alaska, where cold winds blow and storms sometimes roll across the land. But she has learned that God is there too, waiting to willingly heal any hurting heart. Listen:

The Lord will come to save us all.
    He'll take us in His arms.
Satan's reign will finally fall.
    He'll lose his corrupting charms.
The world will burn in cleansing glory.
    I hope you'll learn from this sad story.

A man who won the lottery
    Went home with pride and joy.
But his house, deco'd in pottery,
    And his baby were destroyed.
His tension grew. He got annoyed.
    His head soon filled with fury.
Even though he cashed the check he'd won,
    He spent his life in worry.

The moral here is be prepared!
    For what you fear will make you scared
    Of living life, of loving God.
But through the strife and through the fraud
    The Lord is there. Just trust in Him.
He's there to care when things go wrong.

Heather Austermuhl,
13, Alaska

"SHOOT—IF YOU DARE!"

This court finds you guilty of spying and sentences you to death at dawn." The judge's gavel crashed onto the desk with a fearful *crack*.

The young man standing before him sighed. He'd done everything he could to prove his innocence, but the court wouldn't listen. Born in England, the prisoner had traveled to the United States to gain citizenship there. He'd recently made the mistake of visiting Cuba, a country suspicious of anyone from the U.S.

Ambassadors from both sides of the Atlantic heard of his difficulties and did their best to intercede, but were ignored. When news of the verdict reached them, they panicked. An innocent man was about to die!

The eastern sky was aglow when the gates of the prison yard swung open, and guards marched the young man to a brick wall. Soldiers shouldering powerful weapons took up position and stood waiting for orders. *Only a few moments left*, the prisoner told himself.

Suddenly two riders charged in and leaped from their horses. In seconds they had wrapped something around the condemned man's shoulders. Stepping back, they shouted, "Shoot—if you dare!"

The captain of the guard took one look and ordered his men to their barracks. Encircling the prisoner were the flags of Great Britain and the United States. The captain knew that if he shot through those flags, two very powerful nations would consider that an insult and declare war on Cuba.

Satan takes aim at you, then hesitates when he sees that you're wrapped in the righteous robe of Jesus. "This person is mine," Christ says. "Touch him, and you'll have to fight *Me!*" Satan backs down every time.

BE READY

A friend whose attention will never fail,
    A gracious God who will prevail,
He was bound to the cross with jagged nails
    So we could follow Heaven's trail.

Showering us with His mercy and love,
    He sits on His throne in heaven above.
In glorious fashion, He will come.
    So be ever ready.
For He will take only some.

Nolan Austermuhl,
15, Alaska